teens cook

Teens Cook

How to Cook What You Want to Eat

MEGAN and JILL CARLE
with Judi Carle

TEN SPEED PRESS
Berkeley

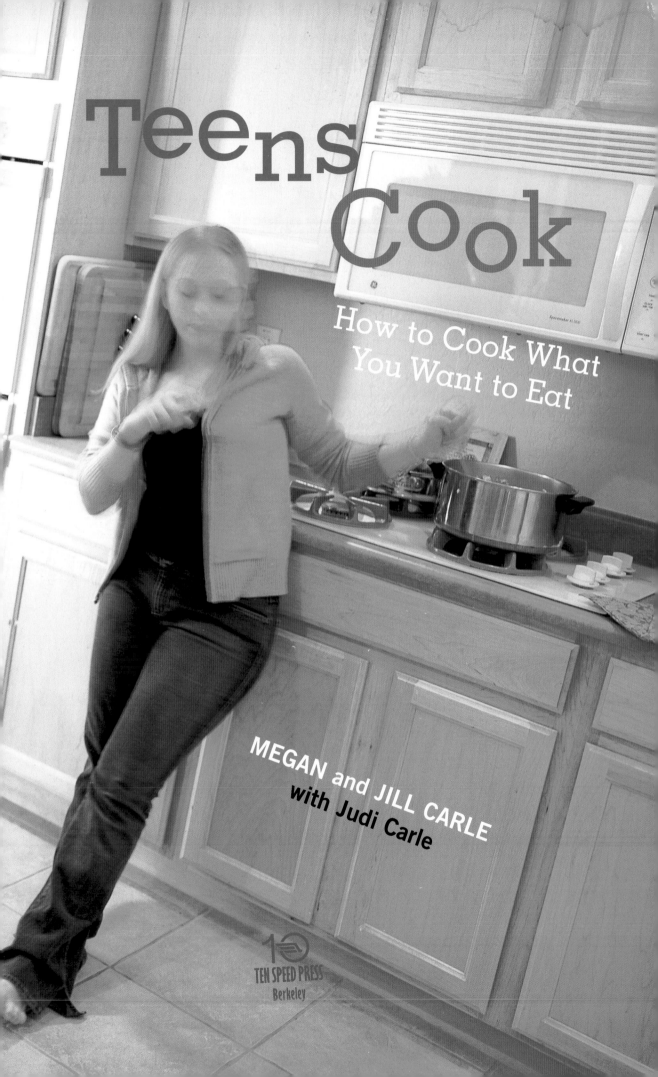

Copyright © 2004 by Megan, Jill, and Judi Carle
Photography © 2004 by Jessica Boone

All rights reserved. Published in the United States by Ten Speed Press, an imprint of the
Crown Publishing Group, a division of Random House, Inc., New York.
www.crownpublishing.com
www.tenspeed.com

Ten Speed Press and the Ten Speed Press colophon are registered trademarks of Random
House, Inc.

Library of Congress Cataloging-in-Publication Data on file with publisher

ISBN 978-1-58008-584-7
Printed in Korea

Cover and book design by Toni Tajima
Food photography and prop styling by Jessica Boone, Los Angeles
Food styling by Susan Draudt, Los Angeles

21 20 19 18

First Edition

This book is for the one person
who matters the most: Mumsernoonernutter,
the Mumsinator, the Mumster, the big Mum, or, as everyone else knows her,
Judi Carle, our mom. Although she probably thinks that we don't realize
how much she does for us (and believe us, it's *a lot*) we really do appreciate
all her work. Besides washing the dishes and cleaning up after we
destroy the kitchen, she is really the brain behind this whole operation
(we just stand there and look pretty). Whether it's going to
debate practices or cutting up thirty-five pounds of cheese for
a choir dinner, she supports us in everything we do.
We know that sometimes we're a little tough to
put up with, so merely living with us is a
feat in itself. Mumsernut,
you're our hero and
we'll always
love you.

Contents

Acknowledgments viii
Introduction x

★ BREAKFAST 1

Banana Bread **2**

Sausage and Egg Bake **4**

Hash Brown Casserole **5**

Cinnamon Rolls **6**

Chocolate Chip Scones **8**

Buttermilk Pancakes with
   Blueberry Syrup **10**

Roman Apple Coffee Cake **12**

Fried Apple Rings **14**

Spinach and Mushroom Quiche **17**

Crepes with Fresh Strawberries
   and Cream **18**

German Apple Puff Pancake **21**

Baked French Toast **22**

Breakfast Burritos **23**

★ SNACKS 25

Potato Skins **26**

Caramelized Onion, Mushroom, and
   Roasted Red Pepper Focaccia **28**

Chili Cheese Dip **31**

Pot Stickers **32**

Vegetable Maki Rolls **34**

Nachos with Salsa and Guacamole **36**

Chicken Empanadas **38**

BLT Dip **39**

Buffalo Wings **40**

Cinnamon Sticks **41**

Strawberries with Marshmallow Dip **43**

Goat Cheese and Tomato Crostini **44**

Deviled Eggs **45**

Crab Rangoons **46**

★ FAMILY MEALS 89

Baked Macaroni and Cheese 90

Chicken Piccata with Rice Pilaf 92

Sloppy Joes 95

Ratatouille with
  Chickpeas and Couscous 96

Cheese and Chile Enchiladas 97

Chicken and Dumplings 98

Vegetable Lasagna 100

Mexican Lasagna 102

Eggplant Parmesan 104

Chicken Pot Pie 106

Chicken Schnitzel with
  Fried Potatoes 108

Potato Chip–Crusted Whitefish with
  Potato Wedges 110

Meatloaf with Scalloped Potatoes 112

Red Beans and Rice with Cornbread 114

Salmon and Vegetables en Papillote 116

★ SOUP/SALAD 49

Split Pea Soup 50

Corn Chowder 51

Baked Potato Soup 52

Broccoli Cheese Soup 54

French Onion Soup 56

Wonton Soup 58

Taco Salad 60

Tuna and Macaroni Salad 62

Steak Cobb Salad 64

Chicken Caesar Salad 66

Spinach Salad with
  Honey-Mustard Dressing 68

★ DESSERTS 119

Banana Cream Pie 120

Cheesecake 122

Peanut Butter Cookies 124

Toffee Bars 125

Peach Turnovers 126

Seven-Layer Bars 129

Apple Crisp 130

Crème Brûlée 132

Snickerdoodles 135

Frozen Bananas with
  Chocolate and Toffee 136

Chocolate Spice Cake 138

Cream Cheese Brownies 140

★ DINNER FOR ONE 71

Spinach and Cheese Ravioli 72

Tuna Melt 74

Vegetable Stir-Fry with Tofu 75

Shrimp Fettuccine Alfredo 76

Chicken Quesadillas 77

Steak Fajitas 78

Fried Rice 80

Egg Salad Tortilla Wrap 81

Grilled Portobello Sandwich 82

Grilled Cheese with
  Bacon and Tomato 83

Vegetable Lomein 84

Turkey-Bacon Puff Pastry Pockets 86

Index 141

Acknowledgments

Many people deserve our very sincere thanks for their help with this book:

m

Lorena Jones, for believing that two teenagers could actually put together a book worth publishing.

Toni Tajima, for listening to all of our scattered thoughts about design and turning them into so much more than we had imagined.

Photographer Jessica Boone and stylist Susan Draudt, for making our food look great, making the photo shoot really fun, and never complaining about the loud music or our singing.

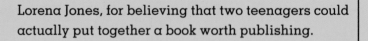

Yvonne Govea, for the countless hours she spent chopping, cooking, and cleaning up after us. (We are particularly grateful for the cleaning up.)

Kristin Rill, Kelly and Kevin Jackson, Paul and Jimmy Casperson, and Tommy Franks, whose input as our teenage recipe testers was invaluable.

And, last, but certainly not least, our Dad, whose years of eating undercooked cakes, gloppy sauces, and blue mashed potatoes without complaint typifies his unwaivering support for everything we do.

Introduction

We began helping in the kitchen when we each turned three years old. We're sure that, at that age, we were more of a hindrance than help, but because our mom thought cooking was a good learning tool, she tolerated all of the mess that we made. Of course, we didn't care about any of that learning stuff, we just thought it was fun, and we still do.

We learned to cook through trial and many, many errors. We can't tell you how many times we have dropped eggs on the floor, coated the kitchen in flour, or boiled things over on the stove. Once Megan even got her head too close to the electric mixer and it yanked out a quarter-size chunk of hair. (She was the only kid in preschool with a comb-over.) The point is, if there is a mistake that could be made, we have made it. But, as our mom always says, mistakes are the best teachers. Through those mistakes we have learned what works and definitely what doesn't.

Our goal in cooking has always been to prepare what we like to eat in the easiest possible way. We take shortcuts that would probably give a chef hives. We get bored just thinking about making stock from scratch. Why do all that work when someone else has already done it? Also, we don't do bones. We only buy boneless chicken and meats. We tell people this is because we are reinforcing the economy by keeping butchers employed, but no one believes us. The truth is, cutting raw meat off the bones gives us the creeps.

We included a variety of our favorite recipes in this book. These recipes have been adapted to our tastes, but feel free to adjust them to yours. We won't be offended. It's what we did. The beauty of cooking is that you can make things exactly the way you like them. Sometimes it's as simple as switching out foods you don't like. We have found that vegetables are pretty much interchangeable, vegetable stock can always be substituted for chicken stock, and one herb will work as well as another. Once you get the hang of it, you won't have to think twice about it. This is particularly useful for vegetarians, like Megan, who almost always require substitutions.

If you are just learning to cook, you may want to follow a recipe at least once, and when you are comfortable with it you can start to change things to your tastes. Even if it doesn't turn out exactly the way you planned, it will probably still taste good. Don't let mistakes stop you from trying again; we make them all the time. Just recently Megan made some pumpkin bread to take to work. Her coworkers loved it and several asked for the recipe. Only later did she realize that instead of using ginger she had inadvertently grabbed the hot mustard powder. The only problem then was whether to give them the recipe with the ginger or the hot mustard.

Many of these recipes started as a mission to re-create something we had in a restaurant. This can be a little more challenging than just adapting a recipe, but the reward comes when you get it right. When we are trying to re-create a dish, we start with recipes for similar dishes. We look at them and decide what the similarities and differences are between the recipes and the dish we are trying to create, and then from there, decide which direction we want to go in first. Seldom do we get it right on the first try, but the process is still fun. Sometimes they are easy, like the Potato Skins. They only took three tries before we got them right. We tried deep-frying them (tasted funny and very messy), baking them after the insides were scooped out (took way too long to get crisp), and finally, we brushed them with oil and broiled them, and they were perfect. Other times it takes much longer to get a recipe just right. The German Apple Puff Pancake took several months of eating pancakes every weekend to perfect. We tried three different recipes for the pancake part before we got it right and then went through at least a dozen versions of when to add the apples, how many to use, and whether we should use white or brown sugar before we were happy with the result. It was like a puzzle that drove us crazy until we figured it out.

At best, this book will teach you some of the basics of cooking and inspire you to explore even further to develop your own personal style. At worst, you'll learn that, without all the cooking lingo, it's not hard to make some great dishes, and that's not bad either.

THINGS YOU SHOULD KNOW ABOUT INGREDIENTS

Although we say **mayonnaise** in the recipes, we use **Miracle Whip**. Either one will work fine. Just use whatever you usually buy.

We use **salted butter**. We know that most cookbooks use **unsalted butter**, but salted is what our mom buys, so it's what we use.

We always buy **lowfat sour cream**, **cream cheese**, and **mayonnaise**. The regular types work fine, but we figure why not save a little fat where we can't taste the difference. The only exception to this rule is in baking. Do not use lowfat cream cheese or sour cream when making the cheesecake or it will come out looking shriveled with big crevasses all over.

When we say **bread**, we mean plain ol' **white bread**. If we like another type better for a recipe we say that specific type, but the reality is, any type will work. Use whatever you have in the house.

Eggs are always large, but everything else is medium unless otherwise stated.

You may notice the lack of **nuts** in our recipes. We like to eat nuts, we just don't like them cooked in cakes, breads, or brownies. If you like them, put them in.

We always use **kosher salt** because it is not as harsh as table salt. But, it is fine to use **table salt** in these recipes. In the few cases when we feel it would work better, we call for kosher salt, but don't let a lack of kosher salt stop you from trying the recipe. It's not that critical.

It doesn't matter whether you use **plain** or **seasoned breadcrumbs** for these recipes. Whatever you have in the house is fine.

We use **thick-sliced bacon**. If you use the regular-slice, you may want to add a little extra when a recipe calls for a specific number of slices. You may notice that sometimes we cook bacon in the microwave and sometimes we cook it on the stove. If we are only cooking a few slices, it is faster and less messy to do it in the microwave, but if we are cooking a whole pound, it's faster on the stove. Use whatever method you prefer.

To us, **buttering a pan** means spraying it with **vegetable cooking spray**. We just use the regular spray, not the one with flour in it.

Although we don't mention it, all **vegetables** and **fruits** should be rinsed under running water before being cooked.

breakfast

We always have bananas in our house, and therefore, we always seem to have a few that are too ripe to eat. What better way to use them up than to turn them into banana bread? Don't let the color throw you. You can use bananas that are still all yellow, but you'll need to mash them with a fork first to break them up. I actually prefer to use the ones that have a lot of brown spots or that are even almost totally black because they are very soft and mix in easily.

m

BANANA BREAD

Makes ONE 9-INCH LOAF

1/2 cup butter

1 cup sugar

2 eggs

3 medium bananas

1 teaspoon baking soda

1/2 teaspoon salt

2 cups flour

1 cup walnuts (optional)

Preheat the oven to 375°F. Lightly butter or spray the bottom and sides of a 9-inch loaf pan.

Place the butter and sugar in a large mixing bowl and beat with an electric mixer on low speed for 1 minute, or until the sugar is completely mixed into the butter. Add the eggs and mix for 1 minute, or until the batter is smooth. Add the bananas and mix for 1 minute, or until no large chunks remain. The batter will be lumpy, but the pieces of banana should all be 1/2 inch or smaller.

Add the baking soda and salt and mix on low speed for 1 minute, or until combined. Add the flour and mix on low speed for 1 minute, scraping the sides of the bowl occasionally, until all of the flour is incorporated. Stir in the walnuts.

Kitchen Vocab

The process of mixing the butter and sugar until it is thoroughly combined is called **creaming**. It can be done by hand, but in most cases it is done with an electric mixer.

2

As part of my constant effort to find shortcuts in cooking, I decided I could save a lot of time by just mixing all of the banana bread ingredients at the same time. I was right, it was faster. The bread was perfect! For a doorstop. My mom explained that wet ingredients are added first is so they can be thoroughly combined before the dry ingredients, especially flour, are added. When flour is mixed with liquid, it activates the gluten in the flour and the more the gluten is mixed, the more elastic it becomes. The elasticity in the flour holds down the gas bubbles formed by the baking soda and keeps the bread from rising, making one very hard and dense loaf. And I *do* mean very hard and dense.

KITCHEN DISASTER

Pour the batter into the loaf pan and bake for 15 minutes. Reduce the oven heat to 350°F and bake for 45 minutes, or until a toothpick inserted in the center of the loaf comes out clean.

Remove the bread from the pan and place it on a cooling rack. (If you let the bread cool in the pan, the bottom will become soggy.)

This is our traditional Christmas morning breakfast. Because it can be put together the night before, it doesn't take time away from the important tasks, like opening presents. We always make two pans, one with just the sausage and egg for Megan and me (she picks out the sausage), and one with sausage or ham and onion, green pepper, and mushrooms for my mom and dad.

SAUSAGE AND EGG BAKE

Serves 6

Place the sausage in a small sauté pan and cook over medium-low heat, turning occasionally, for 15 minutes, or until the sausage is thoroughly cooked. Remove the sausage from the pan and blot on paper towels. Cut the sausages into 1/2-inch pieces and set aside.

Lightly butter or spray a 9-inch-square pan.

Cut the bread into 1/4-inch cubes and spread them evenly in the pan. Place the eggs and evaporated milk in a bowl and whisk until thoroughly combined. Stir in the salt, cheese, and sausage pieces and pour the mixture evenly over the bread. Cover with plastic wrap and refrigerate for at least 30 minutes, or up to 1 day.

Preheat the oven to 350°F.

Bake uncovered for 18 to 20 minutes, or until the top is lightly browned.

6 links pork sausage

2 slices bread

6 eggs

1 cup evaporated milk

1/2 teaspoon salt

3/4 cup shredded Cheddar

HASH BROWN CASSEROLE

Don't let the word "casserole" scare you away from this dish. Believe me, it is nothing like the congealed mass of unappealing ingredients that our parents grew up on. It's just cheesy hash browns. Everyone in our family loves this, and it is a required dish for every family event, whether breakfast, lunch, or dinner. It tastes great and is super easy to make.

Serves 6 TO 8

¼ cup melted butter

1 cup sour cream

3 green onions

1½ cups shredded Cheddar

26 to 30 ounces frozen, shredded hash browns

Preheat the oven to 350°F.

Combine the melted butter and sour cream in a large bowl. Cut off the root ends of the onions and thinly slice the white and about 1 inch of the green parts. Add the sliced green onions and cheese to the bowl and stir until completely combined. Add the hash browns and stir until they are coated with the mixture. (You can put the hash browns in frozen, but they are easier to mix if they are slightly thawed.)

Press the mixture into an ungreased 9-inch-square pan or a large (9 by 5-inch) loaf pan. (It will seem like too much for the pan, but if you press firmly it will all fit.) Bake for 1 hour, or until golden brown.

CINNAMON ROLLS

Cinnamon rolls are a family favorite. We used to make them with yeast and had to let them rise twice. But, while visiting Germany I found this faster method of making the dough. These are best eaten warm for optimal gooeyness (that's the technical term). But don't worry if they get cool, they reheat perfectly in the microwave. These are also really good with a cup of chopped pecans sprinkled in the bottom of the pan.

✳ DOUGH

1 cup cottage cheese

³/₄ cup sugar

2 eggs

¹/₂ cup oil

¹/₂ cup milk

2 tablespoons baking
   powder

4¹/₄ cups flour plus extra for
   dusting

✳ FILLING

2 cups firmly packed brown
   sugar

3 tablespoons cinnamon

¹/₂ cup butter

¹/₂ cup honey

To prepare the dough: **Preheat the oven to 325°F.**

Place the cottage cheese in a blender or food processor and puree until smooth. Add the sugar, eggs, oil, and milk and puree until smooth. Pour the mixture into a large bowl and stir in the baking powder. Add 3¹/₂ cups of the flour and stir until the mixture forms a dough. Using your hands, add the remaining ³/₄ cup of flour a little at a time by sprinkling a little flour over the dough and folding the dough over to mix it in. Repeat this process until the dough is smooth and not sticky. (You may not need all of the flour.)

Spread a thin layer of flour on a flat work surface and roll the dough into a large rectangle, about 20 by 25 inches.

To prepare the filling: **Combine the brown sugar and cinnamon in a small bowl. Melt the butter and brush over the entire surface of the dough. Drizzle the honey over the butter, then sprinkle the sugar mixture evenly over the dough. Starting on the longer side, carefully roll up the dough as tightly as possible.**

Lightly butter or spray the bottom and sides of a 9 by 13-inch baking pan.

Using a serrated knife, cut the roll into 1¹/₄-inch-thick slices with a sawing motion. If you press down while cutting the dough it will smash together and lose the "roll" effect. Arrange the cinnamon rolls in the pan and bake for 35 to 40 minutes, or until done. (To check for doneness, pull up slightly on the center of one of the rolls in the middle of the pan. The dough should pull apart. If it stretches, it needs to cook more.)

Remove the pan from the oven, run a knife around the edges to loosen the cinnamon rolls, and invert the pan onto a serving platter.

The original version of this recipe called for buttermilk.
But, since we never have buttermilk at home, I learned that
if you put 1 tablespoon of vinegar in a measuring cup and
add enough milk to make 1 cup, you have buttermilk. This
is a really easy substitution that I now use all the time.

CHOCOLATE CHIP SCONES

Makes 12 SCONES

1 teaspoon white wine
   vinegar

1/3 cup milk

1 cup butter

1/4 cup plus 2 tablespoons
   sugar

3 eggs

3 cups flour

1 tablespoon baking powder

1/2 cup miniature chocolate
   chips

Place the vinegar in a liquid measuring cup and add
enough milk to make 1/3 cup.

Place the butter and sugar in a large mixing bowl and
beat with an electric mixer on low speed for 1 minute,
or until the sugar is completely mixed into the butter.
Increase to medium speed and mix for 2 to 3 minutes, or
until the mixture is pale and fluffy. Add the eggs, one
at a time, mixing in each egg on medium speed for
1 minute, or until it is completely incorporated into the
batter. Add the milk mixture to the bowl and mix on low
speed for 1 minute, or until combined. Add the flour and
baking powder and mix on low speed for 1 minute, or
until completely combined. Add the chocolate chips
and mix for 30 seconds, or until evenly distributed.

Preheat the oven to 350°F.

Scoop about 1/3 cup of batter at a time and place each
scoop about 2 inches apart on an ungreased baking
sheet. Refrigerate the scones for 15 minutes.

Bake the scones for 15 minutes. Decrease the oven temperature to 325°F and bake for 10 to 15 minutes, or until
the scones are golden brown on the edges. (The scones
can be made smaller if you want, just remember that
the cooking time will be shorter. But, I don't recommend making them any larger. They end up burnt on
the outside before they are cooked in the middle.
Believe me, I tried it, and it wasn't pretty.)

Have you ever taken a cake or, in this case, scones out of the oven thinking they were done, then realized after a few minutes that they were not and put them back in the oven? Well, I have, and it doesn't work. They get really dense on the inside and hard on the outside. Definitely not good. So I checked my reference materials (okay, I asked my mom) and found out that when liquid is added to baking powder or baking soda and heated, it causes a gas to form. The gas forms bubbles that make the baked goods rise. As soon as they are removed from the heat, the bubbles begin to break and the chemical reaction ends. So even if you put it back in the oven, no more bubbles will form and the center will be very solid.

KITCHEN DISASTER

All of my friends think that you have to have pancake mix to make pancakes. I call this successful marketing by the makers of the mixes. Pancakes are so easy to make and are lighter, fluffier, and more tender when made from scratch. They only take about five minutes extra to make, so forget the mix and see how pancakes are really supposed to taste.

BUTTERMILK PANCAKES WITH BLUEBERRY SYRUP

Serves 4

✳ SYRUP

2 cups fresh or frozen
    blueberries

1 cup water

1/2 cup sugar

✳ PANCAKES

1/4 cup butter

1 tablespoon white wine
    vinegar

1 cup milk

2 eggs

1 1/4 cups flour

1 tablespoon sugar

2 teaspoons baking powder

To prepare the syrup: Place the blueberries, water, and sugar in a small saucepan over medium-high heat for 10 minutes, or until it just begins to boil. Decrease the heat to medium-low and simmer, stirring occasionally, for 30 minutes.

Meanwhile, prepare the pancakes: Melt the butter and set it aside to cool. Place the vinegar in a liquid measuring cup and add enough milk to make 1 cup. Place the milk and eggs in a large bowl and whisk until thoroughly combined. Add the cooled butter and mix well. Add the flour, sugar, and baking powder and stir until smooth.

Heat a nonstick griddle or skillet over medium heat. Pour a small amount of oil on a paper towel and rub it over the pan. Pour 1/4 cup of batter at a time onto the griddle, leaving at least 2 inches between the pancakes to allow for spreading. Cook for 3 to 5 minutes,

or until the edges are dry and the pancakes are golden brown underneath. Turn the pancakes over with a spatula and cook for 1 minute, or until light brown.

Serve the pancakes with the blueberry syrup on the side.

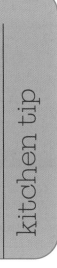

You will notice that whenever there is vinegar in a recipe we use either white wine vinegar or rice vinegar. We think they are interchangeable and use whichever one we happen to have in the cabinet. Regular distilled vinegar also works, but rice or white wine vinegars have milder flavors and aromas. Besides, we have a problem using something in our food that our mom uses to wash windows.

kitchen tip

Roman Apple Coffee Cake is just about the yummiest food in the world. The inside is moist and loaded with apples and the topping is sweet and crunchy, a perfect combination in my book. This is my grandmother's recipe. She serves it for dessert, but we figure that all the apples give us a great excuse to call it coffee cake and eat it for breakfast.

ROMAN APPLE COFFEE CAKE

Makes ONE 8-INCH CAKE

✳ CAKE

1¹/₂ cups flour

1 cup sugar

1 teaspoon baking powder

¹/₂ teaspoon baking soda

¹/₄ teaspoon salt

1 egg

¹/₂ cup milk

1 teaspoon vanilla

¹/₂ cup melted butter

4 medium apples

✳ TOPPING

¹/₄ cup flour

¹/₄ cup butter

1 cup firmly packed brown sugar

To prepare the cake: Preheat the oven to 350°F. Lightly butter or spray an 8-inch-square baking pan.

Stir together the flour, sugar, baking powder, baking soda, and salt in a large bowl. Using a spoon, form a well in the center of the flour mixture. In a small bowl, lightly beat the egg and pour into the well. Add the milk, vanilla, and melted butter to the well and stir until thoroughly combined.

Peel, halve, and remove the cores from the apples. Cut the apples into thin wedges and stir into the batter. Pour the batter into the baking pan and spread evenly.

To prepare the topping: Place the flour, butter, and brown sugar in a small bowl and mix well. Sprinkle the topping evenly over the cake.

Bake for 35 to 40 minutes, or until the top of the cake springs back when gently pressed.

> Fried Apple Rings are a great substitute for donuts. I actually learned to make these in Germany when I was an exchange student. My host family made them for special occasions. Although they are sprinkled with cinnamon sugar, the tart apples keep them from being overly sweet. They are best eaten warm, because when they cool, the juice from the apples can make the batter soggy.

FRIED APPLE RINGS

Makes 12 TO 15 APPLE RINGS

✱ APPLES

3 large Granny Smith apples

2 tablespoons lemon juice

2 tablespoons sugar

½ cup flour

Pinch of salt

1 egg

¾ cup carbonated water

1 egg white

Canola oil for deep frying

✱ TOPPING

¼ cup sugar

1 teaspoon cinnamon

To prepare the apples: Peel the apples and slice into ¼-inch-thick rings. Cut the core out of the center of each slice and place the apple slices in a bowl with the lemon juice and sugar. Gently toss the apples in the mixture until they are completely coated to prevent them from browning.

Place the flour and salt in another bowl. Separate the egg, adding the yolk to the flour and placing the white in a separate bowl. Add the carbonated water to the flour, and mix until smooth. Add the extra egg white to the one in the bowl and whip with a whisk or electric mixer on medium speed for 2 minutes, or until they form soft peaks. (When the beaters are lifted out of the egg whites, the whites will form peaks and the tips of the peaks will flop over as soon as the beaters pull away from the whites.) Gently fold the egg whites into the batter until just combined.

Place 2 inches of oil in a deep fryer or deep saucepan and warm over medium heat to about 300°F. If you don't have a thermometer for the oil, drop a small spoonful of batter into the oil. The batter should take at least 1 minute to brown on the first side and at least

30 seconds on the second side. If it cooks faster than that, the oil is too hot, and if it takes longer than 3 minutes total time, then the oil is too cool.

Dip the apple slices in the batter and carefully place them in the oil. Cook for 1 to 2 minutes, or until golden brown. Using a long-handled slotted spoon, turn them over and cook for 1 minute, or until golden brown. Remove the apple slices from the oil and place them on a paper towel–lined plate to drain.

To prepare the topping: Combine the sugar and cinnamon and sprinkle over the apple rings while they are still warm.

[continued]

kitchen chemistry

When separating eggs, always separate each individual egg white into a small bowl first and then place it in a larger bowl. That way if any egg yolk gets into the white you can throw it away and only have to waste one egg. Egg yolks contain fat and even the smallest bit of that fat will keep the egg whites from getting frothy.

kitchen safety

Always use a pot that is at least four inches deeper than the amount of oil you are using. This allows room for the food and for the oil to bubble up without going over the sides of the pan. If the oil does go over the sides of the pan, immediately turn off the flame and let the stove cool before cleaning. Although the chances are slim, if the oil overflows and starts on fire, do not use water to try to put it out. It will just make it worse. Sprinkling baking soda on a grease fire will put it out very quickly.

APPLE RINGS

FRIED

kitchen tip

Whipped egg whites become frothy because of the air that is forced into them. When the whipped egg whites are mixed with other ingredients, they must be handled gently or they will lose a lot of that air. Always fold in egg whites to add them: simply place them in the bowl with the other ingredients and, using a rubber spatula, scrape along one side of the bowl down to the bottom and come up the other side of the bowl, gently folding the other ingredients over the top of the egg whites and continuing the process until it is fairly well mixed. It is always better to have a few streaks of egg white left than to overmix and deflate the eggs.

SPINACH AND MUSHROOM QUICHE

Although quiche may sound fancy, it is really just an omelet with a crust. Here we use mushrooms and Swiss cheese, but you can use any type of cheese, vegetables, or breakfast meat. Just remember that any meat or vegetables should be cooked before being added to the eggs, because they will not cook much in the quiche.

Serves 6

8 ounces mushrooms

2 tablespoons butter

6 eggs

1 cup evaporated milk

1 1/2 cups Swiss cheese

1/2 cup frozen chopped spinach, unthawed

1/2 teaspoon salt

1 prepared, refrigerated pie crust

Trim the bottoms off of the mushroom stems, discard, and cut the mushrooms into 1/8- to 1/4-inch-thick slices. Melt the butter in a small sauté pan and add the mushrooms. Cook over medium-high heat for 10 to 15 minutes, stirring occasionally, or until golden brown. (It is normal for the mushrooms to release liquid as they cook, but it will cook away before they begin to brown.)

Preheat the oven to 325°F.

Whisk together the eggs and evaporated milk in a large bowl. Stir in the cheese, spinach, salt, and mushrooms.

If using a pie crust that comes folded, gently unfold it and press it into a pie pan. Using a fork, press the tines into the edge of the crust around the rim to make a simple pattern. Pour the egg mixture into the crust and bake for 30 to 35 minutes, or until lightly browned and the center is not jiggly.

Crepes are one of my favorite French desserts, so of course I had to come up with a way to also have them for breakfast. This strawberry filling is light and not too sweet, making it the perfect way to start your day. Crepes can be kept in the refrigerator for several days, so save any extras and eat them with jam, fresh fruit, or chocolate sauce.

CREPES WITH FRESH STRAWBERRIES AND CREAM

Serves 4

✳ CREPES

4 eggs

1 1/3 cups milk

2 tablespoons oil

1 cup flour

1/2 teaspoon salt

✳ FILLING

1 pound strawberries

4 ounces cream cheese

1 1/2 cups heavy cream

1/4 cup powdered sugar, plus extra for dusting

To prepare the crepes: Place the eggs in a blender and pulse a few times to break them up. Add the milk, oil, flour, and salt and blend until smooth.

Heat an 8-inch nonstick sauté pan over medium heat. Place a small amount of oil on a paper towel and rub it over the surface of the pan. Pour in 1/4 cup of the crepe batter and quickly swirl the pan, rolling the batter around until it covers the entire bottom of the pan. Cook for 2 minutes, or until the crepe is set in the center. Loosen the edges with a rubber spatula and turn the crepe over. Cook for 1 minute and remove from the pan. Repeat the process with the remaining batter, oiling the pan between each crepe. Stack the cooked crepes on top of each other and gently pull them apart when you are ready to use them, or separate them with pieces of waxed paper to keep them from sticking together.

To prepare the filling: Wash, stem, and slice the strawberries, draining them well.

Place the cream cheese in a large bowl and mix with an electric mixer on medium speed for 1 minute, or until fluffy. Add the heavy cream and beat on medium-high speed for 2 to 3 minutes, or until it forms a soft whipped cream. As the beaters are lifted out of the cream, they will form peaks, but the tips will flop over as soon as the cream pulls away from the beaters. Add the powdered sugar and mix on medium speed for 30 seconds, or until thoroughly incorporated.

Set aside $\frac{1}{2}$ cup of the sliced strawberries for garnish and gently stir the remaining strawberries into the cream.

Place a crepe in the center of each plate. Spoon about $\frac{1}{3}$ cup of the strawberry cream down the center of each crepe and fold in the sides to form a roll. Gently roll the crepes over so the seam sides are down and continue filling and folding the crepes until there are 3 rolled crepes on each plate. Sprinkle the crepes with powdered sugar, spoon any remaining cream in the center of the crepes, and top with the remaining strawberries.

kitchen tip

Whenever you are mixing cream cheese with other ingredients, always make sure to whip the cream cheese first to smooth it out. If you don't, the cream cheese will stay in small lumps and become almost impossible to get smooth.

The first time I made these I was staring into the refrigerator after school looking for targets of opportunity. (My mom calls this air conditioning the kitchen, but I prefer to think of it as allowing the food to breathe.) We had a couple of leftover baked potatoes and some cheese, so of course I thought potato skins. After that I started cooking extra potatoes on purpose, knowing I would have a great, quick snack the next day.

POTATO SKINS

Makes 12 POTATO SKINS

6 medium potatoes

6 slices thick-sliced bacon

2 tablespoons canola oil

1 1/2 cups shredded Cheddar

1/2 cup sour cream

2 tablespoons milk

2 tablespoons chopped chives

Preheat the oven to 375°F.

Wash the potatoes and poke each one several times with a fork. Bake the potatoes for 45 minutes, or until they are fairly soft when squeezed. Remove the potatoes from the oven and cool slightly.

Meanwhile, cut the bacon slices into 1/8- to 1/4-inch strips. Cook the bacon in a small sauté pan over medium heat for 15 minutes, or until crisp. Transfer the bacon to paper towels to drain.

Kitchen Vocab

When a recipe says chop, it generally doesn't matter what the pieces look like. For example, if you are cutting potatoes that are going to be mashed, it doesn't matter what shape they are, so they can be chopped. But if more precise pieces are required, then it would say diced. We give specific sizes for diced foods, but often recipes just say diced, small-diced, or large-diced. Small-diced is 1/4-inch cubes, large-diced is 3/4-inch cubes, and just "diced" means medium which is about 1/2-inch cubes.

kitchen tip

Hours of watching cooking shows have taught me that you should always snip herbs with kitchen scissors because cutting them with a knife bruises them. Although I have never seen a black-and-blue herb, it is faster and easier to control the size when snipping.

Preheat the broiler and adjust the oven rack to 4 to 5 inches away from the broiler. (If the rack is any closer, the potato skins will get too dark before they get crispy.)

Cut each potato in half lengthwise and scoop out most of the potato with a large spoon. (The insides can be saved to make Baked Potato Soup, page 51). Brush the potato skins inside and out with the oil and place them upside down on a baking sheet. Place under the broiler for 5 minutes. Turn the potato skins over and broil for 5 to 6 minutes, or until the potato skins are crispy.

Remove the pan from the oven and sprinkle some of the cheese and bacon bits into each potato skin. Return the pan to the broiler for 2 minutes, or until the cheese is melted.

Combine the sour cream, milk, and chives in a small bowl. Place the bowl of sour cream in the center of a large plate and arrange the potato skins around the bowl.

CARAMELIZED ONION, MUSHROOM, AND ROASTED RED PEPPER FOCACCIA

Even the thought of making yeast breads can be intimidating, but this recipe is pretty simple and always works. Because of the oil in the dough and all of the toppings, the dough can take a lot of abuse without being a problem. I top the focaccia with whatever we happen to have on hand. It's also great with sliced tomatoes, garlic, thyme, or mozzarella. This is one of those recipes for which the possibilities truly are endless.

Makes ONE 11 BY 17-INCH FOCACCIA

*DOUGH

2 cups warm water
(105°F to 115°F)

2 packages dry quick-rising
yeast

1 teaspoon salt

2 tablespoons olive oil

4 to 4½ cups flour plus
extra for kneading

8 sun-dried tomatoes
packed in oil

2 tablespoons chopped fresh
basil

2 tablespoons chopped fresh
oregano

¼ cup Parmesan

*TOPPINGS

1 red bell pepper

1 small onion

1 tablespoon olive oil

1 tablespoon butter

8 ounces mushrooms, sliced

3 slices provolone

Kosher salt

To prepare the dough: Stir together the water and yeast in a large bowl and let stand for 5 minutes, or until foamy. Stir in the salt and the olive oil. Gradually add the flour until the mixture forms a soft dough.

Lightly sprinkle a work surface with flour and place the dough in the center. Dip your hands in some flour to keep them from sticking to the dough, fold the dough in half, and push forward slightly on it with the heels of your hands. Rotate the dough a quarter turn, fold in half again, and push on it with the heels of your hands, dusting the dough with flour as necessary to keep it from sticking to your hands. (You may need up to ½ cup of additional flour.) Chop the sun-dried tomatoes into ¼- to ½-inch pieces. Add the sun-dried tomatoes, basil, oregano, and Parmesan to the dough and continue the turn, fold, and push process for 5 minutes, or until the dough is smooth and elastic. Spray a large bowl with cooking spray. Shape the dough into a ball and place it in the bowl, rolling the ball around in the bowl to lightly coat it with oil. Place the bowl in a warm spot, cover it with a kitchen towel, and let it rise for 45 minutes (the dough should almost double in size).

To prepare the toppings: Place the red bell pepper directly on the stove burner (or under a broiler if you have an electric stove) and cook over high heat, turning occasionally, for 15 minutes, or until the pepper is almost completely black on the outside. Place the blackened pepper in a small bowl and cover tightly with plastic wrap. Let stand for 10 minutes to loosen the skin. Peel the skin off and cut the pepper in half. Discard the seeds and cut the pepper into ¼-inch-thick strips.

Peel the onion and cut in ¼-inch-thick rings. Cut each ring in half and place them in a small sauté pan with the olive oil and butter. Cook over medium heat for 5 minutes. Add the mushrooms and cook, stirring occasionally, for 10 minutes, or until the onions and mushrooms are golden brown. (It is normal for the

[continued]

mushrooms to release liquid as they cook; the liquid will cook away before the mushrooms begin to brown.) Remove from the heat and set aside.

Lightly butter or spray an 11 by 17-inch baking sheet. Place the dough on the baking sheet and gently pull out the dough until it fills the entire pan in a fairly even layer.

Gently arrange the red pepper, mushrooms, and onion on top of the dough. Rip the provolone in pieces and place it on the dough. Sprinkle the kosher salt over the dough and let it rise for 30 minutes.

Preheat the oven to 400°F.

Bake the focaccia for 30 to 40 minutes, or until golden brown. Remove it from the oven and let it cool in the pan.

Kitchen Vocab

The process of folding, pressing, and turning the dough is called kneading. We checked our sources and found out why it is so important. Kneading causes the gluten strands in the flour to expand and stretch, enabling the dough to hold in the gas formed by the yeast, which helps the dough rise and form the light structure of the bread. Kneading thoroughly is the trick to assure that you won't be baking bricks.

Gluten is a protein contained in most flours. Gluten levels vary in different types of flour, with bread flour having the highest gluten content and cake flour having the lowest. Unless a recipe specifically calls for bread or cake flour, just use all-purpose flour, which falls somewhere in the middle.

Sautéing the onions and mushrooms until they are golden brown is called caramelizing. The natural sugars in the food liquefy during cooking and become golden brown, adding a sweetness and rich flavor that can't be achieved in any other way.

CHILI CHEESE DIP

This dip is so easy it's embarrassing, but we included it anyway because we love it. We usually make it in two smaller pans, one using chili with meat for me and one with vegetarian chili for Megan. This is the perfect after-school snack, taking less than ten minutes from walking in the door to munching away in front of the television.

Makes ONE 10-INCH PAN

8 ounces cream cheese

1 (15-ounce) can chili with beans

1¹/₂ cups Cheddar

Tortilla chips

Spread the cream cheese evenly in the bottom of a 10-inch microwave-safe pan or dish. Spread the chili over the cream cheese and top with the cheese. Microwave on high for 4 to 5 minutes, or until the cheese is completely melted.

Serve with the tortilla chips.

see photo on page 39

kitchen chemistry

Here is some real kitchen chemistry. I got this from my AP Chemistry teacher and thought it was instructions for a lab experiment. It was titled "Edible polymers: A partial thermal degradation of carbon dioxide–foamed saccharides with protein inclusions." The directions were to combine 1¹/₂ cups sucrose, 1 cup glucose solution, and ¹/₂ cup H_2O and bring to a boil. Add 3 tablespoons solidified mixed esters and heat to 250° F. Add 2¹/₄ cups protein pellets and heat to 300°F. Remove from the heat and stir in ¹/₂ teaspoon sodium chloride, ¹/₄ teaspoon sodium bicarbonate, and ³/₄ teaspoon 4-hydroxy-3-methoxy-benzaldehyde. After wracking my brain trying to figure out what solidified mixed esters and protein pellets were, she told me the common names of the ingredients (sugar, corn syrup, water, butter, peanuts, salt, baking soda, and vanilla). It was a recipe for peanut brittle.

Pot stickers are one of my family's favorite appetizers. In fact, my cousins even eat them as the main course. My problem with ordering them from a restaurant is that they never have a vegetarian option, so I prefer to make them at home, where I can sauté chopped cabbage to substitute for the pork.

POT STICKERS

Makes 25 POT STICKERS

✱ POT STICKERS

1 small clove garlic

3 green onions

1½ teaspoons chopped cilantro

1 egg yolk

½ teaspoon salt

8 ounces ground pork

25 3-inch round wonton wrappers

1 tablespoon vegetable oil

✱ SAUCE

2 tablespoons soy sauce

1 tablespoon rice vinegar

1 tablespoon sesame oil

To prepare the pot stickers: Smash the garlic clove by placing it on a cutting board, laying the blade of a large knife flat on top of the garlic, and pressing the knife with the heel of your hand. Remove the papery skin and finely chop the garlic.

Cut off the root ends of the green onions and thinly slice the white and about 1 inch of the green parts. Set aside 1 tablespoon for the sauce and place the remaining onion in a medium bowl.

Add the garlic, cilantro, egg yolk, salt, and ground pork to the bowl and mix well. (I know it sounds gross, but your hands are the best utensil to get this mixed well. Of course, make sure they are clean and be sure to wash them after you've mixed the filling and before you touch anything else.)

Dip your finger in water and wet the entire edge of 1 wonton wrapper. Place a small spoonful of the pork mixture in the center of the wrapper and fold the wrapper in half to enclose the mixture. Firmly press the edges to seal the pot sticker. Just before you seal the pot sticker completely, push gently around the filling

to remove any air pockets. Repeat the process with the remaining wrappers and filling. Lay the finished pot stickers on a baking sheet, keeping them separate. (If the pot stickers touch they will stick together and tear holes in the wrappers.)

Bring a large pot of salted water to a boil. Carefully drop a few of the pot stickers at a time into the water and cook for 2 minutes, or until they float to the top of the pan. Remove the pot stickers with a slotted spoon and place them on the baking sheet.

Heat 1 teaspoon of the vegetable oil in a large nonstick sauté pan over medium-high heat. Place one-third of the pot stickers in the pan and cook for 2 to 3 minutes, or until golden brown on one side. Place the browned pot stickers on a serving plate and repeat the process with the remaining pot stickers.

To prepare the sauce: Place the soy sauce, rice vinegar, and sesame oil in a small bowl and mix well with a fork. Sprinkle the 1 tablespoon of reserved green onions on the sauce and place the sauce on the pot sticker plate.

KITCHEN DISASTER

When my aunt was first learning to cook, she decided to try to make veal scaloppine. She added the two cloves of garlic that the recipe called for and soon the smell of garlic was permeating the entire house. What she didn't know was that when you buy garlic it comes in bulbs. The smaller pieces that make up the bulb are called "cloves." So instead of two cloves she used two bulbs. Needless to say, it was not her best dinner.

VEGETABLE MAKI ROLLS

m

The key to making good maki rolls is to never refrigerate the rice. When rice has been refrigerated it becomes hard, and it completely changes the texture of the rolls. You can buy tied-together sheets of tiny bamboo strips, called "sushi mats," for a few dollars. They make it easier to keep the rolls tight, but if you don't have one, plastic wrap also works pretty well.

Makes 14 TO 16 PIECES

✳ RICE

1 cup sushi rice

1¼ cups water

1 tablespoon sugar

2 tablespoons rice vinegar

To prepare the rice: Place the rice and water in a small saucepan and bring to a boil. Cover and cook over medium heat for 20 minutes. Remove from the heat and let cool to room temperature. Place the sugar and rice vinegar in a small bowl and stir until the sugar dissolves. Sprinkle the vinegar mixture over the rice and toss well to coat the rice thoroughly.

Kitchen Vocab

Wasabi, the spicy green paste used in sushi, is made from the root of an Asian plant and is often called "Japanese horseradish." It can be purchased in paste or powdered form. When used in powder form, as we did here, it can be made into a paste by adding water or soy sauce.

Nori is the paper-thin sheets of dried seaweed used to wrap sushi. Nori is available in many grocery stores and all Asian markets.

✳ ROLLS

1 small carrot

1/2 cucumber

1 avocado

1 teaspoon wasabi powder

2 teaspoons water

2 sheets nori

To prepare the maki rolls: Peel the carrot and cucumber. Scrape the seeds from the cucumber and cut the carrot and cucumber into long strips about 1/4 to 3/8 inch wide. Cut the avocado in half and sink the knife blade a bit into the pit and wriggle the knife slightly to pop the pit out. Beginning at the larger end of the avocado, slide a spoon between the skin and flesh and gently remove the flesh from each half. Cut each half lengthwise into 1/4-inch-thick slices.

Place the wasabi powder and water in a small bowl and stir until smooth.

Lay a sheet of nori on the bamboo sushi mat or plastic wrap and orient it so that you will be able to roll it away from you. Place half of the rice on the nori. Wet your hands to keep the rice from sticking to them and spread the rice over the nori, leaving a 2-inch border at the top spreading all the way to the bottom and extending about 1/4 inch beyond the nori on both sides. Sprinkle half of the wasabi mixture over the rice. Lay 1 row of carrot, 1 row of cucumber, and 2 rows of avocado across the center of the rice. Using the sushi mat or plastic wrap, carefully roll up the maki roll, starting from the bottom. Run your hands over the roll as you go to create a smooth, firm roll. Wet the top border of the nori with water and firmly press the edge to seal the roll. Repeat the process with the remaining ingredients. (If you are preparing these ahead of time, wrap them in plastic wrap and set aside at room temperature for up to 2 hours.)

Trim the ragged ends from the maki roll with a serrated knife and cut each maki roll into 7 or 8 pieces.

NACHOS WITH SALSA AND GUACAMOLE

Serves 6 TO 8

✳ SALSA

4 ripe plum tomatoes

1/2 small red onion

1 jalapeño chile

1 (8-ounce) can tomato sauce

2 tablespoons chopped cilantro

1 tablespoon lime juice

✳ GUACAMOLE

1 small clove garlic

1/2 teaspoon salt

1/2 jalapeño chile

1 tomato

1/4 small red onion

2 avocados

1 1/2 tablespoons lime juice

To prepare the salsa: Cut the tomatoes in half and remove the seeds. Dice the tomatoes into 1/4-inch pieces and place them in a bowl. Dice the onion into 1/4-inch pieces and place them in the bowl. Cut the jalapeño in half and remove the seeds. Finely dice the jalapeño and add it to the bowl. Add the tomato sauce, cilantro, and lime juice to the bowl and stir until combined. Cover the bowl with plastic wrap and place it in the refrigerator until you are ready to serve the salsa.

To prepare the guacamole: Smash the garlic clove by placing it on a cutting board, laying the blade of a large knife flat on top of the garlic, and pressing the knife with the heel of your hand. Remove the papery skin and finely chop the garlic. Place the garlic in a medium bowl and add the salt. Using the back of a spoon, mash the garlic and salt together to form a paste.

Cut the jalapeño in half and remove the seeds. Finely chop half of the jalapeño and place it in the bowl with the garlic.

✳ NACHOS

12 ounces tortilla chips

1 can black beans

2 cups shredded Cheddar

½ cup sour cream

Cut the tomato in quarters and remove the seeds. Finely chop the tomato and add to the bowl. Finely chop the onion and place it in the bowl. Cut the avocados in half and scoop the flesh into the bowl, discarding the pit. Add the lime juice to the bowl and stir well. Smash the avocado with the back of the spoon, until the mixture is fairly smooth.

Place the guacamole in a serving bowl and immediately lay a piece of plastic wrap on the surface. (The avocado will turn a nasty brown color if exposed to the air for too long.) Put the guacamole in the refrigerator until you are ready to serve it.

To prepare the nachos: Preheat the oven to 375°F.

Spread about one-third of the chips on a large ovenproof serving platter. Drain the black beans, spoon some of them over the chips and sprinkle with some of the cheese. Repeat the process, forming 3 layers of chips, beans, and cheese.

Bake for 5 minutes, or until the cheese is melted.

Spoon the sour cream into the center of the nachos and serve with the salsa and guacamole on the side.

We call for plum tomatoes in most of our recipes because they seem to be the most consistent in size, flavor, and texture from season to season. But that doesn't mean you can't use other types of tomatoes. In fact, during the summer when tomatoes are in season, we'd probably use another type, but during the rest of the year when they are out of season and most of them are pale and mealy, plum tomatoes are your best bet.

kitchen tip

An empanada is basically a Spanish turnover that is filled with meat and vegetables. I don't generally like my food too spicy, but this is one place where you should use medium or hot salsa so the filling will stand out over the dough. These are really easy to make, especially if you use leftover chicken, and they look like they were store-bought.

CHICKEN EMPANADAS

Makes 20 3-INCH EMPANADAS

½ boneless, skinless chicken breast

½ cup salsa

½ cup shredded Jack or Cheddar cheese

2 prepared, refrigerated pie crusts

1 egg

Bring a small saucepan of water to a boil. Add the chicken breast and simmer over medium-low heat for 10 minutes. Drain the chicken and let it cool slightly. Cut the chicken into chunks and shred it into small pieces. Combine the chicken, salsa, and cheese in a bowl and set aside.

Preheat the oven to 375°F (unless you plan to bake the empanadas at another time).

If using pie crusts that come folded, gently unfold them and lay them on a flat work surface. Using a 3-inch round cookie cutter, cut 10 circles from each crust. Place a small spoonful of the chicken mixture in the center of one of the dough circles. Using your finger, wet the edge of the dough circle and fold it in half to enclose the chicken mixture. Firmly press the edges with a fork to seal the empanada. Repeat the process with the remaining dough circles. (At this point you may refrigerate the empanadas for several hours or freeze them for up to 1 month.)

Place the empanadas on an ungreased baking sheet. Beat the egg in a small bowl and lightly brush the top of each empanada. (You will not use all of the egg.) Bake for 20 to 25 minutes, or until golden brown. (Frozen empanadas do not need to be thawed before baking, but they will take an extra 10 to 15 minutes to bake.)

BLT DIP

I have been making this for every family party for many years, but it has always puzzled me that it is called BLT when there is no lettuce. I tried calling it BT Dip for a while, but after having to repeatedly explain that it was BLT Dip without the L, I finally gave up. So BLT Dip it is. For you vegetarians, this is just as good made with soy bacon.

Makes APPROXIMATELY 2 CUPS

½ cup mayonnaise

½ cup sour cream

8 ounces thick-sliced bacon

2 plum tomatoes

7 slices bread

Combine the mayonnaise and sour cream in a small bowl and refrigerate overnight. (It is best refrigerated overnight, but in a pinch an hour or two will do.)

Cut the bacon into ¼- to ½-inch strips and place them in a sauté pan. Cook over medium heat, stirring occasionally, for 15 minutes, or until crisp. Transfer to paper towels to drain.

Cut the tomatoes in half and remove the seeds. Dice the tomatoes into ¼- to ½-inch pieces.

Add the bacon and tomato to the mayonnaise mixture and stir well. Place the dip in a serving bowl and set in the center of a serving plate.

Toast the bread, cut each slice into quarters, and arrange on the serving platter.

BUFFALO WINGS

Makes 12 TO 14 WINGS

¼ cup melted butter

¼ cup Louisiana Hot Sauce

1 pound chicken wings

Preheat the oven to 375°F.

Combine the butter and hot sauce in a small bowl. Place the chicken wings on an ungreased baking sheet and pour the sauce over the wings. Toss the wings in the sauce until completely coated. Bake for 30 minutes, turning once, or until the chicken is thoroughly cooked.

CINNAMON STICKS

Cinnamon Sticks are one of the simplest things to make, and they are really tasty. But, I learned the hard way that when dealing with puff pastry, you should actually follow the directions on the box (something I don't do often). Puff pastry should always be thawed in the refrigerator and the sheets should be unfolded as soon as they come out of the refrigerator. The closer they get to room temperature, the more likely they are to stick together.

Makes 10 CINNAMON STICKS

1 sheet puff pastry, thawed

1 egg

1 teaspoon cinnamon

2 tablespoons sugar

Preheat the oven to 400°F. Lightly butter or spray a baking sheet.

Unfold the puff pastry and place it on a large work surface. Beat the egg in a small bowl and brush it over the puff pastry, coating it lightly. (You won't need to use all of the egg.)

Combine the cinnamon and sugar in another small bowl and sprinkle evenly over the puff pastry. Cut the puff pastry into 1-inch-wide strips. Twist each strip several times and place it on the baking sheet. Bake for 12 minutes, or until light brown.

STRAWBERRIES WITH MARSHMALLOW DIP

This is another embarrassingly easy recipe, but again, it's so good we just couldn't leave it out. We always have this for family barbecues because it is light and refreshing and it doesn't break down in the heat. But, since there aren't enough barbecues to suit my tastes, I usually make it as an after-school snack.

Serves 4

1 pound fresh strawberries

4 ounces cream cheese

1 cup marshmallow fluff

Wash the strawberries and drain well.

Whip the cream cheese with an electric mixer on medium speed for 2 minutes, or until fluffy. Add the marshmallow fluff and mix for 1 minute, or until completely combined.

Spoon the fluff mixture into a serving bowl. Set the bowl on a serving plate and arrange the strawberries around the bowl.

I love this dish! I know you're thinking, ewww, goat cheese, but don't knock it 'til you've tried it. It has a great, soft texture and a slightly tangy flavor that is very mild when heated. The warm cheese with the tomato sauce and bread is so good that I can make a meal out of it.

GOAT CHEESE AND TOMATO CROSTINI

Serves 4 TO 6

1-pound French baguette

2 tablespoons olive oil

1 teaspoon kosher salt

4 ounces goat cheese

1 (6-ounce) can tomato paste

1/4 cup cream

1 tablespoon sugar

Preheat the oven to 375°F.

Cut the baguette into 1/4- to 3/8-inch-thick slices and place them on an ungreased baking sheet. Brush both sides of the bread slices with the olive oil and sprinkle with the salt. Bake them for 5 to 7 minutes, or until they are light brown and toasted.

Place a 3-inch round mold, ramekin, or small bowl in the center of a shallow 6-inch microwave-safe bowl and press the goat cheese into it. Quickly turn the mold over and carefully lift it away to leave a round disk of goat cheese. Or, if you don't have a mold, simply shape the goat cheese into a round mound in the center of the microwave-safe bowl.

Combine the tomato paste, cream, and sugar in a small bowl and pour over the goat cheese. Cover the bowl with plastic wrap, and microwave on high for 5 minutes, or until the tomato sauce is hot but the cheese still holds its shape. (When it's overcooked, the edges of the cheese will begin to melt into the sauce. But it won't affect the flavor at all, just the look.)

Serve hot with the toasted bread slices on the side.

DEVILED EGGS

Deviled eggs were the very first thing I learned to make by myself when I was five years old. My mom would boil the eggs for me, and I would peel them and cut them in half using my pumpkin-carving knife. She talks about how many pockmarked, lumpy eggs we ate, but I just remember being really proud of myself.

Makes 12 DEVILED EGGS

6 eggs

1/4 cup mayonnaise

1 teaspoon prepared
    mustard

Salt and pepper

Gently place the eggs in a medium saucepan and cover them completely with cold water. Bring the water to a boil and simmer over medium heat for 10 minutes. Turn the heat off and let the eggs stand in the water until they are cool.

Peel the eggs and slice each in half lengthwise. Separate the egg yolks from the whites, placing the yolks in a bowl and the whites on a serving plate.

Mash the egg yolks with a fork until they are finely crumbled. Add the mayonnaise and mustard to the yolks and stir until smooth. Season to taste with salt and pepper.

Spoon some of the filling into each egg half and set the halves on a serving plate.

We know that everyone knows how to peel an egg, but our mom taught us a trick that makes it easier, especially when you hit the ones whose shells seem to be glued to the inside. Crack the wide end of the egg and roll the end around a little to break up the shell. Pull off some of the cracked shell, slide a spoon between the egg and the shell, and circle it around the egg. On the easy eggs, the shell will pop right off. On the harder eggs, you may cut into the egg white a little, but at least it will still have a nice shape and none of the pits you would get peeling it bit by bit.

kitchen tip

This is another idea that we swiped from our favorite Chinese restaurant. They are extremely easy to make and really tasty. The worst part about these is the oil smell in the house from deep-frying. We have a deep fryer so I just plug it in outside on our patio. If you don't have a deep fryer, keep the air freshener handy.

CRAB RANGOONS

Makes ABOUT 20 RANGOONS

2 green onions

8 ounces cream cheese

1 (6-ounce) can crabmeat

20 3-inch square wonton wrappers

Canola oil for deep-frying

1/2 cup bottled sweet and sour sauce

Cut the root ends off the green onions and thinly slice the white and about 1 inch of the green parts.

Place the cream cheese and onions in a small bowl. Drain the crabmeat and add to the bowl. Using the back of a spoon, mash the onions and crabmeat into the cream cheese until they are completely incorporated.

Dip your finger in water and wet the entire edge of 1 wonton wrapper. Place a small spoonful of the crab mixture in the center of the wrapper and fold in half to form a triangle. Firmly press the edges to seal the rangoon. Just before you seal the last edge, push gently around the filling to remove any air pockets. Repeat the process with the remaining wrappers and filling. (Make sure the edges are sealed really well or the filling will leak out during cooking, and while they will still taste good, it kind of defeats the purpose.)

Place about 1½ inches of oil in a small, deep saucepan or deep fryer and heat to 350°F. (If you don't have a thermometer, fold up an extra wonton wrapper and drop it in the oil. The oil should bubble up and it should take about 1 minute for the wonton wrapper to get golden brown.)

Carefully place a few of the crab rangoons one at a time in the hot oil and cook for 1 minute on each side,

or until they turn light golden brown. Remove them with a slotted spoon and drain on paper towels.

Place the hot crab rangoons on a serving plate and serve with the sweet and sour sauce.

soups & salads

This is Megan's version of split pea soup, my version skips the croutons and includes ham. But, because we occasionally have to make something she will eat, I just add the ham to my bowl. If you don't have a vegetarian in your house, putting ham or a ham bone in the soup while it is cooking adds a great flavor.

SPLIT PEA SOUP

Serves 8 TO 10

✳ SOUP

1 pound dried split peas

2 carrots

1 onion

2 bay leaves

12 cups water

Salt and pepper

✳ CROUTONS

5 slices bread

1/3 cup melted butter

1/2 teaspoon garlic powder

To prepare the soup: Pour the peas into a stockpot and carefully check them for any foreign objects. (I know it sounds weird, but occasionally small stones will slip through during processing.)

Peel the carrots and onion and dice them into about 1/2-inch pieces. Place the carrots, onion, bay leaves, and water into the stockpot and bring to a boil over medium-high heat. Decrease the heat to low and simmer, stirring occasionally, for 1 1/2 to 2 hours, or until the peas have broken down. Season to taste with salt and pepper.

Meanwhile, prepare the croutons: Preheat the oven to 350°F.

Cut the bread into 1/2-inch cubes and place them on a baking sheet. Combine the butter and garlic powder in a small bowl and pour over the bread cubes. Toss the bread cubes until they are evenly coated and bake them for 10 minutes, or until they are golden brown.

Ladle the soup into bowls and top with the croutons.

CORN CHOWDER

When our mom makes corn chowder, she cuts the corn off the cob and cooks the corncobs and husks for hours to make corn broth. I think not. I simply open a can of corn and use the liquid in the can. In my opinion, it's just as good (but don't tell her I said that).

Serves 4

1 small onion

¹/₂ red bell pepper

1 large red potato

3 tablespoons butter

3 tablespoons flour

1 (14-ounce) can corn

3 cups milk

Salt and pepper

Peel the onion and dice it into ¹/₄-inch pieces. Remove the seeds from the red bell pepper, and dice it into ¹/₄-inch pieces. Peel the potato and dice it into ¹/₂-inch pieces.

Place the onion, red bell pepper, potato, and butter in a large saucepan and cook over medium heat, stirring occasionally, for 10 minutes, or until the potatoes are just tender. Stir in the flour and cook for 1 to 2 minutes, or until bubbly. Add the corn and the liquid from the can and stir until the liquid is completely mixed into the flour. Add 1 cup of the milk and stir until smooth. Add the remaining 2 cups of milk and cook, stirring occasionally, for 10 to 15 minutes, or until it just begins to boil. Season to taste with salt and pepper. Decrease the heat to low and cook for 10 minutes.

This is one of my favorite soups. The soup itself doesn't have a ton of flavor, but once you put the cheese and bacon on it, oh man, it's super good. Megan uses Bacos instead of the bacon, and every single time she points out that Bacos were the first soy product ever produced (like I care).

BAKED POTATO SOUP

Serves 4

2 potatoes

2 slices thick-sliced bacon

$^{1}/_{2}$ small onion

3 tablespoons butter

3 tablespoons flour

4 cups milk

Salt and pepper

$^{1}/_{2}$ cup shredded Cheddar

Preheat the oven to 375°F.

Wash the potatoes and pierce several times with a fork. Bake them for 45 minutes, or until they are just soft. Remove them from the oven and let them cool. Peel the potatoes and cut into $^{1}/_{2}$- to $^{3}/_{4}$-inch pieces.

Meanwhile, place a paper towel on a microwave-safe plate and lay the bacon slices in the center. Fold the excess paper towel over the bacon and microwave on high for 2 minutes, or until the bacon is crisp. Allow the bacon to cool and break into small pieces.

Peel the onion and dice it into $^{1}/_{4}$-inch pieces. Place the onion and butter in a large saucepan and cook over medium heat, stirring occasionally, for 5 to 7 minutes, or until the onion is translucent. Stir in the flour and cook for 1 to 2 minutes, or until bubbly. Add 1 cup of the milk and stir until smooth. Add the remaining 3 cups of milk and the potatoes and cook, stirring occasionally, for 7 to 10 minutes, or until it just begins to boil. Season to taste with salt and pepper. Decrease the heat to low and cook for 5 minutes.

Ladle the soup into 4 bowls and sprinkle the cheese and bacon bits over the soup.

kitchen chemistry

Poking holes in the potatoes before cooking is an extremely important step. As they cook, the liquid in the potatoes turns to steam, and without holes to release the steam, they will explode. Not good. Believe us, they will make a huge mess in the oven, and it will smell really bad.

kitchen tip

Figuring out which potatoes to buy can be confusing. The most common types of potatoes found in stores are red, russet (also called Idaho), and Yukon gold. Red potatoes are less starchy so they hold their shape better than the others. They are great just boiled, and they are perfect for potato salad or fried potatoes. (We use them in this recipe because they won't fall apart or make the soup grainy.) Russets, which are high in starch, are great for baking, boiling, or mashing. And Yukon golds, which have medium starch, are good for boiling, mashing, or roasting.

I was intimidated by the prospect of making a broccoli cheese soup, but I like it so much, I had to try. The recipe we came up with turned out to be one of the fastest, easiest soup recipes I've ever tried. Just to clarify, a bunch of broccoli is what you buy rubber-banded together in the store: a stalk is one of the pieces within the rubber band, and florets are the flowery tops.

m

BROCCOLI CHEESE SOUP

Serves 4

½ bunch of broccoli

3 tablespoons butter

3 tablespoons flour

4 cups milk

4 slices American cheese

Salt and pepper

¼ cup shredded Cheddar

Bring a large saucepan of water to a boil. Cut the broccoli florets from the stems and discard the stems. Cut the florets into bite-size pieces and cook in the boiling water for 5 minutes, or until slightly crunchy. Drain and set aside.

Melt the butter in the same saucepan over medium heat and stir in the flour. Cook for 2 to 3 minutes, or until bubbly. Add 1 cup of the milk and stir until smooth. Add the remaining 3 cups of milk and cook, stirring occasionally, for 7 to 10 minutes, or until it just begins to boil.

Reduce the heat to low and add the American cheese, stirring until it is completely melted. Season to taste with salt and pepper. Reserve 4 of the broccoli florets for garnish and stir the remaining broccoli into the soup.

Ladle the soup into 4 bowls. Sprinkle some of the Cheddar in the center of each bowl and top with a piece of broccoli.

Kitchen Vocab

Cooking briefly in boiling water is called **blanching**. It is used either to cook vegetables or just to brighten and set their color. The amount of time for blanching depends on what you want the end result to be, but in the case of green vegetables, they should never be blanched for more than 7 minutes or the color will become pale and the vegetables soggy. If you are blanching vegetables to brighten the color or to just cook them slightly, you will need to **shock** them. This is done by immediately placing them in a bowl of ice water to completely stop the cooking process and avoid residual cooking from the heat already in the vegetables.

m

Cheese, or no cheese, that is the question. I like cheese melted on top of the croutons on onion soup, but I also like the crunchiness you get when you add the croutons just a few at a time. So depending on my mood, I will either melt a couple of slices of provolone or Swiss cheese over the croutons, or not. But for the best of both worlds, I sometimes melt the cheese over the top and then push it into the soup and add more croutons as I go.

FRENCH ONION SOUP

Serves 6

✳ SOUP

3 onions

¹/₄ cup butter

2 (14-ounce) cans beef broth

1 (14-ounce) can chicken broth

Salt and pepper

✳ CROUTONS

5 slices bread

¹/₃ cup melted butter

¹/₂ teaspoon garlic powder

To prepare the soup: Peel the onions and cut into ¹/₈- to ¹/₄-inch-thick rings. Place the butter and onions in a large saucepan and cook over medium heat for 20 minutes, or until the onions begin to brown. Add the beef and chicken broth to the pan and simmer for 30 minutes. Season to taste with salt and pepper.

Meanwhile, prepare the croutons: Preheat the oven to 350°F.

Cut the bread into ¹/₂-inch cubes and place them on a baking sheet. Combine the butter and garlic powder in a small bowl and pour over the bread cubes. Toss the bread cubes until they are evenly coated and bake them for 10 minutes, or until they are golden brown.

Ladle the soup into bowls and sprinkle with a few croutons. Serve the remaining croutons on the side.

We usually use yellow onions because that's what our mom buys. (We'd like to tell you it's more scientific than that, but it's not.) But what we do know is that onions come in three categories: mild, sweet, and strong. Mild onions include green onions, pearl onions, leeks, and shallots. Strong onions include yellow and white onions. And sweet include red, Maui, Spanish, and Vidalia onions. For our recipes, any of the strong or sweet onions will work well. When we use any of the mild varieties, we call for them by name.

kitchen tip

> This is the way the rest of my family makes of wonton soup. When I make this for myself, I use vegetable broth and sauté a cup of cabbage to use instead of the pork. I also like to whisk in a beaten egg before the wontons go in for my own version of egg drop–wonton soup.

m

WONTON SOUP

Serves 4

✻ WONTONS

1 small clove garlic

1 teaspoon chopped cilantro

4 ounces ground pork

12 3-inch-square wonton wrappers

✻ SOUP

8 ounces mushrooms

1 tablespoon canola oil

1 cup shredded Chinese or Napa cabbage

3 (14-ounce) cans chicken broth

Salt and pepper

2 green onions

To prepare the wontons: Smash the garlic clove by placing it on a cutting board, laying the blade of a large knife flat on top of the garlic, and pressing the knife with the heel of your hand. Remove the papery skin and finely chop the garlic.

Place the garlic, cilantro, and ground pork in a small bowl and mix well.

Dip your finger in water and wet the entire edge of 1 wonton wrapper. Place a small spoonful of the pork mixture in the center of the wrapper and fold in half to form a triangle. Firmly press the edges to seal the wonton. Just before you seal the last edge, push gently around the filling to remove any air pockets. Repeat the process with the remaining wrappers and filling.

Although we didn't use this method in any of these recipes, we made this mistake in earlier attempts at making creamed soups, so we decided we better mention it just in case. When you puree hot ingredients, it is a good idea to blend them in small batches and make sure to put a towel over the blender and hold the top down firmly. Because the hot ingredients release a lot of steam when pureed, putting the top on the blender will trap the steam inside; it will build up and eventually blow the top off of the blender and spray hot liquid everywhere, and we do mean everywhere. It will spray all over you, the counter, the walls, and even the ceiling. And believe me, there is nothing fun about standing at the sink running cold water over your burns while soup is dripping on your head.

KITCHEN DISASTER

Lay the finished wontons on a plate or baking sheet, keeping them separate. (If the wontons touch they will stick together and tear holes in the wrappers.)

To prepare the soup: Cut the mushrooms into 1/4-inch-thick slices. Heat the oil in a large saucepan over medium- high heat and add the mushrooms. Cook for 10 minutes, or until the mushrooms are tender. (It is normal for the mushrooms to release liquid as they cook; it will cook away before they begin to brown.) Add the cabbage and cook for 2 minutes, or until the cabbage is wilted. Add the chicken broth to the pan and bring to a boil. Season to taste with salt and pepper. Decrease the heat to medium and add the wontons. Cook for 3 to 4 minutes, or until the wontons float to the top of the pan.

Cut off the root ends of the green onions and thinly slice the white and about 1 inch of the green parts. Ladle the soup into bowls and sprinkle with the green onions over the top.

Serves 4

❄ DRESSING

1 red bell pepper

1 cup sour cream

1 teaspoon Tabasco Sauce

Salt and pepper

❄ SALAD

3 small tomatoes

4 cups salad mix

1 (15-ounce) can black beans

1 (4-ounce) can black olives

1 (14-ounce) can corn

4 tortilla shell bowls

1 cup shredded Cheddar

Sour cream

To prepare the dressing: Place the red bell pepper directly on the stove burner (or under a broiler if you have an electric stove) and cook over high heat, turning occasionally, for 15 minutes, or until the pepper is almost completely black on the outside. Place the blackened pepper in a small bowl and cover tightly with plastic wrap. Let stand for 10 minutes to loosen the skin. Peel the skin off, cut the pepper in half, and discard the seeds.

Place the roasted pepper in a blender with the sour cream and Tobasco sauce and puree until smooth. Season to taste with salt and pepper.

To prepare the salad: Cut the tomatoes in half and remove the seeds. Dice the tomatoes into 1/2-inch pieces and set aside. Place the salad mix in a large bowl. Drain the black beans, black olives, and corn and add to the bowl. Pour the dressing in the bowl and toss until the lettuce is completely coated.

Divide the lettuce mixture among the tortilla bowls and sprinkle some of the cheese on each salad. Place some of the chopped tomatoes in the center of each salad and top with a spoonful of sour cream.

TACO SALAD

Taco Salad is awesome because it is literally a whole meal in one salad—and a vegetarian meal at that. If you want to add meat to the salad, you can cook and drain 1 pound of ground beef, stir in 1 tablespoon of chile powder, and spoon it onto the salad before you add the cheese. Tortilla shell bowls can be difficult to find, but you can just line a bowl with tortilla chips and get the same effect.

This is one of my favorite after-school snacks. It tastes great and it makes a lot, so I can eat it for a few days in a row. Although it tastes better cold, I am usually too impatient (and hungry) to wait for it to chill, so I eat it warm the first day and then cold the rest of the time.

TUNA AND MACARONI SALAD

Serves 4

8 ounces uncooked
   macaroni noodles

1 cup frozen peas

1 (6-ounce) can tuna

1/2 cup mayonnaise

Salt and pepper

Bring a large pot of salted water to a boil and add the macaroni. Cook over medium heat for 7 to 8 minutes, or until just cooked. Place the frozen peas in a colander and drain the macaroni by pouring it over the peas.

Drain the tuna and place it in a large bowl. Add the mayonnaise and stir until well combined. Add the macaroni and peas to the bowl and stir until the macaroni is completely coated with the mayonnaise. Season to taste with salt and pepper. Cover the salad with plastic wrap and put it in the refrigerator until you are ready to serve it.

Kitchen Vocab

A **colander** is shaped like a bowl and has lots of little holes for draining or straining liquid out of foods. A **fine-meshed sieve** is generally smaller and has a metal mesh with very fine holes. Which one we choose to use depends on the amount of food we are draining or how large the stuff is that we are trying to strain out. A colander is larger and works well for draining pasta or vegetables, but a fine-meshed sieve works best for straining lumps out of gravy. (Not that we ever have that problem.)

Okay, the truth is, I'm not a big fan of lettuce, but I love steak. So this recipe was my mom's way of getting me to eat salad. She figured if she put enough stuff on it that I liked, I wouldn't notice the lettuce. Well, I'm not that stupid—I noticed the lettuce. But, her strategy worked, and I will admit (grudgingly) that this salad is good.

STEAK COBB SALAD

Serves 4

* CROUTONS

3 slices bread

¼ cup melted butter

¼ teaspoon garlic powder

* SALAD

4 eggs

10 slices thick-sliced bacon

2 avocados

2 plum tomatoes

8 cups salad mix

1 cup shredded Cheddar

6 ounces sirloin steak

Salt and pepper

To prepare the croutons: Preheat the oven to 350°F.

Cut the bread into ½-inch cubes and place them on a baking sheet. Combine the butter and garlic powder in a small bowl and pour over the bread cubes. Toss the bread cubes until they are evenly coated and bake them for 10 minutes, or until they are golden brown.

To prepare the salad: Gently place the eggs in a medium saucepan and cover them completely with cold water. Bring the water to a boil and simmer over medium heat for 10 minutes. Turn off the heat and let the eggs stand in the water until they are cool. Peel the eggs and dice them into ¼-inch pieces.

Meanwhile, cut the bacon into ¼-inch-thick strips and place them in a sauté pan. Cook over medium heat for 12 to 15 minutes, or until crisp. Transfer to paper towels to drain.

Cut the avocados in half and sink the knife blade a bit into the pit and wriggle the knife slightly to pop the pit out. Beginning at the larger end of the avocado, slide a spoon between the skin and flesh and gently remove the flesh from each half. Dice the avocado into ½-inch pieces.

Cut the tomatoes in half, remove the seeds, and dice the tomatoes into $^1/_2$-inch pieces.

Preheat the grill or broiler to high heat.

Place some of the salad mix in the center of each plate. Working from the center of the plate and leaving space for the steak, form rows of croutons, tomato, and egg on one side of the plate, and avocado, cheese, and bacon on the other side.

✳ VINAIGRETTE

1 large shallot

$^1/_4$ cup balsamic vinegar

$^3/_4$ cup olive oil

Salt and pepper

Season the sirloin with salt and pepper and place it on the grill or under the broiler. Cook for 3 to 4 minutes on each side, or until cooked to the desired doneness. Remove the steak and let it rest for 5 minutes. Cut the steak into $^1/_2$-inch cubes and place them in a row down the center of each plate.

To prepare the vinaigrette: Peel the shallot and dice it into $^1/_8$- to $^1/_4$-inch pieces. Place the shallots and balsamic vinegar in a bowl and slowly whisk in the olive oil. Season to taste with salt and pepper and drizzle over the salads.

Cooking steaks to the doneness you want them can be intimidating because it depends on the thickness of the steak and the temperature of your grill or broiler. We have a gas grill that gets really hot, so we use the rule of thumb that you cook 2 minutes per side for rare, 3 for medium-rare, 4 for medium, 5 for medium-well, and 6 if you like hockey pucks. But if you still aren't sure, stick a knife in it and look.

kitchen tip

I love Caesar salad but, of course, my sister has to ruin it by adding chicken to cover up the taste of the lettuce. I mean really, how can you not like lettuce? This dressing is also really good on pasta salad, and at least Jill doesn't feel the need to add meat to that.

m

CHICKEN CAESAR SALAD

Serves 4

✳ CROUTONS

4 slices bread

$1/3$ cup melted butter

$1/2$ teaspoon garlic powder

2 tablespoons grated Parmesan

✳ DRESSING

2 small cloves garlic

2 teaspoons Dijon mustard

1 teaspoon Worcestershire sauce

$1/2$ teaspoon hot sauce

$1 1/2$ teaspoons fresh lemon juice

$1 1/2$ teaspoons red wine vinegar

$1/4$ cup olive oil

Salt and pepper

To prepare the croutons: Preheat the oven to 350°F.

Cut the bread into $1/2$-inch cubes and place them on a baking sheet. Combine the butter and garlic powder in a small bowl and pour over the bread cubes. Sprinkle with the Parmesan and toss the bread cubes until they are evenly coated. Bake them for 10 minutes, or until they are golden brown.

To prepare the dressing: Smash the garlic cloves by placing them on a cutting board, laying the blade of a large knife flat on top of the garlic, and pressing the knife with the heel of your hand. Remove the papery skin and finely chop the garlic.

Place the garlic in a bowl with the Dijon mustard, Worcestershire sauce, hot sauce, lemon juice, and red wine vinegar. Slowly whisk in the olive oil until completely incorporated. Season to taste with salt and pepper.

✳ SALAD

1 head romaine leaves,
washed and dried

½ cup shredded Parmesan

2 chicken breasts

Freshly ground black pepper

To prepare the salad: Preheat the grill or broiler to high heat.

Tear the romaine into bite-size pieces, place in a large serving bowl, and add the shredded Parmesan and croutons.

Grill or broil the chicken for 4 to 5 minutes on each side, or until it is thoroughly cooked. Remove the chicken from the grill and let it rest for 5 minutes.

Pour the dressing over the salad and toss until the lettuce is completely coated. Place some of the salad on each plate. Cut the chicken breasts into ¼-inch-thick slices and arrange the slices over the salad. Grind pepper over each salad.

Kitchen Vocab

The difference between **grilling** and **broiling** is that grilling heats from underneath and broiling heats from above. We prefer grilling over broiling because it adds flavor, but we have a gas grill that starts by turning a knob and pressing a button. If we had to actually light coals and wait for them to heat, we would be broiling.

SPINACH SALAD WITH HONEY-MUSTARD DRESSING

When I was little, I hated spinach . . . then I actually tried it. Now I love spinach any way at all, but especially in this salad with the honey-mustard dressing. One tip though, buy the triple-washed baby spinach because it's much more tender, and you don't have to hassle with washing it and removing the tough stems.

Serves 4

✳ CROUTONS

3 slices bread

¼ cup melted butter

✳ SALAD

2 eggs

4 slices thick-sliced bacon

2 ounces fresh mushrooms

1 (6-ounce) bag baby spinach leaves

To prepare the croutons: Preheat the oven to 350°F.

Cut the bread into ½-inch cubes and place them on a baking sheet. Pour the butter over the bread cubes and toss them until they are evenly coated. Bake for 10 minutes, or until they are golden brown.

To prepare the salad ingredients: Gently place the eggs in a small saucepan and cover them completely with cold water. Bring the water to a boil and simmer over medium heat for 10 minutes. Turn off the heat and let the eggs stand in the water until they are cool. Peel the eggs and dice them into ¼-inch pieces.

Meanwhile, cut the bacon into ¼-inch-thick strips and place them in a sauté pan. Cook over medium heat for 12 to 15 minutes, or until crisp. Transfer to paper towels to drain.

Wash the mushrooms and cut into ¼-inch thick slices.

✱ DRESSING

¹/₄ cup honey

¹/₄ cup Dijon mustard

To prepare the dressing: Place the honey and Dijon mustard in a small bowl and stir until combined.

Place the spinach in a large bowl and toss with the dressing. Arrange the mushrooms, eggs, bacon, and croutons on top of the spinach.

dinner for one

SPINACH AND CHEESE RAVIOLI

For you non–spinach eaters out there (including me): Don't be turned off by the spinach in this recipe! I always made this with just the cheese filling, but one time, when I had my back turned, my sister added spinach to the filling. She insisted that it would look better and I wouldn't even taste it. Although I hate to admit it, she was right. Besides that, it's worth it just for the shock value of when you ask your mom to buy spinach.

kitchen chemistry

Because air expands as it heats up, too much air in the center of the ravioli can cause it to pop open during cooking. While it is not necessary to vacuum seal them, gently pushing out any visible air pockets will help keep your ravioli intact.

Serves 1

¼ cup ricotta

1 tablespoon Parmesan plus
    extra for garnish

1 egg yolk

2 tablespoons fresh or
    frozen chopped spinach

Pinch of salt

8 3-inch-square wonton
    wrappers

½ cup bottled spaghetti
    sauce

Place the ricotta, Parmesan, egg yolk, spinach, and salt in a small bowl and mix until combined.

Bring a large pot of salted water to a boil.

Lay the wrappers on a flat surface and place some of the cheese mixture in the center of each wrapper. Dip your finger in water and wet the edges of one of the wrappers. Fold the wrapper in half to form a triangle and firmly press the edges to seal in the filling. Just before you seal the last edge, push gently on the center of the ravioli to remove any air pockets. Repeat the process with the remaining ravioli.

Place the spaghetti sauce in a microwave-safe bowl, cover, and heat on high for 1 minute, or until warm.

Place the ravioli in the boiling water and cook for 2 to 3 minutes, or until they float to the top of the pot. Remove the ravioli from the water with a slotted spoon and drain well, keeping the ravioli separate so they don't stick together.

Place one-half of the ravioli in a serving bowl and top one-half with the sauce. Place the remaining ravioli in the bowl, top with the remaining sauce, and sprinkle with Parmesan.

A tuna melt is one of the easiest things to make when you are eating alone. It really doesn't take much more work than a tuna sandwich, but because you eat it with a knife and fork, it always seem more like a meal than just a sandwich.

TUNA MELT

Serves 1

1 (6-ounce) can tuna

1/2 stalk celery

1/4 cup mayonnaise

2 slices Cheddar

1 slice rye bread

Preheat the broiler.

Drain the tuna and place it in a small bowl. Chop the celery into 1/4-inch pieces and add them to the bowl. Add the mayonnaise and stir until completely combined.

Toast the bread in a toaster or under the broiler until golden brown. Place the tuna mixture on the toasted bread and spread it to cover most of the bread. Place the cheese slices over the tuna and place under the broiler for 2 minutes, or until the cheese is melted.

Kitchen Vocab

Stir-frying is similar to sautéing. Both methods cook in oil, but in stir-frying the food is generally cut smaller, cooked over high heat, and kept in constant motion. Foods that take longer to cook are added first, with quicker-cooking items added later.

VEGETABLE STIR FRY WITH TOFU

When I make this dish I buy the Asian-style baked tofu so I don't have to marinate it. It is difficult to find in regular grocery stores, but you can find it at most health food or specialty stores. If you can find it, you can skip the marinating and just stir in the teriyaki sauce at the end. For you meat eaters, a chicken breast can be used instead of the tofu.

Serves 1

✳ RICE

¹/₂ cup white rice

1 ¹/₃ cups water

¹/₄ teaspoon salt

1 teaspoon butter

✳ STIR FRY

4 ounces firm tofu

¹/₄ cup teriyaki sauce

1 tablespoon peanut oil

¹/₂ cup sliced mushrooms

¹/₂ cup broccoli florets

¹/₂ cup shredded Chinese cabbage

10 snow pea pods

To prepare the rice: Place the rice, water, salt, and butter in a small saucepan over medium-high heat and bring to a boil. Decrease the heat to medium-low, cover, and simmer for 20 minutes. Remove the pan from the heat and fluff the rice with a fork.

Meanwhile, prepare the tofu: Cut the tofu into bite-size pieces and place them in a small bowl. Pour the teriyaki sauce over the tofu and gently swirl the bowl until the tofu is completely coated.

Place the oil in a wok or large sauté pan over high heat. Add the mushrooms and cook, stirring frequently, for 3 minutes. Add the broccoli and cabbage and cook for 2 to 3 minutes, or until the mushrooms are almost tender. Add the pea pods and cook for 2 minutes, or until the vegetables are just tender. Add the tofu and sauce and cook, stirring gently, for 2 minutes, or until the tofu is warm.

Place the rice on a plate and top with the vegetables and tofu.

Pasta is one of my favorite foods of all time, and this version is really easy and super good. Although I do occasionally eat shrimp, I probably make this more often without shrimp than with it. It kind of depends on if I am making it for myself, or the whole family. If my parents are eating, then for sure it has shrimp. If it's my sister, I leave the shrimp out because she likes to add (big surprise) grilled chicken.

SHRIMP FETTUCCINE ALFREDO

Serves 1

Bring a large pot of salted water to a boil. Add the fettuccine and cook for 10 to 12 minutes, or until the pasta is just tender. Drain the pasta and set aside.

Meanwhile, heat the oil in a small sauté pan over medium heat. Add the shrimp and cook them for 2 to 3 minutes, or until they turn pink and begin to curl. Remove the shrimp from the pan and set aside. Place the cream and Parmesan in the pan and cook for 3 to 4 minutes, or until it comes to a boil. Decrease the heat to low and stir the shrimp into the sauce. Season the sauce to taste with salt and pepper and remove the pan from the heat. Add the fettuccine to the pan and use 2 forks to toss the pasta until it is thoroughly coated with the sauce.

4 ounces uncooked
   fettuccine noodles

1 teaspoon olive oil

4 ounces peeled shrimp

1/4 cup heavy cream

1/4 cup Parmesan

Salt and pepper

Kitchen Vocab

Sautéing is probably the most common cooking method because it cooks food quickly. Similar to stir-frying, sautéing cooks foods in oil, but the foods are usually cut larger, cooked over medium to medium-high heat, and only stirred or turned occasionally.

CHICKEN QUESADILLAS

I like quesadillas because I can make them just the way I like them. This is one of my favorite combinations, but they are also great with bacon, ham, sausage, and all kinds of peppers. My sister puts other vegetables in hers, but I say, why ruin a good thing?

Serves 1

1 chicken breast

2 green onions

2 10-inch flour tortillas

1 cup shredded Jack cheese

2 tablespoons diced green chiles

Salsa

Sour Cream

Preheat the grill or broiler to high heat.

Grill or broil the chicken breast for 5 minutes on each side, or until thoroughly cooked. Let the chicken rest for 5 minutes, and cut into $1/4$-inch-thick slices.

Cut off the root ends of the green onions and thinly slice the white and about 1 inch of the green parts.

Place 1 tortilla in a large sauté pan over medium heat. Sprinkle half of the cheese over the tortilla and sprinkle with the green chiles and green onions. Arrange the chicken strips on the tortilla and sprinkle with the remaining cheese. Top with the remaining tortilla and cook for 2 or 3 minutes, or until the cheese is melted and the quesadilla holds together. Turn the quesadilla over and cook for 1 minute.

Cut the quesadilla into 6 pieces and serve with the salsa and sour cream.

Fajitas are great because you can put anything you want on them. I like mine with meat, onion, and cheese, but my sister always grills some eggplant or zucchini for hers. They are also really good with refried beans, guacamole, or even Spanish rice.

STEAK FAJITAS

Serves 1

*STEAK

1 small jalapeño chile

1 small clove garlic

1 tablespoon olive oil

4 to 6 ounces sirloin steak

*FAJITAS

1 small onion

1/2 red or yellow bell pepper

1 tablespoon olive oil

3 6-inch flour tortillas

1/2 cup Cheddar

Salsa

Sour cream

To prepare the steak: Cut the jalapeño in half and remove the seeds. Finely dice the jalapeño and place it in a bowl.

Smash the garlic clove by placing it on a cutting board, laying the blade of a large knife flat on top of the garlic, and pressing the knife with the heel of your hand. Remove the papery skin and finely chop the garlic. Add the garlic and olive oil to the jalapeño and stir well. Cut the steak into thin strips, add them to the jalapeño and garlic, and toss the strips until they are completely coated.

To prepare the fajitas: Peel the onion, cut it into 1/4-inch-thick rings, and cut each ring in half. Remove the seeds and ribs from the red bell pepper and cut it into 1/4-inch-thick strips.

Kitchen Vocab

Marinating is a way to add flavor to meats or to tenderize tougher cuts of meat. This recipe uses sirloin, a tender cut of meat, so the marinade is used just to add flavor. Some marinades have a lot of flavor and also make great sauces. Just remember that if the marinade has touched raw meat, before you use it as a sauce it needs to be boiled for a couple of minutes to kill any bacteria it may have picked up from the meat.

Place the oil in a large sauté pan over medium-high heat. Add the onion and pepper and cook, stirring occasionally, for 10 minutes. Push the vegetables to the side of the pan and add the meat mixture. Cook, stirring occasionally, for 2 minutes, or until the steak reaches the desired doneness.

Place a tortilla on a microwave-safe plate and cook on high heat for 15 seconds, or until the tortilla is warm. Arrange one-third of the meat slices down the center of the tortilla. Place one-third of the onion, pepper, and cheese over the meat and top with some of the salsa and sour cream. Fold the tortilla to cup the filling taco-style. Repeat the process with the remaining ingredients.

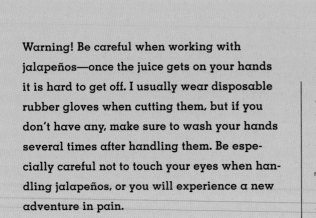

Warning! Be careful when working with jalapeños—once the juice gets on your hands it is hard to get off. I usually wear disposable rubber gloves when cutting them, but if you don't have any, make sure to wash your hands several times after handling them. Be especially careful not to touch your eyes when handling jalapeños, or you will experience a new adventure in pain.

kitchen tip

I love good fried rice. I tried making it many times, but I always ended up with that pale, anemic-looking stuff that they serve at the food court in the mall. After reading about a thousand different fried rice recipes (and that is only a slight exaggeration), I finally figured out that the key is to use day-old rice. So now whenever we have leftover rice, it becomes fried rice the next day.

m

FRIED RICE

Serves 1

½ cup white rice

1½ cups water

1 egg

3 green onions

¼ cup snow pea pods

2 tablespoons peanut oil

¾ cup bean sprouts

¼ cup soy sauce

Place the rice and water in a small saucepan over medium-high heat and bring to a boil. Decrease the heat to low, cover, and simmer for 20 minutes. Remove from the heat and cool slightly. Cover and refrigerate overnight. (If you can't wait until the next day to make the fried rice, you can spread it out on a baking sheet and refrigerate it, uncovered, for an hour or two—or as long as you can stand to wait—to speed up the process.)

Place the egg in a small bowl and beat thoroughly with a fork. Remove the root ends from the green onions and thinly slice the white and about 1 inch of the green part of the onions. Slice the pea pods into ½-inch pieces.

Place 1 tablespoon of the oil in a wok or large sauté pan over high heat. Pour the egg into the hot oil and let it cook for 2 minutes, or until the egg pancake is almost cooked. Add the pea pods, green onions, and bean sprouts, stirring with a wooden spoon to break the egg into small pieces, and cook for 2 minutes. Add the rice and cook, stirring frequently, for 3 minutes. Combine the remaining 1 tablespoon of peanut oil with the soy sauce and pour over the rice. Cook, stirring constantly, for 3 minutes, or until the rice is hot.

EGG SALAD TORTILLA WRAP

When I did an internship at Disney World, one of my coworkers used to eat these for lunch every day. The rest of us always made fun of her until she finally got us to try one. As you probably guessed, pretty soon we were all eating them. This tasty wrap has the egg salad that I have always loved, but the cheese, lettuce, and tomato add a new flavor.

Serves 1

✳EGG SALAD

2 eggs

2 tablespoons mayonnaise

$1/2$ teaspoon mustard

Salt and pepper

✳WRAPS

1 plum tomato

1 10-inch flour tortilla

2 slices Jack cheese

$1/2$ cup shredded or chopped lettuce

To prepare the egg salad: Gently place the eggs in a small saucepan and cover them completely with cold water. Bring the water to a boil and simmer over medium heat for 10 minutes. Turn off the heat and let the eggs stand in the water until they are cool.

Peel the eggs and dice them into $1/4$-inch pieces. Place the eggs, mayonnaise, and mustard in a small bowl and stir until well combined. Season to taste with salt and pepper.

To prepare the wraps: Cut the tomato in half and remove and discard the seeds. Chop the tomato into $1/4$- to $1/2$-inch pieces.

Lay the tortilla in the center of a microwave-safe plate and heat on high for 10 seconds to soften the tortilla. Place the cheese slices down the center of the tortilla, leaving a $2^1/2$-inch border at the bottom. Spoon the egg salad over the cheese. Arrange the lettuce over the egg salad and sprinkle with the tomatoes. Fold up the bottom of the tortilla and tightly fold over the sides to form the wrap.

This sandwich is a little bit of vegetarian heaven that even meat eaters will like. They are healthier than regular hamburgers, yet they lack none of the flavor. The meatiness of the portobello even gives it a texture that makes it seem like a real burger. If you don't want to start up the grill for one mushroom and onion slice, you can sauté them instead.

m

GRILLED PORTOBELLO SANDWICH

Serves 1

1 large portobello mushroom

1 tablespoon balsamic vinegar

2 tablespoons olive oil

1 ¼-inch thick slice onion

Salt and pepper

1 hamburger bun

1 piece leaf lettuce

1 slice tomato

Preheat the grill.

Remove the stem from the portobello. Using a spoon, scrape the gills from the bottom of the mushroom cap and discard them.

Combine the balsamic vinegar and olive oil in a small bowl. Place the portobello and onion on a plate and pour the vinegar mixture over them. Rub the mixture over the onion and mushroom, making sure they are completely coated. Season with salt and pepper and let stand for 5 minutes.

Place the onion on the grill and cook for 5 minutes. Turn the onion over and add the mushroom to the grill. Cook for 3 minutes, turn the mushroom over, and cook for 3 minutes.

Place the lettuce on the bottom of the hamburger bun and top with the mushroom. Arrange the tomato and onion on the mushroom and cover with the top bun.

GRILLED CHEESE WITH BACON AND TOMATO

There are many ways to dress up grilled cheese with different types of bread and gourmet cheeses, but I like it with plain ol' white bread and American cheese. Bacon, ham, or tomato are acceptable additions, but no matter what I put on it, I like to eat it with tomato soup for dunking.

Serves 1

2 slices thick-sliced bacon

2 teaspoons butter

2 slices bread

2 slices American cheese

1 slice tomato

Place a paper towel on a microwave-safe plate and lay the bacon slices in the center. Fold the excess paper towel over the bacon and microwave on high for 2 minutes, or until the bacon is crisp.

Heat a medium sauté pan over medium-low heat. Spread the butter on one side of each bread slice and place them, butter side down, in the pan. Place 1 slice of cheese on each bread slice and cook for 3 to 4 minutes, or until golden brown. Break the bacon slices in half and arrange them on one of the bread slices. Place the tomato on top of the bacon and top with the other bread slice. Remove the sandwich from the pan and cut in half on the diagonal.

kitchen safety

Because we can't see a heat source, we often seem to forget that things get really hot in the microwave. Remember to use hot pads when removing containers, and watch out for the steam. Allow any covered items to cool slightly before removing the covers. Our mom learned this the hard way when she pulled the plastic wrap off of some vegetables and steamed the skin off of two of her fingers. Definitely not good.

I love this dish warm or cold! Just be careful, fresh noodles don't need to cook very long. If they are overcooked, they will get kind of mushy and loose their texture. This is one of my favorite dishes for those bring-a-dish dinners, because even if there is nothing else I like, I can make a meal out of this.

VEGETABLE LOMEIN

Serves 1

6 ounces fresh egg noodles

$^1/_2$ red bell pepper

2 tablespoons sesame oil

1 teaspoon grated fresh ginger

$^3/_4$ cup shredded Chinese cabbage

12 snow pea pods

$^3/_4$ cup bean sprouts

$^1/_4$ cup soy sauce

1 teaspoon cornstarch

Bring a large saucepan of water to a boil. Add the noodles and cook for 3 to 4 minutes, or until just tender. Drain and set aside.

Meanwhile, remove the seeds from the red bell pepper and cut it into $^1/_4$- to $^1/_2$-inch pieces.

Heat the oil in a wok or large sauté pan over high heat. Add the red bell pepper and cook for 2 minutes. Add the ginger and cabbage and cook, stirring constantly, for 2 minutes. Add the pea pods and bean sprouts and cook, stirring constantly, for 2 minutes, or until the cabbage is tender. Combine the soy sauce and cornstarch thoroughly, slowly add the mixture to the pan, and stir until the sauce thickens slightly Add the noodles to the pan and, using 2 forks, toss the noodles until they are completely coated with the sauce and the vegetables are evenly distributed.

Kitchen Vocab

Make sure you don't cook pasta until it is soft. You want to aim for a slight resistance when you bite into it. This is called al dente, which is Italian for "to the tooth."

Puff pastry is very cool stuff. It's easy to work with, and it always turns out really flaky. With one sheet of puff pastry you can make two of these puff pastry pockets and still have enough to make a few Cinnamon Sticks for dessert (see page 41).

TURKEY-BACON PUFF PASTRY POCKETS

Serves 1

2 slices thick-sliced bacon

1 sheet puff pastry, thawed

4 thin slices turkey

Mustard

2 slices Swiss cheese

Preheat the oven to 400°F. Lightly butter or spray an 8- or 9-inch-square baking pan.

Place a paper towel on a microwave-safe plate and lay the bacon slices in the center. Fold the excess paper towel over the bacon and microwave on high for 2 minutes, or until the bacon is crisp.

Unfold the puff pastry and cut it lengthwise into thirds.
Set 1 piece aside for another use. Cut the 2 remaining
pastry strips in half widthwise to form 4 rectangles
measuring about 3 by 5 inches. Lay 2 of the dough rectangles on the baking pan and arrange 1 of the turkey
slices on each piece leaving a ¼-inch border around
the entire edge of the dough. Spread a little mustard
over the turkey and top with the cheese. Break the
bacon slices in half, arrange on top of the cheese, and
top with the remaining turkey. Place the remaining
pieces of dough on top of the turkey and press on all
sides with a fork to seal the edges. Bake the pockets
for 15 to 18 minutes, or until they are golden brown.

family meals

Although it takes longer to make, there is no comparison between real macaroni and cheese and the stuff that comes out of the box with a packet of powdered cheese. (What is that stuff anyway?) I have made it with Cheddar, colby, Jack, and the Mexican cheese mixture with chiles, and they were all great. I even once made it with cream cheese, but I wouldn't recommend that.

m

BAKED MACARONI AND CHEESE

Serves 6

1 pound uncooked macaroni

2 tablespoons butter

2 tablespoons flour

2 cups milk

1 pound sliced American cheese

2 tablespoons Parmesan

Bring a large saucepan of salted water to a boil. Add the pasta and cook, stirring occasionally, for 7 to 10 minutes, or until the pasta is just cooked. Pour the macaroni into a colander and drain off the cooking water.

Preheat the oven to 350°F.

Melt the butter in the same saucepan over medium heat. Add the flour and stir constantly until the mixture starts to bubble. Add 1/2 cup of the milk and stir until smooth. Add the remaining 1 1/2 cups of milk and cook, stirring frequently, for 10 to 15 minutes, or until it comes to a boil.

Remove the pan from the heat, add the American cheese slices, and stir until the cheese is completely melted. Add the macaroni and stir gently until it is completely coated with the cheese.

Place the macaroni in a large baking dish and sprinkle with the Parmesan. Bake for 25 to 30 minutes, or until the cheese is bubbly.

Kitchen Vocab

A **roux** (roo) is a very handy thing to know how to make. It's simply a mixture of flour and fat that is used to thicken soups or sauces. In this recipe you make a white roux by cooking the flour and butter just until it starts to bubble. You could make a blond roux by cooking the mixture a little longer until it is golden brown, or you could make a dark roux by cooking it until it is dark brown with a nutty aroma. The key to making a roux is to cook it slowly over low heat and to stir it constantly.

Béchamel sauce (BEH-shah-mel) is a basic French sauce that is used as a base for many soups and sauces and is quite easy. Here you make a thin béchamel sauce by adding milk to the roux and cooking it until it comes to a boil. Doubling or tripling the amount of butter and flour will make thicker sauces.

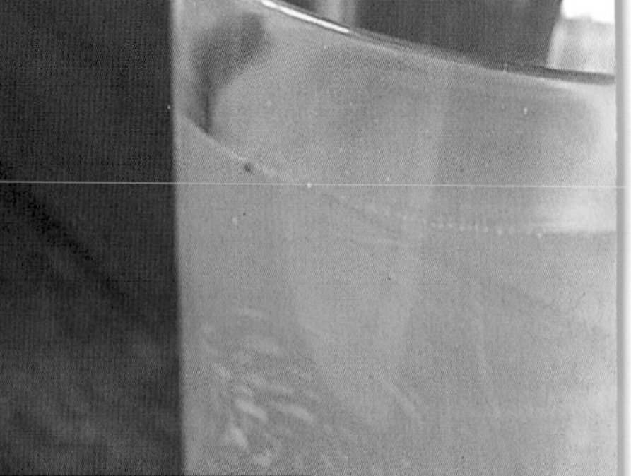

en Vocab

-zoh) is a small rice-
sta that is often found in
can find it in the pasta
he supermarket.

chicken broth to the pan
ny cooked on bits is
lazing the pan. And, if
want to impress people,
he bits that are stuck to
called the **fond**.

The beauty of cooking is that you can make things exactly the way you like them. For example, chicken piccata is usually made with capers, but since I don't like capers, I just use parsley instead. It also means that I can make a double batch of rice pilaf so there are plenty of leftovers. This is not exactly a quick dinner to prepare, but it is so good that I don't mind taking the time to make it.

[continued]

*RICE

1 onion

1 carrot

1 celery stalk

1/4 cup butter

1/2 cup uncooked orzo

1 cup white rice

2 (14-ounce) cans chicken broth

Salt and pepper

*CHICKEN

4 boneless, skinless chicken breast halves

1 egg

1 cup flour

1 teaspoon salt

1/2 teaspoon pepper

1/4 cup olive oil

1 (14-ounce) can chicken broth

2 lemons

2 tablespoons cornstarch

2 tablespoons milk

1/4 cup chopped parsley

To prepare the rice: Peel the onion and carrot. Dice the onion, carrot, and celery into 1/4-inch pieces. (Don't cut them smaller or they will fall apart while cooking.)

Place the butter, onion, carrot, celery, and orzo in a large saucepan and cook over medium heat, stirring on and off, for 10 minutes, or until the orzo is browned. Add the rice and stir until coated with the butter. Add the chicken broth and stir. Cover and cook for 20 minutes, or until the rice is tender. Season the rice with salt and pepper and place it in a serving bowl.

Meanwhile, prepare the chicken: Cut each chicken breast in half lengthwise. Place a chicken breast half in a large resealable bag or between 2 sheets of plastic wrap and pound with a meat mallet (a small saucepan also works well) until it is less than 1/4 inch thick. Repeat the process with the remaining chicken breasts.

Whisk the egg in a shallow bowl. Combine the flour, salt, and pepper in another shallow bowl.

Place a large sauté pan over medium heat and add 2 tablespoons of the oil.

Dip both sides of a chicken breast into the flour, then into the egg, and back into the flour. Carefully place the chicken breast into the hot oil and repeat until the pan is full. Cook for 3 to 4 minutes on each side, or until the chicken is golden brown. Transfer the chicken to paper towels to drain. Drain the used oil out of the pan, wipe out the pan, and add the remaining 2 tablespoons of olive oil. Add the remaining chicken breasts and cook as for the first batch. (If you don't drain off the used oil and add fresh oil to the pan before cooking the second batch, the chicken will taste burnt.)

Pour the chicken broth into the pan and stir to loosen any bits stuck to the pan. Cut the lemons in half, remove any seeds, and squeeze the juice into the pan. Combine the cornstarch and milk in a small bowl and mix until smooth. Pour the mixture into the pan and stir continuously until it comes to a boil.

Arrange the chicken in a shallow serving bowl and pour the sauce over it. Sprinkle the parsley over the chicken and serve immediately with the rice pilaf.

SLOPPY JOES

> I am the queen of Sloppy Joes, and as queen, I get to make the rules:
>
> 1. Sloppy Joes must be served with potato chips and red Jell-O with bananas. Other fruits are acceptable in a pinch, but the Jell-O must be red.
>
> 2. Any meat that falls out of the bun must be scooped up and eaten on a potato chip.
>
> 3. Any leftover Sloppy Joe must be reheated and eaten directly out of the container with potato chips to scoop it up.

Serves 4 TO 6

1 small onion

2 stalks celery

1½ pounds ground beef

1 (6-ounce) can tomato paste

½ cup ketchup

1 teaspoon ground mustard powder

3 tablespoons firmly packed brown sugar

Salt and pepper

4 to 6 hamburger buns

Peel the onion and dice it into ¼-inch pieces. Cut the celery into ¼-inch pieces. Place the onion, celery, and ground beef in a large sauté pan. Cook over medium heat, stirring occasionally, for 10 minutes, or until the ground beef is thoroughly cooked. Dump the meat into a colander and let the fat drain off, washing the grease down the sink with hot running water. Put the drained meat back in the sauté pan.

Add the tomato paste, ketchup, ground mustard, and brown sugar to the pan and stir well. Cook for 20 minutes and season to taste with salt and pepper.

Spoon the meat onto hamburger buns and serve immediately.

Because I am a vegetarian and the rest of my family is not, we are often at odds to come up with a dinner that will make everyone happy. Ratatouille (ra-tuh-TOO-ee) has saved the day more than once. I always make a double batch and freeze the extra in resealable bags. It reheats well in the microwave and is really good on pasta, rice, or whatever starch the rest of your family is eating.

RATATOUILLE WITH CHICKPEAS AND COUSCOUS

Serves 6

*RATATOUILLE

2 small zucchini

2 small summer squash

1 small onion

1 red bell pepper

1 yellow bell pepper

1 eggplant

2 tablespoons olive oil

2 (14.5-ounce) cans crushed tomatoes

1 teaspoon ground thyme

Salt and pepper

1 (14.5-ounce) can chickpeas

*COUSCOUS

2 cups water

2 teaspoons butter

2 cups couscous

To prepare the ratatouille: Stem the zucchini and summer squash and slice them into 1/4-inch-thick rounds. Peel the onion and dice it into 1/4-inch pieces. Cut the red and yellow peppers in half, remove the seeds and ribs, and cut the peppers into 1/2-inch pieces. Stem the eggplant and cut it into 3/4-inch pieces.

Heat the oil in a large sauté pan over medium heat. Add the zucchini, summer squash, onion, and red and yellow peppers to the pan and cook, stirring occasionally, for 10 minutes. Add the eggplant and cook for 10 minutes, or until the vegetables are almost tender. Stir in the tomatoes and thyme and season with salt and pepper. Drain the chickpeas and add to the pan. Cook for 5 minutes, or until the chickpeas are warm.

Meanwhile, prepare the couscous: Place the water and butter in a small saucepan and bring to a boil. Add the couscous, stir quickly, and remove from the heat. Cover, let stand for 5 minutes, and fluff with a fork.

Place some of the couscous in the center of each plate and spoon the ratatouille over the top.

CHEESE AND CHILE ENCHILADAS

This dish is great for families with both vegetarians and meat eaters. You can roll enough enchiladas for the vegetarians and then simply add some cooked chicken to the rest of the filling to make the meat eaters happy. These enchiladas are pretty mild, but using medium or hot salsa and adding a little hot sauce to the filling can easily spice them up.

Serves 4

4 ounces cream cheese

¼ cup sour cream

2 cups salsa

1 (8-ounce) can tomato sauce

1 (14-ounce) can corn

1 (4-ounce) can diced green chiles

½ teaspoon cumin

3 cups grated Cheddar or Jack cheese

Salt and pepper

12 6-inch flour or corn tortillas

Preheat the oven to 325°F.

Place the cream cheese and sour cream in a large bowl and stir until smooth. Combine the salsa and tomato sauce in another bowl and add ½ cup of the mixture to the cream cheese. Drain the corn and add the corn, chiles, cumin, and 2 cups of the cheese to the cream cheese and stir well. Season with salt and pepper.

Spread ½ cup of the salsa and tomato sauce over the bottom of a 9 by 13-inch baking dish. Place the tortillas on a microwave-safe plate and cook on high heat for 30 seconds, or until softened. (Heating the tortillas slightly keeps them from cracking when you roll them.) Place about ⅓ cup of the filling on each tortilla, then roll them up and place them seam side down in the baking dish. Spread the remaining 1½ cups of the salsa and tomato sauce over the enchiladas, coating them well, and bake for 15 minutes. Sprinkle the remaining 1 cup of cheese over the enchiladas and bake for 10 minutes, or until the cheese is melted.

Chicken and dumplings is a great cold-weather dish. When we lived in the Midwest, we would always have this after a day of sledding or building snow forts, but when we moved to Arizona this tradition became a problem. Now when I want chicken and dumplings, I turn down the air conditioning, close the blinds, and pretend it's snowing outside (if I don't close the blinds, the palm trees kind of ruin the effect).

CHICKEN AND DUMPLINGS

Serves 4

*CHICKEN

2 boneless, skinless chicken breasts

3 (14-ounce) cans chicken broth

2 carrots

2 potatoes

1 onion

2 stalks celery

1/4 cup cornstarch

1/2 cup milk

*DUMPLINGS

1 cup flour

1 1/2 teaspoons baking powder

1/2 cup milk

To prepare the chicken: Cut the chicken into bite-size pieces and place them in a large saucepan. Add the chicken broth and place the pan over medium heat.

Peel the carrots, potatoes, and onion, cut them into bite-size pieces, and add them to the pan. Rinse the celery stalks, cut them into bite-size pieces, and add them to the pan. Cook for 30 minutes, or until the potatoes and carrots are tender.

Combine the cornstarch and milk in a small bowl and stir until smooth. Slowly pour the mixture into the pot, stirring gently for 2 to 3 minutes, or until the mixture begins to simmer.

To prepare the dumplings: Place the flour, baking powder, and milk in a small bowl and stir until the flour is completely incorporated. Drop spoonfuls of the dough into the pot, spacing them fairly evenly. Cover tightly and cook for 15 minutes. Do not remove the cover during cooking or the dumplings will become dense and chewy. Remove from the heat and serve immediately.

Stewing is to cook food completely submerged in liquid. This method is usually used for tougher cuts of meat that need longer cooking times.

The first time I made chicken and dumplings I didn't know you have to mix the cornstarch with a little liquid before you add it to

KITCHEN DISASTER

any kind of sauce, so I just dumped it into the hot sauce. It immediately formed nasty gray lumps. After spending about twenty minutes picking out the lumps, I tried it again, this time stirring in cornstarch that I first mixed with milk, and ended up with a nice, smooth sauce. It's amazing what a difference a little premixing can make.

This lasagna is a little different than most because we make it with a Parmesan sauce instead of the traditional tomato sauce. The cheese sauce is a nice complement to the vegetables without overpowering them. One of my favorite things about this recipe is that with all of the juice from the vegetables, you don't even have to cook the noodles first.

VEGETABLE LASAGNA

Serves 4 TO 6

2 tablespoons butter

3 tablespoons flour

1 1/2 cups milk

1/2 cup Parmesan

Salt and pepper

2 red bell peppers

1 small zucchini

1 large tomato

4 ounces mushrooms

6 uncooked lasagna noodles

1 1/2 cups ricotta

1 cup mozzarella

Place the butter and flour in a small saucepan and cook over medium heat, stirring frequently, for 3 minutes, or until bubbly. Add 1/2 cup of the milk and stir until smooth. Add the remaining 1 cup of milk and cook for 7 to 8 minutes, or until it begins to boil. Remove from the heat and stir in the Parmesan. Season to taste with salt and pepper.

Meanwhile, place the red bell peppers directly on the stove burner (or under a broiler if you have an electric stove) and cook over high heat, turning occasionally, for 15 minutes, or until the peppers are almost completely black on the outside. Place the blackened peppers in a small bowl and cover tightly with plastic wrap. Let stand for 10 minutes to loosen the skin. Peel the skin off and cut the peppers in half. Discard the seeds and cut each half into 2 or 3 strips.

Stem the zucchini and cut it lengthwise into 1/8-inch-thick slices. Cut the top and bottom off the tomato and discard them. Cut the remaining tomato into four even slices. Cut the mushrooms into 1/4-inch-thick slices.

Preheat the oven to 350°F.

Spoon ½ cup of the sauce in the bottom of an 8-inch-square baking pan. Cover the sauce with a layer of noodles. Arrange the zucchini slices over the noodles and spread with ¾ cup of the ricotta. Place the roasted red bell peppers over the ricotta and spread with ½ cup of the sauce. Form another layer of noodles and top with the mushrooms. Spread the remaining ¾ cup of ricotta over the mushrooms and top with the remaining sauce. Place the tomato slices over the sauce and cover the pan with aluminum foil. (At this point the lasagna can be refrigerated for up to 1 day.)

Bake the lasagna covered for 40 minutes. Remove the foil and sprinkle the top with the mozzarella. Bake for 10 to 15 minutes, or until the cheese is lightly browned. Remove the lasagna from the oven and let it stand for 10 minutes before serving.

j

MEXICAN LASAGNA

Serves 8 TO 10

1 pound ground beef

1 tablespoon chile powder

2 (14.5-ounce) cans diced
 tomatoes

12 to 15 corn tortillas

2 cups salsa

4 cups Mexican blend
 shredded cheese

Place the ground beef in a large sauté pan and cook, stirring occasionally, over medium heat for 10 minutes, or until thoroughly cooked. Dump the meat into a colander and let the fat drain off, washing the grease down the sink with hot running water. Put the drained meat back in the sauté pan. Add the chile powder and tomatoes to the pan and stir until combined.

Preheat the oven to 350°F.

Spoon one-third of the meat mixture into the bottom of a 9 by 13-inch pan and spread it around the bottom of the pan. (It doesn't need to cover the entire pan; it's just to keep the tortillas from sticking to the pan.) Using 4 or 5 tortillas, form a layer, breaking up the tortillas when necessary to completely cover the meat. Spread another one-third of the meat mixture over the tortillas and spoon about 1/2 cup of the salsa over the meat. Sprinkle 1 1/2 cups of the cheese evenly around the pan. Form another layer of tortillas and top in the same manner with the meat, salsa, and cheese. Form a third layer of tortillas, top with the remaining 1 cup of salsa and 1 cup of cheese. (This can be refrigerated overnight, if desired.)

Bake the lasagna for 30 minutes, or until the cheese is bubbly. (If the lasagna has been refrigerated it will take 10 to 15 minutes longer to cook.) Remove the lasagna from the oven and let it rest for 10 minutes before serving.

My whole family loves this traditional Italian dish except, of course, Jill, who doesn't like eggplant. So she doesn't starve, we usually have to make chicken Parmesan too, which is made the same way but with chicken instead of the eggplant. We always serve this with pasta and extra sauce on the side.

EGGPLANT PARMESAN

Serves 4

1 egg

½ cup flour

1 teaspoon salt

½ teaspoon pepper

1 cup breadcrumbs

1 large eggplant

¼ cup olive oil

Salt and pepper

1 cup bottled spaghetti
   sauce

1½ cups mozzarella

Kitchen Vocab

Dipping the eggplant in the flour and breadcrumbs is called **dredging**. This adds a crispy texture to the foods when they are cooked and helps them retain their moisture.

Beat the egg in a shallow bowl and set aside. Stir together the flour, salt, and pepper in another shallow bowl. Place the breadcrumbs in another shallow bowl. Stem the eggplant and cut it into ¼- to ⅜-inch-thick rounds.

Preheat the oven to 350°F.

Heat 2 tablespoons of the olive oil in a large sauté pan over medium-high heat. Dip both sides of a slice of eggplant in the flour, then in the egg, then in the bread-crumbs. Carefully place the slice in the pan and repeat with the remaining eggplant slices. Cook for 3 to 4 minutes on each side, or until golden brown. If all of the slices will not fit in the pan, cook the first batch, wipe out the pan, and use the remaining 2 tablespoons of oil for the second batch. (If you don't wipe out the pan, the second batch will have a burnt flavor.)

Place the cooked eggplant on a baking sheet and season with salt and pepper. Spread some of the spaghetti sauce on each slice and sprinkle the cheese over the sauce. Bake the eggplant for 10 minutes, or until the cheese is lightly browned.

When placing food into hot oil, always start closest to you and lay it down away from you. This way if the oil splashes, it won't splash toward you.

I am not a big fan of store-bought pot pies because they have too much crust and not enough filling. This version only has crust on the top and uses puff pastry instead of pie dough so it gets all puffy and flaky and looks cool. It's actually kind of interesting to watch it puff up while it bakes. (Yes, I know how to have a good time.)

CHICKEN POT PIE

Serves 4

2 boneless, skinless
    chicken breasts

1 carrot

2 potatoes

1/2 small onion

1 celery stalk

8 green beans

2 (14-ounce) cans chicken
    broth

2 tablespoons cornstarch

2 tablespoons milk

1 sheet puff pastry, thawed

Cut the chicken into bite-size pieces and place them in a large saucepan.

Peel the carrot, potatoes, and onion. Dice them into 1/2- to 3/4-inch pieces and place them in the pan. Dice the celery into bite-size pieces and add to the pan. Snip the ends off the green beans. Cut each bean into 3 or 4 pieces and add to the pan. Add the chicken broth and cook over medium-high heat for 10 minutes, or until it begins to boil. Decrease the heat to medium-low and simmer for 20 minutes, or until the potatoes and carrots are tender. Stir together the cornstarch and milk in a small bowl until smooth. Pour the cornstarch mixture into the pan, stirring constantly, and cook for 3 to 4 minutes, or until it begins to boil.

Preheat the oven to 400°F.

Ladle the filling into 4 ovenproof crocks or bowls. Unfold the puff pastry sheet and cut it in half lengthwise and widthwise to form 4 squares. Place 1 pastry square over each bowl and bake them for 10 minutes, or until the pastries are golden brown.

When I was an exchange student, my German host mom made "hooner schnitzel" every day for my host dad's lunch, but my favorite part was always the *brat kartoffeln* (fried potatoes), and the crispier, the better. This is truly a German dish that is served in almost every restaurant. You can also make *Wiener schnitzel* (veal) and *schnitzel vom schwein* (pork) the same way.

CHICKEN SCHNITZEL WITH FRIED POTATOES

Serves 4 TO 6

* POTATOES

5 potatoes

½ small onion

2 tablespoons olive oil

Salt and pepper

To prepare the potatoes: Place the whole potatoes in a pot of water and bring to a boil. Cook over medium heat for 20 minutes, or until a knife inserted in the potatoes meets slight resistance in the center. (It is better to undercook than overcook the potatoes. They will finish cooking when you fry them, but if they are overcooked they will break into little pieces during frying.) Cool the potatoes slightly and peel.

Peel the onion and dice it into ¼- to ½-inch pieces. Heat the olive oil in a large sauté pan over medium-low heat. Add the onion to the pan and cook, stirring occasionally, for 5 minutes, or until translucent. Cut the potatoes in half lengthwise and then cut into ⅛- to ¼-inch-thick slices. Add the potatoes to the pan and cook, turning occasionally with a spatula, for 30 minutes, or until golden brown. (The potatoes will stick to the pan initially, but as they brown they will be easier to loosen. If the pan becomes too dry after the potatoes have been turned, take the pan away from the heat, drizzle a little more oil around the edges of the pan, and continue cooking.) Season to taste with salt and pepper.

❋ SCHNITZEL

4 boneless skinless chicken breast halves

Salt for seasoning, plus 1 teaspoon

Pepper for seasoning, plus ½ teaspoon

2 eggs

1 cup flour

1 teaspoon salt

Oil for frying

1 lemon

Kitchen Vocab

Cooking the onions the way they are cooked here is called sweating. It is usually done with a small amount of butter or oil over medium or low heat. Unlike sautéing, when you sweat foods you don't want them to brown. In this recipe, we sweat the onions first to bring out their sweetness because they are going to brown with the potatoes, and we don't want them to get burnt.

Meanwhile, prepare the chicken: Cut each chicken breast in half lengthwise. Place a chicken breast half in a large resealable bag or between 2 sheets of plastic wrap and pound with a meat mallet (a small saucepan also works well) until it is less than ¼ inch thick. Repeat the process with the remaining chicken breasts and season with salt and pepper.

Whisk the eggs in a shallow bowl. Combine the flour, the 1 teaspoon of salt, and the ½ teaspoon of pepper in another shallow bowl.

Place a large sauté pan over medium heat and add enough oil to the pan to create a ⅛-inch-thick layer.

Dip both sides of a chicken breast into the flour, then into the egg, and back into the flour. Carefully place the chicken breast into the hot oil and repeat the process until the pan is full. Cook for 3 to 4 minutes on each side, or until the chicken is golden brown. Transfer the chicken to paper towels to drain and continue with the remaining chicken breasts. (If it takes more than 2 batches, drain the used oil out of the pan, wipe out the pan, and start with fresh oil or the chicken will taste burnt.)

Overlap 2 pieces of chicken on each plate and spoon some of the potatoes next to the chicken. Cut the lemon into 8 wedges and place 2 wedges on each plate.

kitchen safety

Cross contamination occurs when raw meat or poultry comes in contact with ready-to-eat foods. Raw meat and poultry can contain bacteria, which are eliminated when they are cooked. But, ready-to-eat foods are not cooked and therefore, the bacteria will remain on the food. In this recipe for example, if you cut the chicken breasts with a knife and later cut the lemon with the same knife or on the same cutting board, you will contaminate the lemon with the bacteria from the chicken. Cross contamination is one of the leading causes of food poisoning, but it is easy to avoid by simply washing any utensils that come in contact with raw food, in this case, the knife, cutting board, and your hands, with hot, soapy water before working with any other foods.

Here I go again: I am not a big fan of fish. Okay, the truth is, I won't eat most types of fish. However, I really do like it when it is made this way, and it's even better with the tartar sauce on it. I mean how can you go wrong with potato chips? This is a super simple dish to make. Just make sure the potato chips get pretty finely crushed, or they will fall off when you take the fish out of the pan.

POTATO CHIP-CRUSTED WHITEFISH WITH POTATO WEDGES

Serves 4

✳ POTATOES

4 potatoes

2 tablespoons olive oil

1 teaspoon salt

✳ FISH

1 tablespoon olive oil

½ cup flour

1 egg

1½ cups crushed potato chips

4 4-ounce tilapia or orange roughy fillets

Salt and pepper

To prepare the potatoes: Preheat the oven to 375°F.

Wash the potatoes and cut each one into 8 wedges. Place the potatoes on a baking sheet and drizzle them with the oil. Toss the potatoes until they are coated with the oil and sprinkle them with the salt. Bake them for 40 to 45 minutes, or until they are golden brown around the edges.

Meanwhile, prepare the fish: Pour the oil into a 9 by 13-inch baking pan and spread to coat the entire pan. Place the flour in a shallow bowl. Whisk the egg in another shallow bowl. Place the crushed potato chips in another shallow bowl.

Dip both sides of the fish in the flour, then the egg, and then the potato chips and place the coated fish in the baking dish. Continue with the remaining fish. Season with salt and pepper. Bake the fish for 10 minutes, or until it pulls apart easily with a fork.

Potatoes will last longest when stored in a cool, dark place that is well ventilated. Prolonged exposure to light can cause potatoes to become green. Green potatoes may contain a substance called "solanine," which has a bitter flavor and can be toxic. Potatoes with greening can still be used, but any of the green should be trimmed before use. Even under perfect conditions potatoes will begin to sprout after a while. Small sprouts can be removed and the potatoes still used, but if the sprouts are large and the potatoes have softened, they are definitely past their prime and should be discarded.

✳TARTAR SAUCE

¹/₄ cup mayonnaise

2 tablespoons pickle relish

¹/₂ teaspoon lemon juice

Dash of Worcestershire sauce

Dash of Tabasco sauce

While the fish is cooking, prepare the tartar sauce: Place the mayonnaise, relish, lemon juice, Worcestershire sauce, and Tabasco sauce in a bowl and stir well.

Place a piece of fish on one side of each plate and arrange the potatoes wedges alongside. Serve the tartar sauce on the side.

> Meatloaf is one of my dad's self-professed specialties. He will spend an hour putting it together, and I swear he adds a pinch of just about every spice in the cabinet. Here we have narrowed down the list substantially, but it is still every bit as good as his. Sorry Dad.

j

MEATLOAF WITH SCALLOPED POTATOES

Serves 6

✳ POTATOES

2 tablespoons butter

2 tablespoons flour

2 cups milk

Salt and pepper

5 potatoes

To prepare the potatoes: Preheat the oven to 350°F.

Melt the butter in a small saucepan over low heat. Add the flour and stir constantly until the mixture starts to bubble. Add 1/2 cup of the milk and stir until smooth. Add the remaining 1 1/2 cups of the milk and cook over medium heat, stirring frequently, for 7 to 10 minutes, or until it comes to a boil. Season to taste with salt and pepper.

Peel the potatoes and, with a slicer or a knife, cut them into 1/16- to 1/8-inch-thick slices. Place one-fourth of the potatoes in a 2-quart baking dish, top with one-fourth of the sauce, and season with salt and pepper. Continue layering the remaining potatoes and sauce, seasoning each layer with salt and pepper. Bake the potatoes for 1 1/2 hours, or until they are dark golden brown and bubbly.

kitchen tip

This béchamel sauce is one of the most versatile sauces, and certainly the one we use most often. We use it as a base for all of the cream soups. We add Parmesan to it and use it in the Vegetable Lasagna. And now it shows up in the potatoes. But, here is yet another variation: simply add a cup of Cheddar to the sauce, and you will have au gratin potatoes.

☀ MEATLOAF

1/2 onion

1 stalk celery

2 slices bread

1 1/2 pounds ground beef

8 ounces ground pork

2 eggs

1 teaspoon salt

1/2 teaspoon pepper

1/2 teaspoon garlic powder

1/2 teaspoon ground mustard powder

1/2 teaspoon ground thyme

2 slices bacon

Meanwhile, prepare the meatloaf: Peel the onion, dice it into 1/4-inch pieces, and place in a large bowl. Dice the celery into 1/4-inch pieces and add them to the bowl. Tear the bread slices into small pieces and place them in the bowl. Add the ground beef, ground pork, eggs, salt, pepper, garlic powder, mustard, and thyme to the bowl and mix with your hands until completely combined. Place the meat mixture into an ungreased 9 by 13-inch baking pan and shape the meat into an oblong loaf. Place the bacon slices lengthwise on top of the meatloaf.

Place the meatloaf in the oven (with the potatoes) and bake for 1 hour and 15 minutes. Let the meatloaf rest for 5 minutes before slicing. Serve with the scalloped potatoes.

When we were on a family vacation in New Orleans we came across a store in the French Quarter that had daily cooking classes. We decided to sign up for a class (it got us out of going to another museum with our dad), and it turned out to be a blast. We learned to make several different Cajun dishes, but this was my favorite. I love the beans, but we also learned the secret to making the best cornbread ever—add lots of milk and sprinkle sugar on the top.

m

RED BEANS AND RICE WITH CORNBREAD

Serves 6

*BEANS

1 pound dried red kidney beans

1 large onion

2 stalks celery

3 tablespoons oil

6 (14-ounce) cans vegetable broth

2 teaspoons garlic powder

1 bay leaf

2 tablespoons Cajun seasoning

Salt and pepper

1/2 cup chopped parsley

To prepare the beans: Soak the beans overnight in water and drain (or see Kitchen Tip below).

Peel the onion and chop the celery and onion into 1/2-inch pieces. Place the oil in a stockpot and add the onion and celery. Cook over medium-high heat for 10 minutes. Add the beans and vegetable stock to the pot and bring to a boil. Add the garlic powder, bay leaf, and Cajun seasoning and simmer uncovered over medium-low heat for 3 hours. Season to taste with salt and pepper. Stir in the parsley just before serving.

kitchen tip

Soaking beans overnight softens them slightly and removes some of the starch. The only problem is, I never plan a meal that far in advance. I asked a chef friend of mine if there was a shortcut, and his answer was to drop the beans in boiling water, cook until the water comes back to a boil, and then drain and cook as directed. It works great.

✳CORNBREAD

1 1/2 cups milk

2 eggs

1/3 cup canola oil

3 tablespoons melted butter

1 1/2 cups flour

2/3 cup sugar plus extra for dusting

1/2 cup cornmeal

1 tablespoon baking powder

1/2 teaspoon salt

✳RICE

1 1/2 cups white rice

3 1/3 cups water

3/4 teaspoon salt

1 tablespoon butter

To prepare the cornbread: Preheat the oven to 350°F. Lightly butter or spray an 8- or 9-inch-square pan.

Combine the milk, eggs, oil, and melted butter in a large bowl. Add the flour, sugar, cornmeal, baking powder, and salt and mix until just combined (overmixing will make the cornbread tough). Pour the batter into the pan and sprinkle a light dusting of sugar over the top. Bake the cornbread for 20 to 25 minutes, or until a toothpick inserted in the center comes out clean. Cool slightly and cut into 9 squares.

Meanwhile, prepare the rice: Place the rice, water, salt, and butter in a small saucepan over medium-high heat and bring to a boil. Decrease the heat to medium-low, cover, and simmer for 20 minutes. Remove the pan from the heat and fluff the rice with a fork.

Place some of the rice on each plate and top with some of the beans. Serve the cornbread on the side.

SALMON AND VEGETABLES EN PAPILLOTE

Serves 4

✳ VEGETABLES

½ head cauliflower

1 stalk broccoli

1 carrot

12 green beans

4 teaspoons butter

8 sprigs thyme

Salt and pepper

To prepare the vegetables: Preheat the oven to 350°F.

Place 4 sheets of parchment paper on a work surface. Trim the cauliflower and broccoli florets from the stems, discarding the stems, and divide the florets among the parchment sheets.

Peel the carrot and cut into ¹/₁₆- to ⅛-inch-thick round slices. Place some of the carrots on each parchment sheet. Cut the ends off the green beans and cut each bean into 3 or 4 pieces. Arrange some of the beans on each parchment sheet and top with 1 teaspoon of butter. Place 2 thyme sprigs and 1 teaspoon of water on each parchment sheet. Season with salt and pepper. Bring the sides of the parchment to the middle and fold over three times, about ½ inch each time. Fold the ends of the parchment and tuck them under the package to loosely enclose the vegetables. Place the vegetable packets on an ungreased baking sheet and bake for 25 minutes.

✳ SALMON

4 5-ounce salmon fillets

3 lemons

Salt and pepper

8 sprigs thyme

Meanwhile, prepare the salmon: Lay 4 sheets of parchment paper on a work surface and place 1 salmon fillet in the center of each sheet. Cut 2 of the lemons in half, remove the seeds, and squeeze the juice from 1 lemon half on each salmon fillet. Season with salt and pepper and top each fillet with 2 thyme sprigs. Bring the sides of the parchment to the middle and fold over three times, about ½ inch each time. Fold the ends of the parchment and tuck them under the package, loosely enclosing the salmon. Add the salmon packets to the baking sheet and bake them for 10 minutes. (If your pieces of salmon are thicker than ¾ inch, you will need to cook them up to 5 minutes longer.)

Cut the remaining lemon into 8 wedges.

Remove the salmon and vegetables from the parchment and arrange them on plates with the lemon wedges.

Desserts

desserts

I love all banana cream pies, but this one is absolutely the best ever. Although this recipe is a little time-consuming, it is really not difficult to prepare. You spend most of your time just waiting for things to boil or cool, and the result is an awesome desert that will impress your family and friends.

BANANA CREAM PIE

Makes ONE 9-INCH PIE

✳ FILLING

5 egg yolks

¹/₄ cup cornstarch

3 cups half-and-half

1³/₄ cups granulated sugar

2 teaspoons vanilla

✳ CRUST

1¹/₂ cups crushed vanilla wafers

¹/₄ cup melted butter

3 bananas

1¹/₂ cups heavy cream

3 tablespoons powdered sugar

To prepare the filling: Fill a large bowl about halfway with ice cubes and add enough water to just cover the ice. Set aside.

Whisk together the egg yolks, cornstarch, and 1 cup of the half-and-half in a medium bowl. Place the remaining 2 cups of half-and-half and the sugar in a large saucepan and bring to a boil. Slowly whisk about ¹/₂ cup of the hot half-and-half mixture into the egg yolks, and then whisk the egg yolks and half-and-half into the hot half-and-half. Cook over medium-high heat, whisking constantly, until the mixture just comes to a boil. Continue to cook, whisking constantly, for 1 minute, or until thickened. Add the vanilla and whisk until smooth. Strain the custard through a fine-meshed sieve into a medium bowl. Place the bowl of custard into the ice water and stir occasionally until cool. Refrigerate until thoroughly chilled.

To prepare the crust: Preheat the oven to 350°F.

Place the vanilla wafers and melted butter in a 9-inch pie pan and mix until all of the vanilla wafers are moistened. Firmly press the mixture to cover the bottom and sides of the pan and bake the pie crust for 20 minutes, or until it is lightly browned. Remove the pan from the oven and let it cool to room temperature.

Kitchen Vocab

The process of whisking a little hot liquid into the eggs is called **tempering** the eggs. This is necessary whenever you are adding eggs to a hot liquid. Tempering allows the eggs to slowly increase in temperature without cooking them. If the eggs were added directly to the hot liquid they would cook and you would end up with scrambled eggs floating in the half-and-half.

To prepare the pie: Peel the bananas and slice them into ¼-inch-thick rounds. Arrange half of the bananas in an even layer in the bottom of the crust. Spoon half of the cooled custard over the bananas and spread smooth. Place the remaining bananas in an even layer over the custard and top with the remaining custard. Refrigerate the pie for at least 2 hours or overnight.

To prepare the topping: Whip the cream with an electric mixer on medium speed for 1 minute. Add the powdered sugar and whip on medium-high speed for 2 to 3 minutes, or until soft peaks form. (Test for soft peaks by pulling the beaters straight up. The cream should pull up with the beaters and form a peak, and when it releases, the tip should fold over and be slightly soft.) Spoon the whipped cream over the custard and refrigerate the pie until you are ready to serve it.

Ice water baths are used to quickly cool foods to a safe temperature. Perishable foods, in this case the eggs and milk, should be kept below 40°F or above 140°F. Ice water baths shorten the time in the "danger zone" (between 41°F and 139°F) where bacteria growth can occur.

kitchen safety

121

> This cheesecake is a cross between a New York style and the creamier, no-bake versions. It is really good and really impressive looking (and really big). We usually save this for family parties since it serves twelve people, but if you are making it for your family, it can be refrigerated for four or five days or sliced, individually covered in plastic wrap, and frozen.

CHEESECAKE

Makes ONE 9- OR 10-INCH CAKE

❋ CRUST

1 1/2 cups graham cracker crumbs

1/4 cup melted butter

1/4 cup sugar

❋ FILLING

32 ounces cream cheese

1 cup sugar

4 eggs

2 teaspoons vanilla

1/4 cup heavy cream

1/4 cup sour cream

To prepare the crust: Preheat the oven to 325°F.

Place a large sheet of aluminum foil over the base of a 9- or 10-inch springform pan. Place the sides on the base over the foil and attach to the base. Fold the excess foil up around the outside of the pan so when it is placed in a water bath, the water will not leak into the cheesecake. (If you don't have a springform pan, use a 9 by 13-inch pan and omit the foil.)

Place the crust ingredients into the foil-lined springform pan and stir until combined. Firmly press the mixture into the bottom and sides of the pan and refrigerate it until you are ready to add the filling.

To prepare the filling: Place the cream cheese in a large bowl and beat with an electric mixer on medium speed for 2 minutes, or until completely smooth. Add

Kitchen Vocab

A springform pan has a spring-loaded latch on the side so the top can be removed from the bottom. These are great for times, as with this cheesecake, when you want to remove the cake from the pan to serve it, but it is too fragile to remove from a regular cake pan.

kitchen math

the sugar and beat, scraping the sides of the bowl occasionally, for 2 minutes, or until combined. Add the eggs and vanilla and mix for 2 to 3 minutes, or until smooth. Add the heavy cream and sour cream and stir with a spoon until just incorporated. (Using an electric mixer for this step causes a lot of air bubbles to form in the batter. The air bubbles float to the top of the cheesecake and pop during baking, leaving little craters all over the top.) Pour the filling into the springform pan and place it in a larger baking pan. Place the pans in the oven and pour enough hot water into the larger baking pan to come halfway up the sides of the springform pan. Bake for 1 hour. Turn off the oven and leave the cheesecake inside until the oven is completely cool. Take the cheesecake out of the oven and refrigerate for at least 4 hours, or overnight.

I like to make these cookies small, using a scoop so they are all the same size, whereas Jill uses a spoon and makes them huge and all different sizes. Either way, they are one of our favorite cookies. They are great the way they are, but sometimes I like to add butterscotch chips for something different.

see photo on page 135

PEANUT BUTTER COOKIES

Makes 72 COOKIES

½ cup butter

¾ cup peanut butter

1¼ cups firmly packed brown sugar

1 egg

2 tablespoons milk

¾ teaspoon baking soda

2 cups flour

2 tablespoons granulated sugar

Preheat the oven to 350°F.

Place the butter, peanut butter, and brown sugar in a large bowl and mix with an electric mixer on medium speed for 2 minutes, or until completely combined. Add the egg and milk and mix on medium speed for 2 minutes, or until light and fluffy. Add the baking soda and mix for 30 seconds. Add the flour and mix until completely incorporated.

Place the granulated sugar in a small bowl. Drop teaspoonfuls of the dough onto an ungreased baking sheet at least 2 inches apart. Dip a fork into the cookie dough to make it sticky. Dip the fork in the sugar and press down twice on each cookie in a crisscross pattern, dipping the fork in the sugar after each press.

Bake the cookies for 7 to 10 minutes, or until they are lightly browned on the edges.

KITCHEN DISASTER

Every time we make cookies we have the same problem. Everything goes like clockwork, getting the trays in the oven, taking out the finished ones, taking them off the tray to cool, setting up the next tray. And then we get to the last tray. No matter how many times we remind ourselves, we always forget to set the timer for the last tray, and they end up burnt to a crisp. We now actually stick a note on the oven door to remind us to set the timer. Sometimes it even works!

TOFFEE BARS

Toffee Bars were the first things I learned to bake. These are my standard fare for those, "Oh man, I forgot I was supposed to bring cookies" times. They're super easy and quick to make. Ten minutes to prep, twenty minutes to cook, done.

j

Makes ONE 11 BY 17-INCH PAN

1½ cups butter

1½ cups firmly packed brown sugar

1½ teaspoons vanilla

3 cups flour

1 cup chocolate chips

Preheat the oven to 350°F.

Place the butter, brown sugar, and vanilla in a large bowl and mix with an electric mixer on medium speed for 2 minutes, or until completely combined. Add the flour and mix on low speed for 2 minutes, or until the flour is incorporated. Stir in the chocolate chips.

Place the dough on an ungreased 11 by 17-inch baking sheet and press into an even layer covering the entire pan. Bake the bars for 20 to 25 minutes, or until they are light golden brown. Let them cool for 5 minutes and then cut them into squares. (If they cool too much they will crack when you cut them.)

PEACH TURNOVERS

Peeling peaches with a knife can be a pain, but blanching them first makes it much easier. Lowering the peaches into a pan of boiling water for two or three minutes loosens the skins enough that you can easily peel them with your fingers. This works even better on tomatoes, which are impossible to peel otherwise.

j

[continued]

3 peaches

1 cup sugar

1/2 cup water

1 vanilla bean or 1 teaspoon
  vanilla extract

2 sheets puff pastry, thawed

1 egg

1/2 cup heavy cream

Peel the peaches, cut in half, and remove the pits. Cut each peach half into 1/2-inch-thick wedges.

Place the sugar and water in a large sauté pan over medium heat and cook for 10 to 15 minutes, or until the sugar is golden brown. Do not stir the sugar and water mixture. Stirring after the sugar is melted can cause the sugar to crystallize (become grainy). If the sugar becomes crystallized, there is no way remelt it, you have to throw it away and start over.

Preheat the oven to 350°F. Lightly butter or spray a baking sheet.

Add the peach wedges to the sugar and stir until the peaches are coated with the sugar. Cut the vanilla bean open lengthwise and scrape out the seeds with the knife. (If you are using the vanilla extract, add it after the pan has been taken off the heat.) Add the seeds and bean to the pan and cook, stirring occasionally, for 5 minutes. Remove the pan from the heat and let it cool slightly. Strain through a fine-meshed sieve, reserving the liquid and the peaches and discarding the vanilla bean.

Unfold the puff pastry sheets and cut them in thirds lengthwise and widthwise, forming 9 squares from each sheet. Place 1 or 2 peach slices in the center of each pastry square and fold the squares in half diagonally, pressing firmly on the point to seal the front of the turnovers. Place the turnovers on the baking sheet.

In a small bowl, beat the egg with a fork and brush over the turnovers. Bake them for 15 to 18 minutes, or until golden brown.

Meanwhile, place the sugar back in the pan and cook over medium heat for 5 minutes, or until it begins to simmer. Remove the pan from the heat. Add the cream and stir until well combined.

Place 2 or 3 turnovers in the center of each plate and drizzle the sauce over the turnovers and around the plate.

SEVEN-LAYER BARS

These bars are one of the easiest and most-loved desserts in our repertoire. All of our friends (and many of our teachers) request them with great regularity. We won't name names, but these bars have even gotten us out of a few after-school detentions for being tardy. They have mutated over the years and don't have seven layers any more. We know that one layer we eliminated was nuts, but we can't even remember what the seventh layer was any more.

see photo
on page
125

Makes ONE 9 BY 13-INCH PAN

2 cups graham cracker crumbs

¹/₂ cup melted butter

1 cup chocolate chips

1 cup butterscotch chips

1¹/₂ cups sweetened coconut

1 (14-ounce) can sweetened condensed milk

Preheat the oven to 350°F.

Stir together the graham cracker crumbs and butter in an ungreased 9 by 13-inch pan and firmly press the mixture to cover the bottom of the pan.

Evenly sprinkle the chocolate chips, butterscotch chips, and coconut over the crust. Drizzle the sweetened condensed milk evenly over the entire pan. Bake the bars for 30 to 40 minutes, or until they are golden brown.

j

I love apple crisp, and this version is the best ever. It's really easy to make and almost impossible to ruin. This recipe is also great with peaches, pears, blueberries, or raspberries, but if you use berries, put all of the crumble mixture on top, or it will get soggy. No matter what fruit you use, eat it warm with some vanilla ice cream, and oh man, it is the best!

APPLE CRISP

Makes ONE 9 BY 13-INCH PAN

✱ CRUMBLE

2 cups flour

1 cup firmly packed brown sugar

1/2 cup oatmeal

3/4 cup melted butter

✱ FILLING

6 apples

1 cup sugar

3 tablespoons cornstarch

1/4 teaspoon salt

1 cup water

1 teaspoon vanilla

To prepare the crumble: Place the crumble ingredients in a bowl and stir with a fork until the mixture is completely combined.

To prepare the filling: Preheat the oven to 350°F.

Peel the apples and cut them in half. Remove the cores and cut the apples into 1/4-inch-thick wedges. Place the sugar, cornstarch, salt, water, and vanilla in a large bowl and stir until combined. Add the apples and toss until coated.

Place one-half of the crumble mixture in an ungreased 9 by 13-inch pan and pat it down to form a crust. Pour the apple mixture into the pan and spread the apples evenly over the crust. Sprinkle the remaining crumble mixture over the apples and bake for 40 to 45 minutes, or until the topping is golden brown.

There are zillions of different kinds of apples out there, and it can get really confusing trying to figure out which ones to use for what. Here is a quick rundown on the eight most popular types. The best eating apples are Red Delicious, Gala, and Fuji. The best cooking apples are Granny Smith, McIntosh, and Rome Beauty. And then there are Golden Delicious and Jonathan, which are good for both eating and baking.

kitchen tip

m

I'm sure you are probably thinking you could never make something as fancy-schmancy as crème brûlée, but let me clue you in on a little secret—it's not hard to make. The thing to remember when you are dealing with custard is to never let the eggs get too hot or they will scramble. But if you pour the half-and-half into the eggs very slowly and be sure to pull the custard out of the oven when it still jiggles slightly in the center, it will turn out perfectly every time.

CRÈME BRÛLÉE

Serves 4

½ cup half-and-half

1 vanilla bean or 1 teaspoon vanilla extract

4 egg yolks

⅓ cup sugar plus extra for dusting

1½ cups heavy cream

Preheat the oven to 325°F.

Place the half-and-half in a small saucepan over medium heat. Cut open the vanilla bean lengthwise and scrape out the seeds with a knife. (If you are using the vanilla extract, add it after the pan has been taken off the heat.) Place the seeds and bean in the pan and cook for 5 minutes, or until it begins to boil.

Kitchen Vocab

The pan of water that the crème brûlée is baked in is called a **water bath**. A water bath is used to cook custards gently so they don't curdle (when egg-based batters are heated too much and too quickly, they turn into scrambled eggs, all curdy and, in this case, sweet too). Be very careful not to splash yourself with the hot water in the water bath when you take the pan out of the oven. Leave the **ramekins** (individual ceramic baking dishes) sitting in the water bath while the water cools and remove them when the baking dishes and water are cool. Custards are delicate and may collapse if they cool too quickly.

Whisk together the egg yolks and sugar in a medium bowl. Very slowly pour the hot half-and-half into the eggs, whisking constantly. Whisk in the cream and discard the vanilla bean.

Pour the custard into 4 ramekins or crème brûlée dishes and place the dishes into a baking pan. Place the pan in the oven and add enough hot water to the pan to come halfway up the dishes. Bake the custards for 35 minutes, or until their edges are set and their middles are slightly jiggly.

Cool slightly and refrigerate until ready to serve.

Evenly coat the top of each crème brûlée with a thin layer of sugar and, under a gas broiler, melt the sugar until a golden brown caramelized crust forms.

SNICKERDOODLES

Megan and I absolutely love Snickerdoodles, but neither of us likes to roll them into balls. So, one of us will mix the dough, and then we begin "let's make a deal" with our parents. Offering to do chores seems to be our most effective bargaining chip to trade for rolling: we have washed dishes, cooked dinner, cleaned the litter box, and when it's a double batch, even cleaned our rooms.

Makes APPROXIMATELY 72 COOKIES

✴ DOUGH

1 cup butter

1½ cups sugar

2 eggs

1 teaspoon vanilla

1 teaspoon cream of tartar

½ teaspoon salt

2⅔ cups flour

✴ TOPPING

2 tablespoons sugar

2 teaspoons cinnamon

To prepare the dough:
Preheat the oven to 400°F.

Place the butter and sugar in a large bowl and mix with an electric mixer on medium speed for 2 minutes, or until completely combined. Add the egg and vanilla and mix for 2 minutes, or until the mixture is fluffy. Add the cream of tartar and salt and mix for 30 seconds. Add the flour and mix on low speed until the flour is completely incorporated.

To prepare the cookies: Combine the 2 tablespoons sugar with the cinnamon in a small bowl. Drop a teaspoonful of the dough into the cinnamon sugar and shake the bowl slightly to coat the dough. Place the dough on an ungreased baking sheet and roughly form it into a ball with your fingers. (The balls don't have to be perfect, just vaguely round.) Continue with the remaining dough, placing the cookies about 2 inches apart on the baking sheet. Press down on the cookies to flatten them slightly. Bake them for 8 to 10 minutes, or until their edges just begin to brown.

m

After a seven-month internship at Walt Disney World, I can say with some authority that people love frozen bananas. You can't even imagine how many times I said, "The nut wagons in Adventureland and Fantasyland are the only places to get frozen bananas in the Magic Kingdom." I love them like this, with toffee, but they are also good with coconut or nuts.

FROZEN BANANAS WITH CHOCOLATE AND TOFFEE

Makes 6 BANANAS

3 bananas

1 cup chocolate chips

½ cup toffee chips

Line a baking pan with parchment or waxed paper.

Peel the bananas and cut each one in half crosswise. Insert a skewer or Popsicle stick 2 to 3 inches into one end of each banana half. Place the bananas on the pan and freeze for 30 minutes.

Place the chocolate chips in a microwave-safe bowl and cook on high for 2 minutes, or until completely melted.

Holding a banana over the bowl, spoon the chocolate over the banana, spreading quickly to cover the entire outside. Sprinkle the banana with the toffee chips and place it on the baking sheet. Repeat with the remaining bananas. Freeze the bananas for at least 30 minutes, or up to several days.

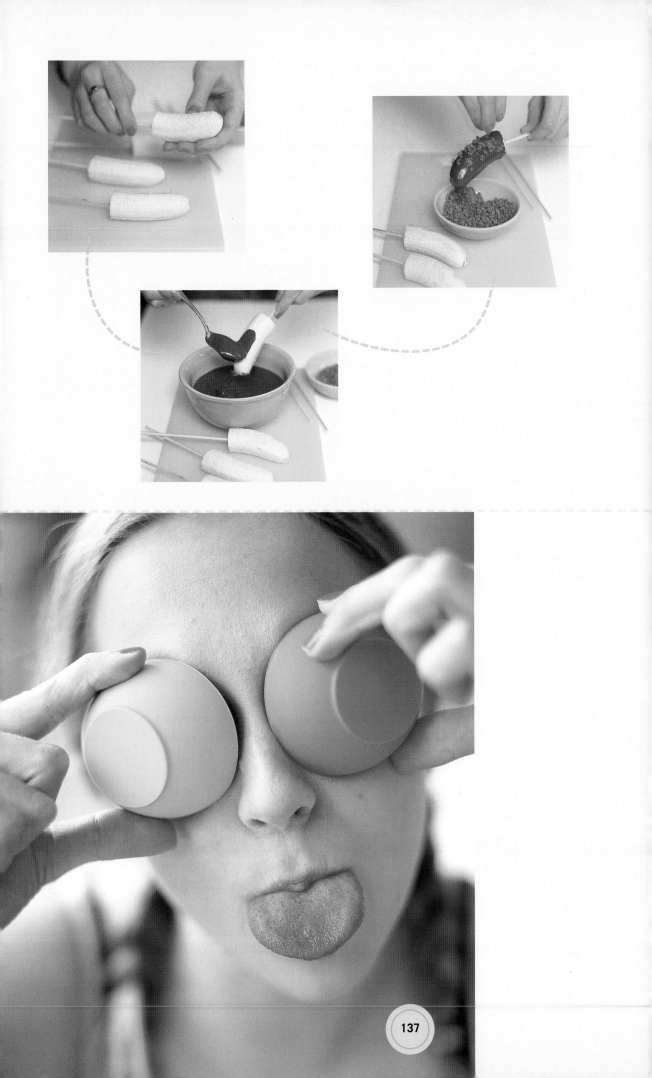

This was my great-grandmother's recipe and has been the traditional Carle family birthday cake for four generations. That means that for four generations we have argued about how many raisins should be in the cake. My grandfather liked it like a fruitcake, loaded with raisins and other dried fruit, and my oldest sister, Mindy, likes it with none. But, since we are writing the book, it's 1 cup.

CHOCOLATE SPICE CAKE

Makes ONE 8-INCH 2-LAYER CAKE

✳ CAKE

1 tablespoon white wine vinegar

1 cup milk

1/2 cup butter

1 egg

1 cup sugar

1 teaspoon baking powder

1/4 teaspoon salt

1 teaspoon ground cinnamon

1 teaspoon ground allspice

1 teaspoon ground cloves

1 teaspoon baking soda

2 tablespoons unsweetened cocoa powder

2 cups flour

1 cup raisins

To prepare the cake: Preheat the oven to 350°F. Lightly butter or spray two 8-inch round cake pans.

Place the vinegar in a liquid measuring cup and add enough milk to make 1 cup. Set aside.

Place the butter and egg in a large bowl and beat with an electric mixer on medium-high speed for 2 minutes, or until the mixture is fluffy. Add the sugar and mix on medium speed for 1 minute.

Add the baking powder, salt, cinnamon, allspice, cloves, baking soda, and cocoa and mix for 1 minute, or until the batter is completely even in color. Add the flour and mix on low speed for 2 minutes, or until completely incorporated. Add the milk and mix for 1 minute, or until smooth. Add the raisins and mix until evenly distributed.

Spoon half of the batter into each cake pan and spread evenly. Bake the cakes for 20 to 25 minutes, or until a toothpick inserted in the center of each cake comes out clean. Place a wire cooling rack on top of each cake pan. Hold both the wire rack and the pan, turn them over, and remove the pan. Cool the cakes to room temperature.

kitchen chemistry

Here is a little tidbit that surprised me when I heard it. If you have a problem with cakes or muffins not rising enough, it is probably not because you aren't using enough baking powder or baking soda, but because you are using too much. When liquid is added to baking powder and soda they create a gas that forms air bubbles. If there is too much of either one, the overproduction of small bubbles breaks up the larger bubbles which will make cakes heavier and more dense. The rule of thumb is 1 teaspoon of baking powder or $\frac{1}{4}$ teaspoon baking soda per cup of flour.

✳ FROSTING

3 ounces unsweetened
   chocolate

1 cup butter

1 egg

3 cups powdered sugar

1 teaspoon vanilla

1½ tablespoons milk

Pinch of salt

To prepare the frosting: Place the unsweetened chocolate in a small microwave-safe bowl. Microwave on high for 2 minutes, or until the chocolate is completely melted.

Place the butter and egg in a large bowl and beat with an electric mixer on medium speed for 2 minutes, or until fluffy. Add the sugar and melted chocolate and mix until completely even in color. Add the vanilla, milk, and salt and mix until combined.

Place one of the cakes upside down on a serving plate and cover the top and sides with half of the frosting. Place the remaining cake upside down on top of the frosted cake and spread the remaining frosting on the top and sides, blending the upper and lower portions of the sides as you go.

As we mentioned earlier, this recipe has been in our family for almost a hundred years. Back then they didn't know that the raw egg in the frosting may contain harmful bacteria that may not be safe for young children, the elderly, or people with weakened immune systems. Pasteurized eggs (found in the dairy case in most grocery stores) are a safe substitute and work just as well as fresh eggs in this recipe.

kitchen tip

These are my favorite kind of brownies. I like chocolate, but I'm not into the serious fudgy-chocolate kind of stuff. With these brownies I can pick out the ones with more cream cheese and leave the more chocolaty ones for someone else (like my mom).

m

CREAM CHEESE BROWNIES

see photo on page 125

Makes ONE 9 BY 13-INCH PAN

✳ BROWNIES

4 ounces unsweetened chocolate

3/4 cup butter

2 cups sugar

1 cup flour

3 eggs

1 teaspoon vanilla

✳ CREAM CHEESE

8 ounces cream cheese

1/3 cup sugar

1 egg

2 tablespoons flour

To prepare the brownies: Preheat the oven to 350°F. Lightly grease a 9 by 13-inch pan.

Place the chocolate and butter in a microwave-safe bowl and cook on high for 2 minutes, or until completely melted. Stir in the sugar until well combined. Add the flour, eggs, and vanilla and stir until combined. Spread the mixture into the baking pan.

To prepare the cream cheese: Place the cream cheese in a bowl and, using an electric mixer on medium speed, whip the cream cheese until smooth. Add the sugar, egg, and flour and mix until smooth.

Drop spoonfuls of the cream cheese batter on top of the chocolate and swirl it into the chocolate by running a knife back and forth across the pan. Bake the brownies for 35 minutes, or until the cream cheese is light brown. Cool completely before cutting.

Index

★ A

Apples
    Apple Crisp, 130–31
    Fried Apple Rings, 14–15
    German Apple Puff Pancake, 21
    Roman Apple Coffee Cake, 12–13
    types of, 131
Avocados
    Guacamole, 36–37
    Steak Cobb Salad, 64–65
    Vegetable Maki Rolls, 34–35

★ B

Bacon
    BLT Dip, 39
    cooking, xii–xiii
    Grilled Cheese with Bacon and Tomato, 83
    Potato Skins, 26–27
    Spinach Salad with Honey-Mustard Dressing,
        68–69
    Steak Cobb Salad, 64–65
    substitute, 52
    thick-sliced, xii
    Turkey-Bacon Puff Pastry Pockets, 86–87
Bacterial contamination, 109, 121, 139
Baked French Toast, 22
Baked Macaroni and Cheese, 90
Baked Potato Soup, 52
Baking powder, 139
Baking soda, 139
Bananas
    Banana Bread, 2–3
    Banana Cream Pie, 120–121
    Frozen Bananas with Chocolate and Toffee,
        136–137
Beans
    Nachos with Salsa and Guacamole, 36–37
    Ratatouille with Chickpeas and Couscous, 96
    Red Beans and Rice with Cornbread, 114–15
    soaking, alternative to, 114
    Taco Salad, 60–61
Bean sprouts
    Fried Rice, 80
    Vegetable Lomein, 84
Béchamel sauce, 91 112
Beef
    Meatloaf with Scalloped Potatoes, 112–13
    Mexican Lasagna, 102–103
    Sloppy Joes, 95
    Steak Cobb Salad, 64–65
    Steak Fajitas, 78–79
    steaks, cooking, 65
Bell peppers
    Caramelized Onion, Mushroom, and Roasted Red
        Pepper Focaccia, 28–30
    Ratatouille with Chickpeas and Couscous, 96
    Vegetable Lasagna, 100–102
Blanching, 55, 127
BLT Dip, 39
Blueberry Syrup, 10
Bread. **See also** Sandwiches
    Baked French Toast, 22
    Banana Bread, 2–3
    BLT Dip, 39
    Caramelized Onion, Mushroom, and Roasted Red
        Pepper Focaccia, 28–30
    Chocolate Chip Scones, 8–9
    Cinnamon Rolls, 6–7
    Cornbread, 114
    Goat Cheese and Tomato Crostini, 44
    kneading, 30
    mixing ingredients for, 3, 13
    types of, xii
    yeast for, 30
Breadcrumbs, xii

Breakfast
    Baked French Toast, 22
    Banana Bread, 2–3
    Breakfast Burritos, 23
    Buttermilk Pancakes with Blueberry Syrup, 10–11
    Chocolate Chip Scones, 8–9
    Cinnamon Rolls, 6–7
    Crepes with Fresh Strawberries and Cream, 18–19
    Fried Apple Rings, 14–15
    German Apple Puff Pancake, 21
    Hash Brown Casserole, 5
    Roman Apple Coffee Cake, 12–13
    Sausage and Egg Bake, 4
    Spinach and Mushroom Quiche, 17
Broccoli
    Broccoli Cheese Soup, 54
    bunches vs. stalks of, 54
    Vegetable Stir Fry with Tofu, 75
Broiling, 67
Brownies, Cream Cheese, 140
Buffalo Wings, 40
Burritos, Breakfast, 23
Butter
    creaming sugar and, 2
    salted vs. unsalted, xii
Buttermilk
    Buttermilk Pancakes with Blueberry Syrup, 10–11
    substitution for, 8

★ C

Cabbage
    Vegetable Lomein, 84
    Vegetable Stir Fry with Tofu, 75
    Wonton Soup, 58–59
Caesar Salad, Chicken, 66–67
Cakes
    Cheesecake, 122–23
    Chocolate Spice Cake, 138–39
    mixing ingredients for, 13
    rising problems with, 139
    Roman Apple Coffee Cake, 12–13
Caramelized Onion, Mushroom, and Roasted Red
        Pepper Focaccia, 28–30
Caramelizing, 30
Cheese. **See also** Cream cheese
    Baked Macaroni and Cheese, 90
    Breakfast Burritos, 23
    Broccoli Cheese Soup, 54
    Cheese and Chile Enchiladas, 97
    Cheesecake, 122–23
    Chicken Empanadas, 38–39
    Chicken Quesadillas, 77
    Chili Cheese Dip, 31
    Cinnamon Rolls, 6–7
    Eggplant Parmesan, 104–105
    Egg Salad Tortilla Wrap, 81

Goat Cheese and Tomato Crostini, 44
    Grilled Cheese with Bacon and Tomato, 83
    Hash Brown Casserole, 5
    Mexican Lasagna, 102–103
    Nachos with Salsa and Guacamole, 36–37
    Potato Skins, 26–27
    Sausage and Egg Bake, 4
    Spinach and Cheese Ravioli, 72–73
    Spinach and Mushroom Quiche, 17
    Steak Cobb Salad, 64–65
    Steak Fajitas, 78–79
    Taco Salad, 60–61
    Tuna Melt, 74
    Turkey-Bacon Puff Pastry Pockets, 86–87
    Vegetable Lasagna, 100-01
Chicken
    Buffalo Wings, 40
    Chicken and Dumplings, 98–99
    Chicken Caesar Salad, 66–67
    Chicken Empanadas, 38–39
    Chicken Piccata with Rice Pilaf, 92–93
    Chicken Pot Pies, 106–07
    Chicken Quesadillas, 77
    Chicken Schnitzel with Fried Potatoes, 108–09
Chickpeas, Ratatouille with Couscous and, 96
Chiles
    Breakfast Burritos, 23
    Cheese and Chile Enchiladas, 97
    handling, 79
    Salsa, 37
    Steak Fajitas, 78–79
Chili Cheese Dip, 31
Chocolate
    Chocolate Chip Scones, 8
    Chocolate Spice Cake, 138–39
    Cream Cheese Brownies, 140
    Frozen Bananas with Chocolate and Toffee,
        136–37
    Seven-Layer Bars, 129
    Toffee Bars, 125
Chopping, 26
Chowder, Corn, 51
Cinnamon Rolls, 6–7
Cinnamon Sticks, 41
Coffee Cake, Roman Apple, 12–13
Colanders, 62
Cookies
    Cream Cheese Brownies, 140
    Peanut Butter Cookies, 124
    Seven-Layer Bars, 129
    Snickerdoodles, 135
    Toffee Bars, 125
Cooking spray, vegetable, xiii
Corn
    Cheese and Chile Enchiladas, 97
    Corn Chowder, 51
    Taco Salad, 60–61

Cornbread, 114
Cornstarch, thickening with, 99
Couscous, Ratatouille with Chickpeas and, 96
Crab Rangoons, 46–47
Cream cheese
    Cheese and Chile Enchiladas, 97
    Cheesecake, 122–23
    Chili Cheese Dip, 31
    Crab Rangoons, 46–47
    Cream Cheese Brownies, 140
    Crepes with Fresh Strawberries and Cream, 18–19
    lowfat, xii
    Marshmallow Dip, 43
    mixing, with other ingredients, 19
Creaming, 2
Crème Brûlée, 132–33
Crepes with Fresh Strawberries and Cream, 18–19
Crisp, Apple, 130–31
Cross contamination, 109
Crostini, Goat Cheese and Tomato, 44
Custards, 132–133

★ **D**
Deglazing, 92
Desserts
    Apple Crisp, 130–31
    Banana Cream Pie, 120–21
    Cheesecake, 122–23
    Chocolate Spice Cake, 138–39
    Cream Cheese Brownies, 140
    Crème Brûlée, 132–33
    Frozen Bananas with Chocolate and Toffee, 136–37
    Peach Turnovers, 126–28
    Peanut Butter Cookies, 124
    Seven-Layer Bars, 129
    Snickerdoodles, 135
    Toffee Bars, 125
Deviled Eggs, 45
Dicing, 26
Dinners for one
    Chicken Quesadillas, 77
    Egg Salad Tortilla Wrap, 81
    Fried Rice, 80
    Grilled Cheese with Bacon and Tomato, 83
    Grilled Portobello Sandwich, 82
    Shrimp Fettuccine Alfredo, 76
    Spinach and Cheese Ravioli, 72–73
    Steak Fajitas, 78–79
    Tuna Melt, 74
    Turkey-Bacon Puff Pastry Pockets, 86–87
    Vegetable Lomein, 84
    Vegetable Stir Fry with Tofu, 75
Dips
    BLT Dip, 39
    Chili Cheese Dip, 31

Guacamole, 36–37
Marshmallow Dip, 43
Disasters
    burnt cookies, 124
    doorstop breads and cakes, 3, 89
    explosions, 52, 59
    fires, 15
    food poisoning, 109, 121, 139
    garlic, excessive, 33
    jalapeño juice in the eyes, 79
    lumpy sauces, 99
    oil-clogged drains, 47
Dredging, 104
Dumplings, Chicken and, 98–99

★ **E**
Eggplant
    Eggplant Parmesan, 104-5
    Ratatouille with Chickpeas and Couscous, 96
Eggs
    Breakfast Burritos, 23
    Deviled Eggs, 45
    Egg Salad Tortilla Wrap, 81
    peeling, 45
    Sausage and Egg Bake, 4
    separating, 15
    size of, xii
    Spinach and Mushroom Quiche, 17
    Steak Cobb Salad, 64–65
    tempering, 121
    whites, whipping, 16
Empanadas, Chicken, 38–39
Enchiladas, Cheese and Chile, 97
Explosions, preventing, 52, 59

★ **F**
Fajitas, Steak, 78–79
Family meals
    Baked Macaroni and Cheese, 90–91
    Cheese and Chile Enchiladas, 97
    Chicken and Dumplings, 98–99
    Chicken Piccata with Rice Pilaf, 92–93
    Chicken Pot Pies, 106
    Chicken Schnitzel with Fried Potatoes, 108–09
    Eggplant Parmesan, 104–05
    Meatloaf with Scalloped Potatoes, 112–13
    Mexican Lasagna, 102–103
    Potato Chip Crusted Whitefish with Potato Wedges, 110–11
    Ratatouille with Chickpeas and Couscous, 96–97
    Red Beans and Rice with Cornbread, 114–15
    Salmon and Vegetables en Papillote, 116–117
    Sloppy Joes, 95
    Vegetable Lasagna, 100-101
Fettuccine Alfredo, Shrimp, 76
Fires, putting out, 15

Fish
    Potato Chip Crusted Whitefish with Potato
        Wedges, 110–11
    Salmon and Vegetables en Papillote, 116–17
    Tuna and Macaroni Salad, 62
    Tuna Melt, 74
Flour
    gluten in, 3, 30
    mixing, with liquids, 3
    types of, 30
Focaccia, Caramelized Onion, Mushroom, and
    Roasted Red Pepper, 28–30
Fond, 92
Food poisoning, 109, 121, 139
French Onion Soup, 56–57
French Toast, Baked, 122
Fried Apple Rings, 14–15
Fried Potatoes, 108
Fried Rice, 80
Frozen Bananas with Chocolate and Toffee, 136–37
Fruits, xiii. **See also individual fruits**

★ **G**
Garlic, 33
German Apple Puff Pancake, 21
Gluten, 3, 30
Goat Cheese and Tomato Crostini, 44
Grilled Cheese with Bacon and Tomato, 83
Grilled Portobello Sandwich, 82
Grilling, 67
Guacamole, 36–37

★ **H**
Hash Brown Casserole, 5
Herbs, snipping, 27

★ **I**   ★ **K**
Ice water baths, 121
Kneading, 30

★ **L**
Lasagna
    Mexican Lasagna, 102–03
    Vegetable Lasagna, 100–01
Lomein, Vegetable, 84

★ **M**
Macaroni
    Baked Macaroni and Cheese, 90
    Tuna and Macaroni Salad, 62
Maki Rolls, Vegetable, 34–35
Marinating, 78
Marshmallow Dip, 43
Mayonnaise, xii
Measurements
    equivalent, 22, 50
    liquid vs. dry, 123

Meatloaf with Scalloped Potatoes, 112–13
Mexican Lasagna, 102–03
Microwave safety, 83
Miracle Whip, xii
Mixing
    batters for muffins and cakes, 13
    cream cheese with other ingredients, 19
    wet and dry ingredients, 3
Muffins
    mixing ingredients for, 13
    rising problems with, 139
Mushrooms
    Caramelized Onion, Mushroom, and Roasted Red
        Pepper Focaccia, 28–30
    Grilled Portobello Sandwich, 82
    Spinach and Mushroom Quiche, 17
    Spinach Salad with Honey-Mustard Dressing,
        68–69
    Vegetable Stir Fry with Tofu, 75
    Wonton Soup, 58–59

★ **N**
Nachos with Salsa and Guacamole, 36–37
Noodles. **See** Pasta and noodles
Nori
    buying, 35
    Vegetable Maki Rolls, 34–35
Nuts, xii

★ **O**
Oil, hot
    disposing of, 47
    fires from, 15
    placing food in, 105
Onions
    Caramelized Onion, Mushroom, and Roasted Red
        Pepper Focaccia, 28–30
    French Onion Soup, 56–57
    types of, 56
Orzo, 92

★ **P**
Pancakes
    Buttermilk Pancakes with Blueberry Syrup,
        10–11
    German Apple Puff Pancake, 21
Pans
    buttering, xiii
    deglazing, 92
    springform, 122
Pasta and noodles
    Baked Macaroni and Cheese, 90
    Chicken Piccata with Rice Pilaf, 92–93
    cooking al dente, 84
    orzo, 92
    Shrimp Fettuccine Alfredo, 74
    Tuna and Macaroni Salad, 62

Vegetable Lasagna, 100–101
Vegetable Lomein, 84
Peaches
    Peach Turnovers, 126–28
    peeling, 127
Peanut Butter Cookies, 124
Peas. **See also** Snow peas
    Fried Rice, 80
    Split Pea Soup, 50
    Tuna and Macaroni Salad, 62
Pie, Banana Cream, 120–121
Pork. **See also** Bacon; Sausage
    Meatloaf with Scalloped Potatoes, 112–113
    Pot Stickers, 32–33
    Wonton Soup, 58–59
Portobello Sandwich, Grilled, 82
Potatoes
    Baked Potato Soup, 52
    exploding, 52
    Fried Potatoes, 108
    green, 111
    Potato Chip Crusted Whitefish with Potato
        Wedges, 110–11
    Potato Skins, 26–27
    Scalloped Potatoes, 112
    storing, 111
    types of, 53
Pot Pies, Chicken, 106
Pot Stickers, 32–33
Puff pastry
    Chicken Pot Pies, 106
    Cinnamon Sticks, 41
    Peach Turnovers, 126–28
    thawing and using, 41
    Turkey-Bacon Puff Pastry Pockets, 86–87
Pureeing, 59

★ Q

Quesadillas, Chicken, 77
Quiche, Spinach and Mushroom, 17

★ R

Ratatouille with Chickpeas and Couscous, 96
Ravioli, Spinach and Cheese, 72–73
Red Beans and Rice with Cornbread, 114–15
Rice
    Chicken Piccata with Rice Pilaf, 92–93
    Fried Rice, 80
    Red Beans and Rice with Cornbread, 114–15
    Vegetable Maki Rolls, 34–35
    Vegetable Stir Fry with Tofu, 75
Rolls
    Cinnamon Rolls, 6–7
    Vegetable Maki Rolls, 35–36
Roman Apple Coffee Cake, 12–13
Roux, 91

★ S

Safety tips
    for bacterial contamination prevention, 109,
        121, 139
    for hot oil, 15, 47, 105
    for microwaves, 83
Salads
    Chicken Caesar Salad, 66–67
    Egg Salad, 81
    Spinach Salad with Honey-Mustard Dressing,
        68–69
    Steak Cobb Salad, 64–65
    Taco Salad, 60–61
    Tuna and Macaroni Salad, 62
Salmon and Vegetables en Papillote, 116–17
Salsa, 36
Salt, xii
Sandwiches
    Egg Salad Tortilla Wrap, 81
    Grilled Cheese with Bacon and Tomato, 83
    Grilled Portobello Sandwich, 82
    Sloppy Joes, 95
    Tuna Melt, 74
Sauces
    béchamel, 91, 112
    Tartar Sauce, 111
    thickening, 91, 99
Sausage
    Breakfast Burritos, 23
    Sausage and Egg Bake, 4
Sautéing, 76
Scalloped Potatoes, 112
Schnitzel, Chicken, with Fried Potatoes, 108–09
Scones, Chocolate Chip, 8–9
Seven-Layer Bars, 129
Shocking, 55
Shrimp Fettuccine Alfredo, 76
Sieves, 62
Sloppy Joes, 95
Snacks
    BLT Dip, 39
    Buffalo Wings, 40
    Caramelized Onion, Mushroom, and Roasted Red
        Pepper Focaccia, 28–30
    Chicken Empanadas, 38–39
    Chili Cheese Dip, 31
    Cinnamon Sticks, 43
    Crab Rangoons, 46–47
    Deviled Eggs, 45
    Goat Cheese and Tomato Crostini, 44
    Nachos with Salsa and Guacamole, 36–37
    Potato Skins, 26–27
    Pot Stickers, 32–33
    Strawberries with Marshmallow Dip, 43
    Vegetable Maki Rolls, 34–35
Snickerdoodles, 135

Snow peas
  Vegetable Lomein, 84
  Vegetable Stir Fry with Tofu, 75
Soups
  Baked Potato Soup, 52
  Broccoli Cheese Soup, 54
  Corn Chowder, 51
  French Onion Soup, 56–57
  Split Pea Soup, 50
  thickening, 91
  Wonton Soup, 58–59
Sour cream, xii
Spinach
  Spinach and Cheese Ravioli, 72–73
  Spinach and Mushroom Quiche, 17
  Spinach Salad with Honey-Mustard Dressing,
    68–69
Split Pea Soup, 50
Springform pans, 122
Squash
  Ratatouille with Chickpeas and Couscous, 96
  Vegetable Lasagna, 100–01
Steaks
  cooking, 65
  Steak Cobb Salad, 64–65
  Steak Fajitas, 78–79
Stewing, 99
Stir-frying, 74
Strawberries
  Crepes with Fresh Strawberries and Cream, 18–19
  Strawberries with Marshmallow Dip, 43
Sugar, creaming butter and, 2
Sweating, 109
Syrup, Blueberry, 10-11

★ T
Taco Salad, 60–61
Tartar Sauce, 111
Tempering, 121
Toffee
  Frozen Bananas with Chocolate and Toffee, 136
  Toffee Bars, 125
Tofu, Vegetable Stir Fry with, 75
Tomatoes
  BLT Dip, 39
  Goat Cheese and Tomato Crostini, 44
  Grilled Cheese with Bacon and Tomato, 83
  Mexican Lasagna, 102–103
  peeling, 127
  Ratatouille with Chickpeas and Couscous, 96
  Salsa, 36
  Steak Cobb Salad, 64–65

  Taco Salad, 60–61
  types of, 37
Tomato sauce
  Cheese and Chile Enchiladas, 97
  Eggplant Parmesan, 104–105
  Spinach and Cheese Ravioli, 72–73
Tortilla chips
  Cheese and Chile Enchiladas, 97
  Chili Cheese Dip, 31
  Nachos with Salsa and Guacamole, 36–37
  Taco Salad, 60–61
Tortillas
  Breakfast Burritos, 23
  Chicken Quesadillas, 77
  Egg Salad Tortilla Wrap, 81
  Mexican Lasagna, 100–01
  Steak Fajitas, 78–79
Tuna
  Tuna and Macaroni Salad, 62
  Tuna Melt, 74
Turkey-Bacon Puff Pastry Pockets, 86–87
Turnovers, Peach, 126–28

★ V
Vegetables. **See also individual vegetables**
  blanching and shocking, 55
  rinsing, xiii
  Salmon and Vegetables en Papillote, 116–17
  Vegetable Lasagna, 100–01
  Vegetable Lomein, 84
  Vegetable Maki Rolls, 34–35
  Vegetable Stir Fry with Tofu, 75
Vinegar, 11

★ W
Wasabi, 35
Water baths
  hot, 133
  ice, 121
Wonton wrappers
  Crab Rangoons, 46–47
  Pot Stickers, 32–33
  Spinach and Cheese Ravioli, 72–73
  Wonton Soup, 58–59
Wrap, Egg Salad Tortilla, 81

★ Y ★ Z
Yeast, 30
Zucchini
  Ratatouille with Chickpeas and Couscous, 96
  Vegetable Lasagna, 100–101

CREATIVE HOMEOWNER PRESS®

THE COMPLETE GUIDE TO
WALLPAPERING

by David M. Groff

CREATIVE HOMEOWNER PRESS®, Upper Saddle River, New Jersey

Editorial Director: Timothy O. Bakke
Art Director: W. David Houser

Senior Editor: Mike McClintock
Associate Editor: Craig Fahan
Copyeditors: Bruce Wetterau, Paul Rieder
Editorial Assistants: Craig Clark, Laura DeFerrari
Technical Reviewers: Jim Turner, Deborah Roos

Graphic Designer: Jan H. Greco
Illustrators: Jim Randolph, Vincent Alessi, Clarke Barre

Cover Design: W. David Houser
Front Cover Photography: Stephen E. Munz
Back Cover Photography (left to right): William Zinsser & Co.; William Zinsser & Co.; Thibaut Historic Homes

Printed in the United States of America

Current Printing (last digit)
10 9 8 7 6 5 4 3 2 1

The Complete Guide to Wallpapering, Second Edition
Library of Congress Catalog Card Number: 98-070208

ISBN: 1-58011-019-3

CREATIVE HOMEOWNER PRESS®
A Division of Federal Marketing Corp.
24 Park Way
Upper Saddle River, NJ 07458

Web site: http://www.creativehomeowner.com

Acknowledgments

I would like to extend special thanks to my wife, Cynthia, for her encouragement and support; and our sons, Daniel and D.J., who have been very patient. Special thanks to my Dad, Bob Groff, who took the time to train me from the time I was seven. Without his patience this book could not have been written.

Safety First

Though all the methods in this book have been reviewed for safety, the importance of using the safest possible work methods cannot be overstated. What follows are reminders—some do's and don'ts of work safety. They can not substitute for your own common sense, however.

■ *Always* use caution, care, and good judgment when following the procedures described in this book.

■ *Always* be sure that the electrical setup is safe; be sure that no circuit is overloaded and that all power tools and electrical outlets are properly grounded. Use GFCI-protected circuits whenever possible, and do not use power tools in wet locations.

■ *Always* read the toolmaker's instructions for using a tool, and pay special attention to how the tool works so that you can avoid injury. Know the limitations of your tools, and do not try to force them to do what they were not designed to do.

■ *Always* read container labels on paints, solvents, and other products; provide ventilation, and observe all other warnings.

■ *Always* be aware that there is seldom enough time for your body's reflexes to save you from injury from a power tool in a dangerous situation; everything happens too fast. Be alert! Never work with tools when you are tired or under the influence of alcohol or drugs.

■ *Always* wear the appropriate rubber or work gloves when handling chemicals, moving or stacking lumber, or doing heavy construction. Wear a disposable face mask when you create dust by sawing or sanding. Use a special filtering respirator when working with toxic substances and solvents. Always wear eye protection, especially when using power tools or striking metal on metal or plaster; a flying chip, for example, can severely injure your eye. Never work where lighting is insufficient.

■ *Never* work while wearing loose clothing, long-hanging hair, open cuffs, or jewelry.

■ *Never* work with dull tools. Have them sharpened, or learn how to sharpen them yourself. Never carry sharp or pointed tools, such as utility knives, awls, or chisels in your pocket. Use a special purpose tool belt with leather pockets and holders instead.

Special Safety Tips for Wallcovering

Even though installing wallpaper is basically cosmetic work, not heavy-duty construction with complicated power tools, safety is still a top priority. Use these tips to help keep your work area safe.

■ *Never* set up in a high traffic zone such as an entrance foyer or hall, especially when other workers are present. Allow room to work efficiently and safely—even if it means taking time to rearrange furniture.

■ *Always* keep small children and pets clear of the work area.

■ *Always* set up a sturdy worktable that can't be tipped over easily, and keep your tools and supplies well organized and close at hand. Cover the floor surface under the worktable and the surrounding furniture with clean dropcloths or plastic. Use a slip-resistant dropcloth when working on slick floors.

■ *Always* keep a trash container to discard scraps at the worktable and at the wall where you're working. Cover the edges of used razor blades if you discard them in the trash, or store them in a box until the job is done. Tape the box shut before throwing it away.

■ *Always* cut off power by removing the appropriate fuse or tripping the right circuit breaker before removing or replacing an electrical fixture. Then use a current tester to double-check whether electricity is present before you touch exposed wires.

■ *Always* turn off water supply valves before removing a toilet or wall-mounted plumbing fixture. If there is no cutoff valve, either turn off the main water valve or do not remove the fixture.

■ *Always* set up ladders and planks on a secure footing. When a scaffold plank or other scaffolding equipment is needed, fasten the components together with elastic straps. Don't allow anyone to walk under ladders or scaffolding while you are working on them.

■ *Never* leave a tool belt with razors or other dangerous tools lying around where curious children could pick them up. The same goes for cans of adhesives and primer-sealers. Make sure they're securely closed and stored out of the way.

Contents

Chapter One
Wallpaper Old & New   8

King Henry IV granted an official charter to the Guild of Paperhangers in 1599. From the Middle Ages to present day, wallpaper has never gone out of style.

Chapter Two
Tools & Supplies   14

Whether you are a do-it-yourselfer or a professional paperhanger, here is what you'll need to install wallpaper successfully.

Protection 16
Preparation 16
Application 18
Mainly for contractors 21

Chapter Three
Estimating Materials   22

With so many sizes, patterns, and styles available, it's important to estimate quantity accurately. This chapter shows you how to estimate for walls, ceilings, and stairways.

Design guidelines .23
Basic types 26
Sizes and packaging variables 28
Estimating 29
   Small-pattern repeats 30
   Large-pattern repeats 31
   Count-strip method 32
   Stairways and cathedral walls 34
   Ceilings 35
   Borders 36
Commercial wallcoverings 36
Murals 37
Mainly for contractors 37

Chapter Four
Preparing Walls   38

From drywall to concrete block, careful wall preparation is key to achieving a pleasing result.

Preparation products 40
Clearing and cleaning 42
Painted wall surfaces 45
How to repair a hole in drywall 46
Preparing special surfaces 47
Removing wallpapers 48
Mainly for contractors 51

Chapter Five
Patterns & Seams   52

Learn how to distinguish between the five different pattern types of wallpaper, how to match even the most complex patterns, and how to create almost invisible seams.

Pattern matches 54
   Random match .54
   Random texture .54
   Straight across .56

Half drop 56
Multiple drop 58
Fractional drops 59
Seam and seaming techniques 60
Types of seams .62
Seam placement 64
Prepasted wallpapers 65
Adhesives 67
Mainly for contractors 69

Chapter Six
Basic Installation   70

This chapter covers installation techniques, from applying paste on the first strip to making multiple-mitered relief cuts, rounding inside and outside corners, and working around obstructions.

Papering walls 72
Planning the first strip 72
Applying adhesive 72
Installing the first strip 74
Trimming allowance edges 77
Multiple-mitered relief cuts 77
Inside corners 77
Testing for squareness 78
Outside corners .79
Parallels and guidelines 80
Working around door frames 82
Covering electrical plates 85
Working around fixtures 86
Papering ceilings 86
Installing wallpaper on a ceiling 87
Liner papers 88
Prepasted wallpapers 88
Preparing prepasted paper 89
Dry-hanging paper .90
Untrimmed wallpapers 91
Mainly for contractors 93

Chapter Seven
Special Areas   94

Here, you'll find instruction for dealing with borders, chair rails, windows and doors, ceilings, cathedral walls, stairways, soffits, archways, dormers, concrete block, and prefinished paneling.

New paper over old .96
Borders 97
Installing borders on painted walls 99
Special border applications 101
Cathedral walls 105
Stairways 106
Murals 107
Installing partial wall murals 107
Installing photo murals 108
Soffits 109
Recessed windows 113
Archways 117
Dormers 118
Concrete block or brick walls 120
Prefinished paneling 121

Chapter Eight
Trouble-shooting   122

From paper printed out of bias to puckering seams, this chapter covers, in detail, what can go wrong and how to avoid problems when hanging wallpaper.

Patch repairs 124
Material problems .125
Problems with wall preparation 130
Problems with seams 132
Problems with adhesives 134

Glossary   136

Index   142

Chapter 1

Wallpaper Old and New

Wallpaper sample books are packed with so many patterns and colors that it's difficult to zero in on one style in general and one paper in particular. This is not a new problem. More than 200 years ago, when a Boston merchant looked into the possibilities for decorating his shop, he said, "There are so great a variety of Fashions, I am totally at a loss as to what to get." Even in colonial days there were almost too many choices—wallpapers decorated with flowers, animals, colorful abstracts, and patriotic scenes of recent historical events. And it didn't matter whether you lived in the New World or the Old; if you had any wealth or position at all in those days, your house just had to have at least one papered room.

Unfortunately, not many of the earliest papers have been preserved, and when you peel off a layer of wallpaper today you'll probably find plain-painted drywall underneath. But imagine a renovation where you peel away sheet after sheet, one dated design after another, decade after decade like an archeological dig that reveals both the different styles of the times and a complete history of the room's decoration. In a perfectly preserved house, you could peel off enough layers to reach back to the 1500s, when the first known wallpapers, painted sheets, were used in European and Chinese homes.

We don't know much about how people used the earliest wallpaper because, unlike tapestries and screens, it was not easily moved from one house to another. And it was fragile, often printed on cheap, flimsy paper. Even if it survived everyday wear, it ended up covered by paneling, more paper, or paint. Until the invention of the wall steamer, in fact, paperhangers generally removed only badly damaged portions before applying the new layer.

We do know that the decorating technique was popular and gave rise to the craft of hanging paper that was officially recognized in England by Henry IV in 1599, when he granted a charter to the Guild of Paperhangers. By the eighteenth and nineteenth centuries, the Golden Age of wallpaper, elaborate designs and exotic materials were used to create exquisite papers prized by kings and merchant princes with enough money to buy them.

Before then, back in the Middle Ages, the upper classes hung their castle walls with thick tapestries and velvets to shut out the cold wind and add beauty to a room, while the poor made do by gluing patterned paper squares to their walls. The squares often were painted with religious

images that provided decoration, covered cracks, and served as talismans against bad luck.

Oddly enough, the earliest documented use of wallpaper as we know it wasn't on walls at all. In 1509, a printer named Hugh Goes created a black and white block print on paper sheets—a popular design that featured a cross section of the fruit and seeds of a pomegranate surrounded by leaves and his printer's mark, an H for Hugh and a small but alert-looking goose for Goes. Printed on the reverse side of previously printed paper, this ancestor of modern wallpaper somehow wound up applied to the ceiling of the Master's Lodging at Christ's College at England's Cambridge University.

The revolutionary breakthrough in wallpaper came in 1688 when a Frenchman named Jean Papillon made printed papers with a continuously repeating pattern—a very simple but completely new idea. Like today's wallpapers, they could be joined to create an unbroken design that wrapped around a small room or swept down a long hall. Papillon's innovation created so much interest that by the 1700s wallpaper was replacing whitewash as the most common interior wall decoration. The increase in wallpaper's popularity also was brought on by the opening of trade routes to the East and to the Americas, which not only introduced new goods but inspired new styles. At the same time, the middle class was growing—and becoming wealthy enough to want walls as elegant and expensive as the exotic furnishings and fabrics in the homes of aristocrats. Even royalty gave wallpaper the nod. In 1720, English decorator William Kent covered the Salon at Kensington Palace—as far as we know, wallpaper's first appearance in a royal building anywhere in Europe.

Stronger, more durable papers encouraged experimental techniques and materials. Black and white block

1800 Before the advent of the Industrial Revolution, wallpaper was painstakingly created by hand using labor-intensive methods on custom-made printing presses. As the popularity of wallpaper and demand increased, this seventeenth-century technique would soon be superseded by nineteenth-century machines.

1830 As printing technology advanced, wallpaper patterns became more detailed. This era was known for its intricate designs, full of detailed flowers and intertwining vines, or dense geometric patterns.

prints were still in use, but more manufacturers began imitating velvets, woods, and marbles in their paper designs. Japanese and Chinese patterns festooned with birds, animals, and panoramic landscapes became popular novelties in the early 1700s, and by the mid-eighteenth century flocking was the new rage. In this process, wallpaper artisans used adhesive to lay out a design on paper or canvas. They then applied colored, powdered wool to the surface. When the wool powder was blown away, a fuzzy, raised pattern that looked and felt like expensive cut velvet remained on the paper.

People clamored for these new flocked papers in a variety of colors and began demanding levels of craftsmanship that eventually rivaled those of the fine arts. Wallpapers were printed with sharp line etchings, were silk-screened and hand-painted, and were even embellished with bits of mica to create a sparkling surface in sunlight and candlelight.

When it came to actually hanging wallpaper, the French led the way in ingenuity and extravagance. Instructions drawn up in 1792 for the first general-information encyclopedia show seven ways to join each wallpaper panel to the next, and even more ways to bor-

der floors, windows, and doors. Ceilings, walls, stairwells, chimneys, and even banisters became candidates for the most innovative and stylish decoration of the time.

As early as the seventeenth century, wallpaper evolved from individual sheets to hand-joined rolls, and factories turned out color- and edge-matched wallpaper almost identical to those we use today. The first American wallpaper factory was set up in 1790 by John B. Howell in Albany, New York. But it wasn't until 1840 that the material was truly mass-produced by machines, reducing the cost so much that the product

1880 The first American wallpaper factory dates from 1790, but it wasn't until the 1800s that wallpaper was mass-produced on machines. William Orr invented one of the earliest devices; a later model is shown here. Similar to a cylindrical printing press, it automatically decorated, rolled, and packaged wallpaper.

1887 Late in the nineteenth century, embossing techniques were applied to heavy-weight wallpaper. The highly intricate, textured designs became extremely fashionable.

could be purchased by the vast majority of Americans.

William Orr, who came to America from Belfast in 1811, invented one of the first production-line devices, basically a cylinder with raised ribs in the shape of the repeating design. It could print the decoration as paper rolled by underneath—and was equipped with a mechanism for wrapping the paper into packages at the end of the line.

Lower costs and wider availability brought on by mass production arrived just in time to satisfy the fascination for highly decorative detail that marked the Victorian period. By the time of wallpaper's last great era in the 1880s, special patterns existed on both sides of the Atlantic for specific purposes, from covering chimneys and fireplaces to gracing entrance halls. Decorators used paper almost everywhere, and they developed combinations that might seem busy by today's standards. They mixed flowered landscapes with bold stripes and used marble-like pillars and columns to divide papered walls into panels. Some papers reproduced works of art, complete with printed frames to simulate walls hung with real paintings. Decorators might use radically different designs in the same house, and it was not unusual for a dozen different patterns to meet—or maybe collide—in a single space.

By the start of the twentieth century, the wallpaper printing process was so efficient that the Sears, Roebuck and Company catalog could boast, "at no time in the history of wallpaper were they so beautiful and cheap as now." It's extensive low-cost line included such items as "White-back papers printed in color, silver illumination, in scroll, floral, stripes and geometrical designs." Wallpapering experienced a nostalgic revival at the time, as owners of America's substantial stock of aging, period homes began looking for historically accurate patterns to

1893 People in the Victorian period loved colors and patterns, as shown here not only by the Oriental rugs and painted detailing on the drawers but also in the ornate floral wallpaper that rivals the rug for intricacy.

1915 Wallpaper was used in increasingly novel ways: as a frieze highlighting the upper wall (as shown here), as panels decorating dadoes, or as a covering for chimneys and fireplaces, sometimes with several different patterns in one room.

redecorate their walls. The demand encouraged manufacturers to develop a new area of specialization: historic wallpaper designs, which cost six to ten dollars per roll—very expensive when you consider that Sears sold its cheapest brand for just pennies a roll at the time.

Prices have changed just a bit since then—and styles, too—but most of the equipment used by workers to hang traditional wallpaper is basically unchanged today: brushes, sponges, scissors, paste, and water. In other trades, the old-fashioned hand tools have been replaced by pneumatic or electronic equipment that handles repetitive jobs faster and often more accurately. But there are no battery-powered smoothing machines for wallpaper—not yet.

Some of the do-it-yourself advice hasn't changed much either, such as these wallpapering tips from a prominent American homeowner, George Washington. When specifying an installation on the walls of his home in Mount Vernon, he wrote, "The paste must be made of the finest and the best flour, and free from lumps. The paste is to be made thick and may be thinned by putting water in it. The paste is to be put upon the paper and suffered to remain about five minutes, to soak in before it is put up, until all parts stick. If there be wrinkles anywhere, put a large piece of paper thereon and rub them out with a cloth." He makes it all sound so easy, doesn't he?

today Wallpaper is now rarely made from plain paper. The majority of the designs available today are manufactured with a thin vinyl coating for durability, protection, and easy clean-up. And for high-moisture areas, where even vinyl-coated paper is subject to deterioration, there is practically indestructible, thick-skinned vinyl—most of it already prepasted and ready to hang.

1948 By the mid-twentieth century, wallpapers that once had to be printed by hand (at prohibitive cost) could be mass-produced, giving any home a nostalgic look at an affordable price.

1974 Vinyl wallpapers, developed later in the twentieth century, are designed to be long-lasting, so you can keep enjoying them indefinitely. Fortunately, they are also strippable, so you can alter rooms as the years go by to satisfy changing tastes.

Chapter 2

Tools & Supplies

L ike every building trade, the craft of paperhanging has its fair share of specialized tools and equipment. The strangest might be a syringe—an oversized version of the dreaded doctor's needle that some pros use to fix air bubbles. Instead of marring a finished wallpaper surface by cutting open a bubble and spreading fresh glue with a brush, they puncture the air pocket and give it a quick shot of adhesive.

The scary-looking needle is not a do-it-yourself item. But most paperhanging tools are commonplace in well-stocked home shops and even where the household toolbox is a big drawer in the kitchen. You need basic prep tools like a paint scraper and drywall knife; layout tools like a ruler and chalk-line box; a utility knife, scissors, and other trimming tools; plus a typical collection of do-it-yourself clean-up supplies from sponges to buckets. You don't need a lot of complicated and expensive equipment because paperhanging isn't a high-tech business. It's a traditional trade where you do things the old-fashioned way, by hand.

If you're planning to use an unprepasted or exotic paper such as grasscloth, you'll need some extra tools and supplies, including a wide brush for paste and a big table on which to paste. But most residential jobs use prepasted paper. It's the favorite by far because the manufacturer applies the paste, and that makes the application straightforward: You dunk it and hang it.

Whatever wallcovering you install, of course, the quality of the tools you use will have an impact on the finished job. But it's not necessary to spend top dollar for the heavy-duty contractor's version of every scraper and roller—not unless you're in the business. If you use the tools every day and your livelihood depends on satisfied customers, it pays to buy durable, professional equipment. But for typical do-it-yourselfers—people who might hang a few rolls of paper every few years—a mid-range of price and quality is the best bet. Avoid the extremes of top-end contractor models and bargain-basement throwaways, and use tools that match your how-to experience and do-it-yourself skills. Remember, a tool doesn't produce professional results; it's the skill of the hand holding the tool that counts.

Here is a look at the equipment and supplies you'll need for most paperhanging projects—with a twist. At the end of the basic list (and throughout the book), you'll find a small section with information mainly for contractors.

If you're a novice, expect a few unfamiliar terms and difficult operations in these sections. Even handy do-it-yourselfers may find some of them challenging. And several entries won't really apply to jobs in your home. For instance, you probably won't need to stock up on flood lamps and the hardware to hang them so you can create a brightly lit work area in an otherwise dark house. But if you read these sections, you may pick up a

few good ideas—such as using bright lights—that make sense no matter how much paper you hang.

Protection

Dropcloths. Protect floors, furniture, appliances, and everything else with dropcloths when preparing walls and installing wallpaper. Use the rubber-backed type to prevent spills from soaking through and to help prevent slips and falls on slick floor surfaces. Thin plastic drops are fine for wrapping furnishings such as audiovisual equipment to prevent fine dust from getting inside, but they tear too easily to provide adequate under-foot protection.

Current tester. Use this tool to check whether the electrical current is off before removing or replacing electrical fixtures—even after you think you've cut the power at the appropriate breaker or fuse. This tool is inexpensive and is highly recommended for use by novices and professionals.

First-aid kit. It's wise to have one of these on hand in case of an accident. A basic kit includes first-aid cream, bandages, gauze, small scissors, waterproof tape, disinfectant, and tweezers. Remember, for deep cuts or wounds always see a physician.

Masking tape. Protect small fixtures that are not easily removed with masking tape before you begin repairing and sanding walls.

Preparation

Bleach. Clean mildew and mold, and temporarily control mildew growth, by washing with a mix of bleach and water. Spray the area with disinfectant after bleaching to help prevent mildew from recurring.

Liquid dish-washing detergent. Use liquid detergent mixed with warm water (or a proprietary mixture) to remove wallpaper. It will penetrate existing wallcoverings that have been scored with abrasive sandpaper or a specialized scarifying tool.

Electrical tape and wire connectors. These supplies are used to cover hot (live) electrical wires that are left exposed temporarily during some wallpaper preparation or installation procedures when power for light is still needed

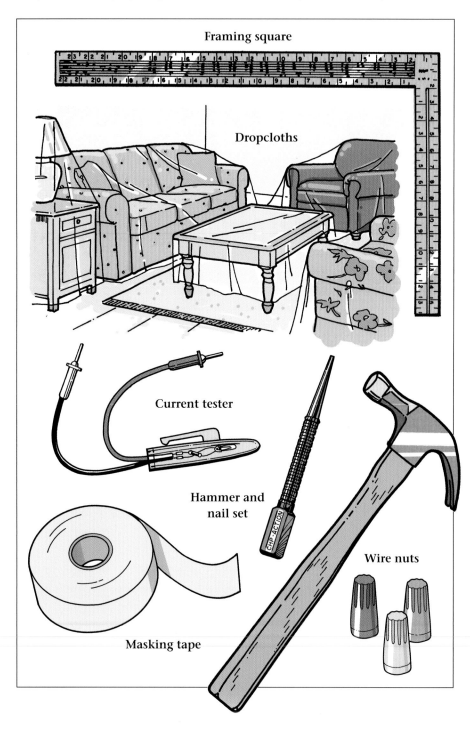

Framing square

Dropcloths

Current tester

Hammer and nail set

Wire nuts

Masking tape

Framing square. Normally used in carpentry, this L-shaped tool helps you check patterns for squareness, both horizontally and vertically; it's also used to form parallel guidelines.

Hammer and nail set. Use these to re-secure loose or protruding nails in paneling before installing wallpaper or liner paper. Over drywall, it's wise to pull loose nails and replace them with threaded drywall fasteners that can't work loose under the new paper.

Fiberglass mesh tape. Mend large holes or cracks in walls with this tape and layers of joint compound. Fiberglass works well over areas that are chronic repair problems because of seasonal shifting and stress in the structure.

Pliers, screwdrivers, and wrenches. You will need these tools to remove light fixtures, nails, picture hooks, staples, and other types of fixtures. These are basic tools found in a standard home toolbox.

Scarifiers. These tools are used for perforating and cutting through wall-paper to make it more porous and easier to strip with a removing agent (sometimes just soap and water) or steam. Most of these hand-held tools have wheels with little teeth at the base that do the cutting and make dozens of perforations in a single pass.

Scrapers. These tools remove different surface materials depending on the type of blade. A putty knife with a narrow, stiff blade is good for digging excessive caulking from around countertops and thick layers of rough paint from around architectural trim. Taping knives with wider, more flexible blades are needed for spreading filler in cracks and holes and for peeling soaked paper off walls. A wall scraper, typically a razor blade mounted on a handle, is good for removing dry wallpaper from hard finished surfaces.

Steamers. Usually a rental item, this machine has a tank for heating water and a shallow pan with a perforated face for spreading steam over the

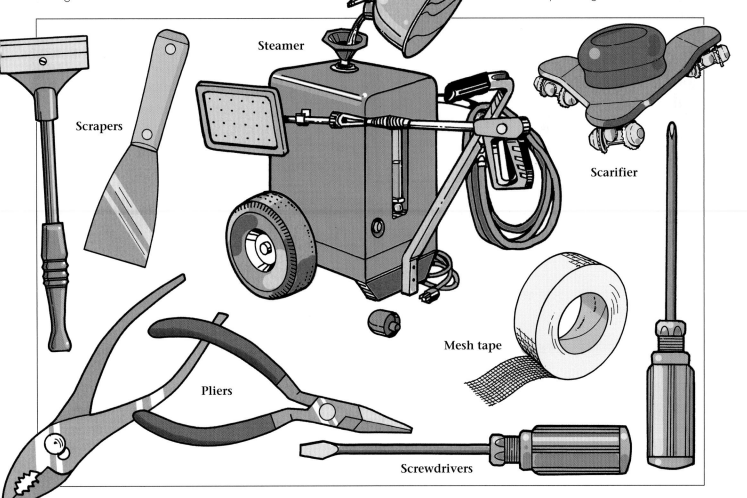

Steamer

Scrapers

Scarifier

Mesh tape

Pliers

Screwdrivers

Extension handle

Roller with sleeve

Sandpaper

Ruler

Measuring tape

Spray bottle

Roller pan

painted surfaces, new drywall, and patched areas; A sandpaper holder (or small, square-edged block of wood) helps protect your hands, increases productivity, and keeps you from sanding irregular depressions in the wall.

Spray bottle. This common household item is handy to test the effects of different remover agents on the paper's stripability. You can also use it to spray a 50-50 solution of bleach and water on mildewed walls.

Application

Caulk (and gun). Generally dispensed from cartridges with a gun, caulk is used to seal around the edges of wallpaper where the material will be exposed to excessive moisture.

Chalk-line box. Use this tool to establish a long straight line between two fixed points, horizontally or vertically. Use a light-colored white and yellow chalk combination (not the typical deep blue variety carpenters use to mark lumber) so that the color won't show through semi-transparent wallcoverings. Never snap a chalk line directly on a seam area. Always locate it at least $\frac{1}{4}$ inch to one side of the actual seam to prevent chalk from bleeding between the two strips after they're joined.

Clamp light. This fixture provides a handy way to make light available wherever needed. You can also position it to simulate conditions once the light fixtures are back in place.

Fans. Getting the air circulating in your work area will speed up the drying cycle of primer-sealers and

wallpaper surface. If the paper is properly prepared and porous, the steam will release the adhesive underneath.

Rollers. A sleeve, pan, and extension handle will be needed with the roller, which is used for applying primer-sealers and adhesives. Disposables are fine and reduce cleanup time. A one-gallon pan is recommended, and remember to clean it after each use. An extension handle that threads into the end of a roller makes it easier to apply primer-sealers and adhesives in high or hard-to-reach places.

Rulers. For large-scale projects, a 30-foot retractable steel tape with $\frac{1}{16}$-inch increments is recommended. Use it to

measure long strips of wallpaper and borders. Yardsticks are used to measure strips on the wallpaper table, to calculate placement, and sometimes to smooth wallpaper in difficult locations. Folding rulers (carpenter's rulers) also are used to calculate wallpaper seam placement and to measure the length of strips before cutting.

Sandpaper. You'll need sandpaper to smooth wall surfaces and rough drywall joint repairs. The several types you may use include 4-grit (floor sandpaper) to score vinyl-coated wallpaper so that wallpaper remover solution can penetrate the vinyl coating; 50-grit to roughen enamel paints and hard laminates so that they provide better adhesion; 80- to 100-grit for latex-

joint compound. Fans also will help reduce humidity in rooms where existing wallpaper has been removed using hot water.

Heat gun. Soften heavy vinyls using a heat gun so that they will easily adhere to tight corners, especially on soffits, recessed windows, open doorways, and the like. Heating will also give vinyls some extra flexibility when you're trying to secure edges in a tight seam. A hair dryer will work in a pinch.

Ladder and stepstool. You will use ladders alone and sometimes in combination with planks (specially rated timbers, not standard 2-bys) so that you can work close to the wall and even in stairwells. For most people, a three- or four-rung stepstool provides enough extra reach in typical rooms with 8-foot-high walls. To reduce the risk of accident, never use a ladder with a damaged step or worn hardware that allows the ladder to wobble. And don't overextend yourself when you're working from a ladder or scaffold plank. Move your setup instead of leaning to smooth a few more inches of paper.

Levels. These indispensable tools are used to establish a plumb (vertical) line to guide the edge of wallpaper. Levels provide the alternative to a string and plumb bob for most do-it-yourselfers. The rule of thumb is the longer the level, the more accurate the line. So if you don't have a 4-footer (the standard length for construction), extend the useful scale of a 2-foot level by holding it against a straight 2x4. Don't expect a high degree of accuracy over long lengths from very short levels or the gadget

Chalk-line box

Caulk gun

Level

Clamp light

Paint-brushes

Ladder

Heat gun

levels built into some multipurpose tools.

Paintbrushes. Use brushes for cutting-in (edging) around trim work with more accuracy than a roller can provide, use them with primer-sealer or adhesive the same way you would with paint. A 3-inch sash brush is a good all-around size. Traditionally, a special 8-inch

brush is used to apply wallpaper paste—one of the tools you won't need if you work with prepasted material. If your job doesn't turn out perfectly (and no one's does), you might want an artist's brush to dab adhesive into small tears or peeling corners.

Paste bucket. The bucket is used with the 6-inch paste brush when pasting

Paste bucket and brush

Razor knife and blade

Plumb bob

Scissors

Smoothing brush

Seam roller

Trimming knife

Smoothing brush (sweep). With this brush you can smooth out wrinkles and disperse air pockets in newly applied wallpaper before the adhesive sets. It's the tool that most directly expresses your hand movements—and makes the most progress getting rolls of paper in position on the wall. A 12-inch-long bristle brush works well with most wallpapers. A brush with short bristles is handy for working heavyweight vinyls. On papers with more delicate surfaces you can use a plastic wallpaper smoother. On pre-pasted papers you may get better results smoothing with a natural sponge.

Drywall knife. This versatile tool is used for a variety of jobs, including repairing damaged surfaces, scraping off old wallpaper, trimming paper (as a guide for a razor knife), and smoothing out adhesive wrinkles during installation. Pick one with a comfortable handle and a little flex to the blade.

Sponges. Use a soft sponge to clean adhesive from the surface of the wallpaper. A natural sponge has more capacity and works better than the man-made version.

Straightedge. More than just a measuring device, the straightedge provides a cutting guide for trimming wallpaper. Pros might carry a room-scale straightedge 6 or 7 feet long. The DIY model should be at least 36 inches, but the longer the better.

Strainer. Another common household item, this one helps remove debris from primer-sealers and adhesives that could create bumps under the paper. A metal kitchen strainer works well; so does a nylon stocking.

sheets of wallpaper the old-fashioned way. The process is used mostly on high-cost, somewhat exotic materials that are not available prepasted.

Plumb bob. With this tool you can locate a point that is precisely below the point where the bob is suspended; in other words, a truly vertical line.

Razor knife. Handy for various trimming jobs, razor knives are available in many styles and sizes. Some people like the feel of a substantial handle (your basic utility knife); others like the small scale of a single-edged razor blade. As long as the blade is sharp, it doesn't matter much which type you use. Pick one that feels comfortable in your

hand—and safe. Instead of working with a razor blade freehand, for example, it's wise to use a blade holder. Never hold razor blades in your mouth.

Scissors. These common tools are used to cut wallpaper, often to the exclusion of all other cutters. Some people find scissors the most comfortable to use. For best results, try 6-inch stainless-steel blades with plastic handles, and keep them clean.

Seam roller. A flat or oval-shaped (convex) roller is used to secure the seams between sheets of wallpaper. Do not use a seam roller on embossed materials or on grasscloths, stringcloths, or flocks because rolling can burnish and flatten the seam.

Trim guide. Any tool with a reliable edge (normally a metal ruler or triangle) can be used to guide your cutting blade when trimming wallpaper. Triangular guides are good for creasing paper where it must be cut against ceilings and baseboards.

Water box. Submerge prepasted papers at the wall just prior to installation in this plastic water trough. If you have some paperhanging experience, you will save time by using a large box that accommodates two strips at once.

Wire whisk. Another implement stolen from the kitchen, this one is ideal for mixing paste.

MAINLY FOR CONTRACTORS

Canvas tool bags. For storing and carrying the most frequently used tools and supplies, these bags make loading and unloading a lot easier.

Cleaning supplies. Finish the job with the professional touch of a thorough cleanup using your own supplies. You'll need a broom and dustpan, trash bags, paper towels, sponges, and a supply of household cleaners.

Extension cords. You will need these to get power to the work site when the electricity has been disconnected.

Foam-rubber padding (ladder pads). Cushion the ends of ladders where they rest against the wall to prevent marring.

Light bulbs. Used in a clamp light, a bright light is the best way to create shadows that highlight defects on the wall surface during preparation. A 150-watt bulb in a clamp light provides better lighting during wallpapering than most household lamps can offer.

Mollys, toggles, and expansion shields. Because these may drop into the wall cavity as you remove a towel rack or other fixture, keep several different sizes on hand to eliminate a trip to the hardware store.

Offset screwdriver. Use this small, S-shaped screwdriver to turn screws in tight places.

Palette knife. Use this tool to mix watercolors with a pigmented primer-sealer base when coloring seams that have pulled apart during drying.

Paneling nails. Another handy item; you should carry them to secure loose seams or bows in paneling.

Pliers, screwdrivers, and wrenches. These are essential for removing fixtures and fittings. Professionals should have several sizes available. You should also carry a set of hex wrenches to remove setscrews on towel brackets and handrails.

Scaffold planks (extension planks). Generally, you will use scaffold planks when installing wallpaper in stairwells, ceilings, and any surface beyond the reach of a stepstool.

Business supplies. Contractors who want to make a professional presentation keep these items on hand, even though they may be conducting business out of a truck. You should always carry a map book—so that you don't get lost and arrive late for business appointments—and key tags to keep track of clients' keys. Use contract and estimate forms to record pertinent information about a job, with room to identify the pattern numbers, dye-lot numbers, type of primer-sealer, estimated preparation time, and total price for each room you estimate.

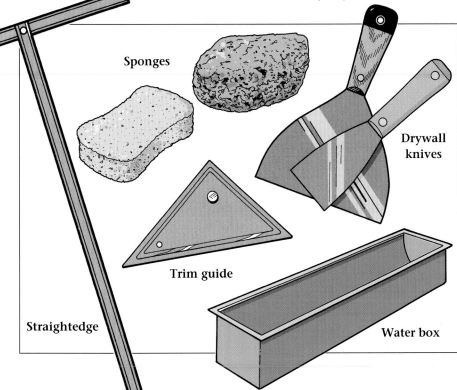

Sponges

Drywall knives

Trim guide

Straightedge

Water box

Chapter 3

Estimating Materials

I t's easy to dwell on decisions about wallpaper because there are so many colors and patterns. And no matter what you decide, you're never really wrong—even if no one else in the world can appreciate your scheme of blue plaids and brown stripes. It's a question of personal taste, of course, and there's no better place to express it than in your own home. But you might want to consider a few design guidelines almost everyone agrees on, because they hold true for many types of finishing materials inside and outside the house, not just wallpaper.

Design Guidelines

Light versus dark. Remodeling projects can make one room seem bigger than another even though they have the same floor plan. For instance, by bumping out a bay window, you can increase the space visually with no real increase in floor space. But given the same proportions, lighter-colored surfaces generally make a space look bigger, while darker-colored surfaces generally make it look smaller. That holds true whether it's mahogany versus pine on kitchen cabinets or light-and-airy versus dark-and-dense patterns on wallpaper. In some areas—say, a den where you want the feeling of privacy and seclusion—a dark

paper could be the best choice. But the same paper could make a narrow hallway look like a tunnel and feel uncomfortably claustrophobic.

Horizontal versus vertical. You have probably noticed how a short, stocky guy tends to look a little leaner dressed in a suit with vertical pinstripes. Your house works the same way. With siding, for example, vertical board-and-batten makes a building look taller, while horizontal clapboards help it hug the ground. Because wallpapers with horizontal patterns emphasize width and those with vertical patterns emphasize height, a small entryway with a low ceiling might benefit from a vertical pattern. But the same paper could make an open stairwell seem cavernous.

Contrast versus blend. Most people perceive space as a single unit first, then subconsciously start sorting out different elements—the ceiling, the floor, and sections of wall. If your paper pattern is a subtle combination of light tan colors and the surrounding wood trim is cream color, the room will seem more like one big space—a little larger. If your paper is a bold contrast of red and black surrounded by bright white trim, the room will seem more like several connected spaces—a little smaller.

Large pattern versus small pattern. Given the same color, large-scale patterns make rooms seem smaller, while miniprints make them appear larger. That's because your eye can recognize the bold shape of a big pattern from a distance and focus in on the perimeter of the room. But you see a miniprint pattern as a vague, multicolor surface somewhere beyond pieces of furniture that catch your focus instead of the walls. A large-scale pattern might not shrink a room if it has a predominantly light background that you pick up in the trim,

LIGHT versus DARK

HORIZONTAL versus VERTICAL

but the pattern could loom in the same space with dark trim.

These are basic principles, which means there are exceptions and contradictions. A space that seems crowded to one person may seem roomy to someone else. Or perhaps you live in a house where the rooms are so big that the shrinking effect of a huge pattern is just what you need.

However you handle the subjective questions about design, you need to be practical about two other key decisions: what type of wallcovering to use and how much to buy. Before you

CONTRAST versus BLEND

LARGE PATTERN versus SMALL PATTERN

tackle the task of estimating, here is a quick look at the types of paper used most often in homes—plus some special cases, such as exotic grasscloths you need to handle with kid gloves and fireproof fiberglass weaves so strong they can bridge cracks in masonry walls.

Basic Types

Color and pattern make the first impression, but other characteristics of wallpaper may loom larger over time, say, when someone leaves grimy hand prints and you find out the surface isn't scrubbable or when it's time for a new wallcovering and you discover that the old one isn't strippable. When you're flipping through sample books and preoccupied by patterns, take a second to read the fine print on the back side of the sample. Like care labels in clothing, the sample usually provides information on the product's content, cleaning, and removal.

The directions vary as much as the products themselves because wallpaper isn't just paper. The more accurate description is wallcovering, which includes very lightweight papers made from pulp, heavyweight commercial products laminated to clear plastic, a wide range of fabrics, plus exotic finishes such as cork and suede that have unique properties aside from a staggering price. But there are fundamental differences even among the most ordinary types.

Common papers. Inexpensive, untreated paper is the most likely to rip during installation, and degrade from abrasion or staining during cleaning. It's akin to like having a giant paper napkin spread flat on the wall just waiting to soak up dirt, grease, and natural oils from your hands. Vinyl-coated papers have a thin protective coating that helps, without losing the look of paper.

Heavy-duty papers. Anaglypta, Supaglypta, and Lincrusta (old-fashioned papers that are still produced today) are thick enough to be embossed with a pattern. Some have surprising definition and create what amounts to three-dimensional, bas-relief wallpaper. Many of these papers have the toughness of cardboard and enough strength to span small cracks in the underlying surface. They can take several coats of paint, so you can change the color over the years if not the imprinted pattern.

Fiberglass weaves. They won't burn, rot, or mildew, and they're highly durable and long-lasting. Many different weaves are available, from open, gauzelike patterns to tightly-knit designs that resemble vinyl. Like heavy-duty natural papers, fiberglass weaves can be painted. But the glass strands are stronger than paper fibers—so much so that you can apply this material directly over concrete block. A major manufacturer, Tasso, recommends using a plastic applicator.

HEAVY-DUTY PAPERS

FIBERGLASS WEAVES

VINYL PAPER

TEXTILE PAPER

Vinyl paper. This is the most popular wall-covering with do-it-yourselfers, particularly for kitchens and baths because it stands up well to grease, moisture, and water. Interior paints have improved a lot, but few wash up as easily as vinyls. Here is a quick look at the distinctions.

■ Fabric-backed vinyl has a vinyl top layer over cloth or non-woven synthetic. This beefy material is generally washable, strippable, and basically indestructible. It's generally too heavy to manufacture prepasted.

■ Paper-backed vinyl is a good alternative that is typically prepasted, peelable, washable, and light, which makes it easier to handle. There are thousands of colors and patterns, and an extensive range of raised vinyls with surface tex-

ture. The patterns may not do the best job of simulating natural materials like stone, but they do help conceal problems with irregular and cracked walls.

■ For heavy screen-printed vinyls (not prepasted) you can't afford to overlook the fact that you need vinyl adhesive instead of standard paste. Because vinyl isn't porous like paper, moisture trapped in the wall can cause mold and mildew problems unless you use vinyl adhesive with a fungicidal agent.

Textile paper. This category covers an enormous range of colors, patterns, and textures, including weaves of cotton, linen, synthetics, heavyweight burlap, and unusual finishes such as woven grasscloth, made with real strands of long grass. Many

types come bonded to a backing paper for support. Some are so delicate they must be installed over liner paper—a soft, plain white paper that provides a smooth subsurface. Only experienced paperhangers should install textiles and other fragile coverings.

Flocked papers. This wallcovering was a sensation in the eighteenth century because it looks like expensive velvet. This paper may feature silhouette scenes and ornate patterns with a raised, fuzzy-feeling surface that changes appearance in different kinds of light.

Foils. Their reflectivity is a bonus in small dark spaces, and their resistance to steam makes them useful in

bathrooms. But foils can be difficult to install. Most aren't nearly as rugged as the foil you wrap around turkey legs and stick in the refrigerator. The decorative variety is a fairly flimsy sheet of metalized plastic on a paper backing. It wrinkles easily and mirrors every imperfection of the wall surface. You might want to tape up a sample before making a permanent installation on a wall that gets direct sunlight. The glare can be blinding.

Size & Packaging Variables

Most building and finishing materials are manufactured in standard sizes so that they fit together with other materials and don't make the jobs of estimating and ordering needlessly complex. Not wallcoverings. They are manufactured

and packaged in many different widths and lengths, figured in inches and centimeters, sold in rolls of different sizes—all kinds of variations to foul you up.

The standard metric single roll contains between 28 and 30 square feet and ranges from 13½ and 16½ feet in length and from 20½ to 28 inches in width. The standard American single roll contains between 34 and 36 square feet and ranges from 12 to 24 feet in length and from 18 to 36 inches in width. The American roll, once quite common, is now rarely seen; a few manufacturers make special silk-screened papers in American rolls. Most residential and lightweight commercial wallcoverings are sold by the metric single roll, although they are packaged in double- or triple-roll bolts. Heavyweight commercial wallcoverings are commonly sold by the

linear yard and packaged with 30 yards in a continuous bolt, generally either 48 or 54 inches in width. It seems like a crazy system, but there is some method to the madness. The manufacturer wants to provide more usable full-length strips per bolt (a double- or triple-roll package), which reduces the amount of waste during the installation.

Consider a single roll that is 24 inches wide and 15 feet long. One floor-to-ceiling strip on a standard, 8-foot-high wall leaves a lot of waste every second strip. But a double roll that is 24 inches wide and 30 feet long provides three full lengths, and less waste every fourth strip.

Fortunately, the wallcovering roll tag (and swatches in sample books), generally include a table to help you translate a square-foot measurement

FLOCKED PAPERS

FOILS

of area into the number of rolls needed for the job.

Pattern and dye-lot numbers. Even if you sort out the size problems, there is still room left for unexpected variations that can wreck a wallcovering project. The trouble stems from color changes during the manufacturing process.

The manufacturer may decide to reprint the pattern, but with slightly different colors. The papers can look almost the same at a glance, and their product numbers can be similar. But pattern CK1001 may include red, green, and bits of yellow, while pattern CK1002 includes red, green, and bits of orange. Because the pattern is the same and only some colors are different, you should check each roll of an order to ensure complete uniformity.

Yet one more variable is the dye-lot number. It represents a particular group of rolls that is printed at the same time. The dye-lot number will change whenever there is an alteration in the printing process—an alert to subtle changes of color tone, a change in the vinyl coating or consistency, or a change in the embossing process.

Estimating

Running short of materials is a nuisance on any remodeling job. But when you unexpectedly run out of wallpaper, you could be in for a long wait while the local dealer orders more. And when the paper finally arrives, it may be from a different dye lot that doesn't quite match.

To avoid problems like these, estimate accurately. Measure the wall area you want to cover, and divide by the number of square feet in one roll of the paper you're using. This fairly

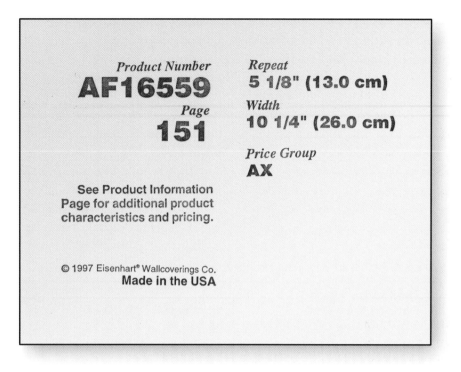

A wall covering roll tag like this, found in wallpaper sample books, provides important information on the type of wallpaper and the pattern repeat.

obvious formula will work on a plain-face or random-pattern paper over a flat, uninterrupted wall, but it has its limitations. You still need to account for the length of the wallpaper per roll, and how many full floor-to-ceiling strips it provides. You can check the roll tag or sample book for help in translating your overall area measurement into the right number of rolls.

To measure stairwells where the height varies, you can split up the space into single- and double-story rectangles or figure the wall height by averaging the lowest and highest wall dimensions. If you use nonpattern papers, you can simply deduct the area for window and door openings. That method is risky with patterns, though, particularly large-scale designs that don't repeat frequently within the roll. You may find yourself with many leftover pieces and a roll short. (The back of a wallpaper sample also generally

contains information on the size of its pattern repeat.)

The more complicated the room and the paper, the more complicated the estimate, unless you play it safe and plan for a significant amount of waste. But if you want to be close, you have to account for pattern repeats, doors and windows, oddly shaped rooms, special areas such as archways, and other variables that can skew estimates.

Before you start calculating, here is the information you should try to assemble about the wallpaper in question: the pattern repeat, the pattern match (random, straight-across, half-drop, or multiple-drop), the length and width of the wallpaper, the square footage per single roll (whether metric or American), and the available packaged bolts (double rolls or triple rolls). All of these factors can affect the final order, whichever estimating system you use.

Small-Pattern Repeats

Measure along each wall, including doors and windows, and multiply by wall height to get the total wall surface in square feet. Next, divide that total by 23, the average amount of usable square footage that a standard metric single roll will yield. Although there are approximately 28 to 30 square feet in a single roll, about 5 square feet will be wasted when matching patterns from one strip to another and when trimming around obstacles such as windows, doors, moldings, and baseboards. After dividing by 23 to get the number of single rolls needed, subtract half a roll for each normal-sized window and door. Don't subtract the entire opening; there will be some waste involved in keeping the pattern sequence.

Here's how it works on a 12x12-foot room with two windows and one door. Each wall measures 12x8 feet, or 96 square feet, times four walls for a total of 384 square feet. When you divide by 23, it equals 16.7 single rolls. Subtracting 1.5 rolls for the three openings equals 15.2, which you then round up (remember to always round up for ordering) to 16 rolls.

To convert this figure to American rolls, subtract one roll for every four figured in metric-size single rolls. Remember that an American-size single roll has 34 to 36 square feet per single roll, and a metric roll has only 28 to 30 square feet per single roll, about 25 percent less.

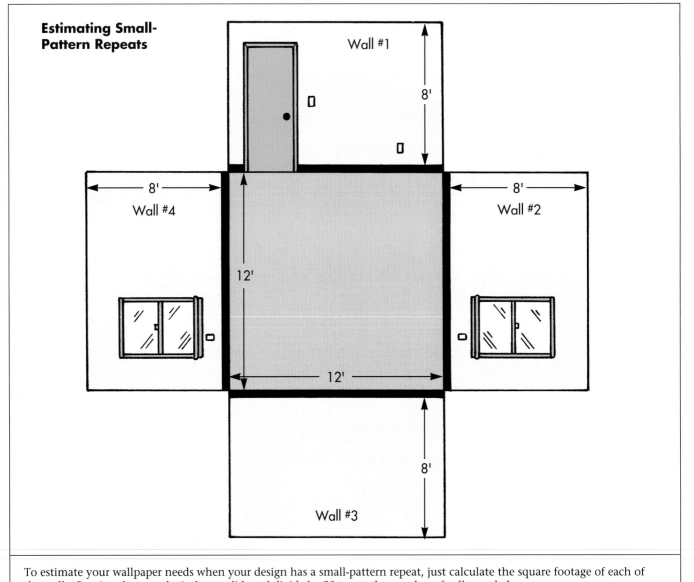

Estimating Small-Pattern Repeats

Wall #1

8'

Wall #4   8'

Wall #2   8'

12'

12'

Wall #3   8'

To estimate your wallpaper needs when your design has a small-pattern repeat, just calculate the square footage of each of the walls, figuring doors and windows solid, and divide by 30 to get the number of rolls needed.

Large-Pattern Repeats

When wallpaper has uniform texture and color, it doesn't matter where one piece joins another. Patterned papers are different. Move a strip up or down even 1 inch, and the beautiful pattern of flowers looks fractured, as though you're seeing it through the glass wall of a fish tank.

Some small, tight patterns need only a minor adjustment to make images align across seams. But when wallpaper has an 18-inch or larger vertical repeat, use either the square-foot or percentage method to determine if you will need additional wallpaper.

Square-foot method. Check information on the original estimate as follows:

■ The number of single (metric) rolls originally required.

■ Wall height in inches. (Note: Include an allowance of 3 inches top and bottom for trimming.)

■ The pattern repeat and pattern match, either straight across or half-drop, of the wallpaper. (Note: This information is provided on the back of samples.)

In this example, we'll use 20 single rolls, standard 96-inch wall height, a 30-inch pattern repeat, and a straight-across match.

STEP 1: Divide the wall height in inches by the pattern repeat in inches to determine how many times the pattern will reoccur in each strip. **Example:** 96-inch height divided by 30-inch repeat equals 3.2 repeats, rounded up to 4 repeats per strip.

STEP 2: Multiply the number of repeats by the inches of repeat to determine

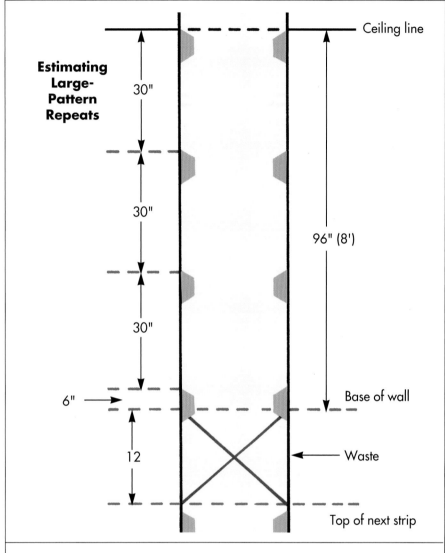

Estimating Large-Pattern Repeats

Ceiling line
30"
30"
96" (8')
30"
6"
Base of wall
12
Waste
Top of next strip

With an 18-in. or larger pattern repeat, use the square-foot or percentage method to determine how much wallpaper to purchase.

how long each strip must be to allow for the usable yield and waste. **Example:** 4 repeats times 30 inches (the repeat distance) equals 120 inches required per strip for usable yield and waste.

STEP 3: Subtract the wall height from the required inches per strip to find the waste per strip. **Example:** 120 inches per strip minus 96-inch wall height equals 24 inches of waste for matching. (Note: If a half-drop match is being used, the amount of waste can be cut in half by alternating rolls when

cutting strips; waste would be less than the 18-inch maximum. During the original estimate, a maximum of 18 inches of waste should have been allowed for matching patterns per strip. Any amount over 18 inches means recalculating for extra waste. Because the waste in this example is 24 inches, you must continue with the following steps.)

STEP 4: Convert the length of each strip from inches back to length in linear feet—the new height needed to recalculate the room. **Example:** 120

inches divided by 12 inches per foot equals 10 feet.

STEP 5: Convert the amount of metric rolls to the usable square footage required to do the room. **Example:** 20 metric single rolls times 23 square feet per roll equals 460 square feet originally required.

STEP 6: Divide the original square footage by the wall height to determine the distance around the room. **Example:** 480 square feet divided by 8 feet equals a 57.5-foot perimeter.

STEP 7: Multiply that distance by the new wall height figured in Step 4. **Example:** 57.5 feet times 10 feet (wall height) equals 575 new square feet.

STEP 8: Divide the new square footage by the usable yield of a metric single roll. **Example:** 575 square feet divided by 23 square feet equals 25 metric single rolls— the new amount required to do the room. Be sure to convert this figure to American if the wallpaper originally figured was American size.

Percentage method. Gather the same information listed under Step 1 of the square-foot method. In this example we'll use 24 single rolls, 96-inch wall height, a 42-inch vertical repeat, and a straight-across match.

STEP 1: Divide the wall height in inches by the pattern repeat in inches to determine how many times the pattern will reoccur in each strip. **Example:** 96 inches divided by 42 inches equals 2.29 repeats, rounded up to 3 repeats per strip.

STEP 2: Multiply the number of repeats by the inches of repeat to determine how long each strip must be to allow for the usable yield and waste. **Example:** 3 repeats times 42 inches equals 126 inches required per strip for usable yield and waste.

STEP 3: Subtract inches of wall height from the required inches per strip to find the waste per strip. **Example:** 126 inches minus 96 inches equals 30 inches of waste. *(Note: Because the waste is 30 inches, well over the 18-inch maximum noted previ-*

ously, continue with the following steps, and recalculate the estimate.)

STEP 4: Divide inches of waste per strip by inches of wall height to figure the percentage of waste. **Example:** 30 inches of waste per strip divided by 96 inches of wall height equals 31.25, or 32, percent waste. (*Note: This means that 32 percent more wallpaper will be wasted than originally figured for the estimate and that 32 percent more wallpaper will be required to complete the job.*)

STEP 5: Refigure the estimate. **Example:** 24 estimated rolls plus 32 percent additional rolls (8) equals 32 single rolls. (*Note: With the percentage method, it isn't necessary to convert metric to American to recalculate the estimate.*)

Count-Strip Method

The count-strip method is the most accurate way of calculating the required number of standard metric-size rolls with a vertical repeat of 18 inches or less. There are two

Large-Pattern Repeat Waste					Strip 5	
Strip 1	Strip 2	Strip 3	Strip 4		24"	Strip 1
					24"	Strip 2
					24"	Strip 3
24"	24"	24"	24"		24"	Strip 4

A metric triple roll, 42 ft. long, yields five full-length (8-ft.) strips. A pattern repeat of 18 in. plus allowance cuts of 6 in. results in waste per strip of 24 in., or the entire fifth strip of each roll.

variations to this system: one to figure 8-foot strips for standard walls and one to figure longer strips.

First, you should review the 18-inch pattern-repeat rule. It is important to understand why 18 inches is used as a maximum pattern repeat when you are employing the count-strip method for estimating standard 8-foot-high walls.

When a metric double roll contains 33 linear feet, it will yield four full-length strips. If the pattern has a vertical repeat of 18 inches or less and there is any waste involved in matching, the usable yield will be only three strips per double roll, instead of the usual four.

Even if a strip has exactly the maximum allowance of 18 inches, you have to add the 3-inch allowance to the top and bottom of each strip, which brings the total to 24 inches. This waste will have to come from the fourth strip every time a new strip is cut from the roll. After three consecutive strips are cut to match, there will be a total of 96 inches wasted—the entire fourth strip. If there are more than 24 inches of waste per strip (including matching and the allowance cuts of 6 inches), you should refigure the estimate.

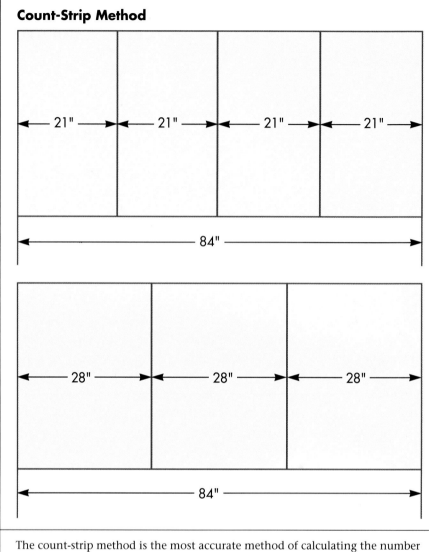

Count-Strip Method

The count-strip method is the most accurate method of calculating the number of rolls required to complete a job. Simply measure the distance, and divide by the width of the roll to determine the number of strips.

STEP 1: For 8-foot-long strips, measure the distance around the room in inches, and divide by 21 to determine the number of strips required. *(Note: Every four strips 21 inches wide by 8 feet long equals one metric double roll, and every three strips 21 inches wide by 5 feet long equals one metric single roll. However, some wallcoverings will not yield as many 8-foot-long strips per bolt [packaged roll] as others; you have to check the usable yield of the rolls.)*

STEP 2: Deduct one single roll for every two standard doors or windows on 8-foot-high walls.

STEP 3: Deduct one single roll for every three standard doors or windows when installing wallpaper only over chair rails. *(Note: Deduct for door and window openings only if you have included them when counting individual strips.)*

For strips over 8 feet long. Use the following steps to determine by the

count-strip method the number of usable strips more than 8 feet long that a double or triple roll will yield according to its width and length. In this example, the paper has a random match pattern and is 21 inches wide with 33 linear feet per double roll on a job with 9-foot-high (108-inch) ceilings.

STEP 1: Add 6 inches for the top and bottom allowance cuts to the wall height. **Example:** 108 inches plus 6 inches equals 114 inches.

STEP 2: Divide the total by 12 inches to get the average length per strip in feet. **Example:** 114 inches divided by 12 inches equals 9.5 feet per strip.

STEP 3: Divide that length into the double-roll or triple-roll length (in feet) to determine how many strips each bolt will yield. **Example:** 33 feet divided by 9.5 equals 3.5—or 3 usable strips per double roll.

Once you know this yield factor (3 strips), you can find the number of bolts required by dividing this number into the number of strips needed for the room. This example does not account for waste.

Stairways & Cathedral Walls

These locations are tricky because you have to allow for extra waste for the slope of the steps in a stairwell or the slope of the roof above a cathedral wall. To measure a stairway or cathedral wall, the best approach is to divide the surface area into rectangles that make it easy to determine the square footage.

In a stairwell 15 feet long, where first and second stories have 8-foot walls, the upper section is 8x15 feet, or 120 square feet. The corresponding lower section is split along the diagonal of the rectangle by the steps. But you can't simply reduce this part of the estimate by 50 percent, because extra wallpaper is required to reach the lower section of each strip. This will require about 15 percent more wallpaper in addition to the 50 percent, so you must multiply 120 square feet times 65 percent, which is 78 square feet. Add that

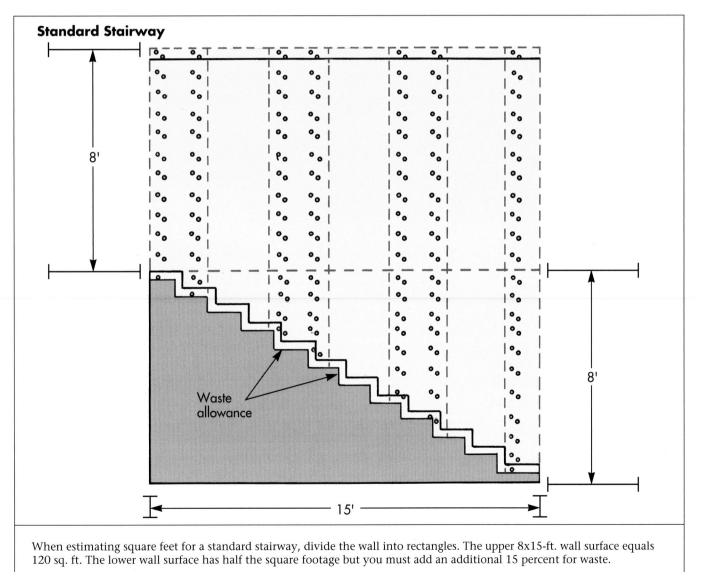

Standard Stairway

8'

8'

Waste allowance

15'

When estimating square feet for a standard stairway, divide the wall into rectangles. The upper 8x15-ft. wall surface equals 120 sq. ft. The lower wall surface has half the square footage but you must add an additional 15 percent for waste.

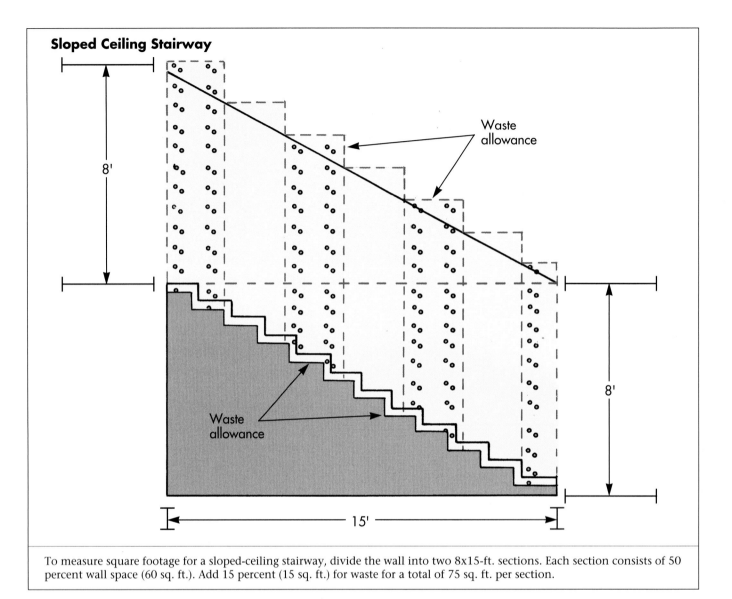

Sloped Ceiling Stairway

8'

Waste allowance

Waste allowance

8'

15'

To measure square footage for a sloped-ceiling stairway, divide the wall into two 8x15-ft. sections. Each section consists of 50 percent wall space (60 sq. ft.). Add 15 percent (15 sq. ft.) for waste for a total of 75 sq. ft. per section.

figure to the 120 square feet of the upper section.

In a stairwell through two stories where the ceiling slopes over the stairs use the extra 15 percent waste allowance (65 percent instead of 50 percent) for both upper and lower sections.

Ceilings

Here's how to use the count-strip method to estimate ceilings. If you use a texture pattern, it may yield more usable strips in one direction than the other. It is usually undesirable to splice ceiling strips because of appearances

and waste that amounts to two-thirds of a strip per bolt. That's why the count-strip method is the best system.

First, determine the direction of the wallpaper and the length of each strip. Add the allowance cuts and vertical repeat waste (if applicable) to determine the exact length of each strip, including waste. Next, determine how many usable full-length strips are available per double- or triple-roll bolt. Finally, divide this into the number of strips needed for the ceiling to find the number of double or triple rolls required.

In this example, we'll use the following: length of ceiling—15 feet; width of ceiling—15 feet; vertical repeat distance—19 inches; width of wallpaper—20½ inches; length of double roll—33 feet.

STEP 1: Determine the length of each strip in inches: 15-foot room length times 12 inches per foot equals 180 inches overall.

STEP 2: Include 6-inch allowance cuts: 180 inches plus 6 inches equals 186 inches required per strip.

STEP 3: Divide the repeat distance into the length required to find the number of repeats per strip: 186 inches divided by 19 inches equals 9.79, or 10 repeats per strip.

STEP 4: Multiply the number of repeats times the repeat in inches to find the length required per strip to allow for matching patterns: 10 repeats times 19 inches equals 190 inches per strip for matching. *(Note: Whenever textures or non-matching patterns are used, there are no repeats or waste for matching.)*

STEP 5: Convert this figure to feet: 190 inches divided by 12 inches per foot equals 15.83 feet, rounded up to 16 feet.

STEP 6: Divide the length of the double roll by this figure to determine how many usable strips it will yield: 33 feet divided by 16 feet equals 2.06. This means that the double roll will yield only two full-length strips, and every strip will equal a single roll. The fraction (.06) will be wasted. A ceiling 15 feet (180 inches) wide would require 8.78, rounded up to nine 20½-inch-wide strips. Because each strip is equal to a single roll, this ceiling would require nine single rolls.

For the sake of comparison, here is a look at the same example using the standard, square-foot method: 15 feet times 15 feet equals 225 total square feet. If the standard rule of 23 usable square feet per roll had been used for this estimate, this ceiling would have required only 9.8, or 10 single rolls: 225 square feet divided by 23 square feet equals 9.8. To complete the job based on this estimate, strips would have to be spliced, which is an unattractive option.

Mural borders must be carefully matched all the way around the room. Check the pattern carefully before trimming or installing.

Borders

Borders are packaged in 5-yard or 7-yard spools, although continuous strips and odd lengths are sometimes available. This information is just one of the variables in estimating borders, because each spool must be matched during the installation. You should add a minimum of one-half yard for each spool required to allow for matching.
Example: For a room requiring 15 yards of border material, you would need three 5-yard spools plus 1½ yards for matching during installation. This totals 16½ yards, and means that you should purchase four spools.

If the border is packaged in a continuous strip, add 2 yards to compensate for crooked corners and damage to the ends of the roll. Add an extra foot to allow for miter cuts whenever border paper is installed around door or window frames.

Commercial Wallcoverings

Wallcovering contractors should be aware that commercial wallcoverings are generally sold by the linear yard, as opposed to square feet and single rolls, and are packaged in 30-yard

bolts. This provides a high usable yield over large areas, such as in office buildings.

Follow these steps to estimate an area in linear yards. In this example, 54-inch untrimmed wallcovering is estimated for a 10x15-foot space with 9-foot-high walls.

STEP 1: Determine the distance around the space in inches, including doors and windows. In this example, the distance equals 600 inches.

STEP 2: Divide this distance by the width of the wallcovering, either 48 or 54 inches, to find the number of strips required for the space. *(Note: If the material is untrimmed, deduct four inches from the width to allow for double cutting—using two inches at each edge. The result is the usable yield of width in inches.)*
Example: 54 inches minus 4 inches equals 50 inches usable width; 600 inches divided by 50 inches equals 12 strips to cover the room.

STEP 3: Multiply the number of strips required times the height of the wall in

feet to find the total linear feet required. **Example:** 12 strips times 9 feet equals 108 linear feet for the room.

STEP 4: Divide total linear feet by three to determine the number of linear yards required. **Example:** 108 feet divided by 3 equals 36 linear yards required. *(Note: Do not subtract for normal-sized doors or windows that are no wider than the width of the wallcovering.)*

To use the conversion method, divide the total square footage of the room by 12.75 to find linear yards when using 54-inch-wide random-patterned paper. Divide by 11.25 to find linear yards if it is 48-inch-wide random paper.

Here's how the conversion method works using the example above—a space measuring 15x10 feet with 9-foot wall height. **Example:** 10 feet plus 15 feet equals 25 feet, times 2 equals 50 feet around the room, times the 9-foot wall height equals 450 total square feet for the room. Divide 450 by 12.75 (the conversion factor for 54-inch material), which is 35.29, rounded up to 36 yards.

Murals

To estimate for a mural, you need to know if it has extra background or filler paper available to complete a large room and whether the mural repeats like a pattern—say, with a four-panel vista of mountains that can easily become an eight-panel scene without an obvious splice. Of course, there is always room to experiment, by mixing panels from two similar murals to create a larger picture. Some designs lend themselves to a repeat while others do not.

When estimating for photo murals, be sure to check the same information. Photo murals are usually full height on the wall and are divided into quarter panels.

MAINLY FOR CONTRACTORS

Contractors also must be able to estimate wallcoverings from blueprints before there are any physical walls to measure. Almost all architectural plans are drawn at $\frac{1}{4}$ scale, which means that a $\frac{1}{4}$-inch space on the drawing equals a 12-inch space when the structure is finally built. Always check the scale of a blueprint before making your calculations.

To figure linear feet, you can check the measurements on the floor plans. To convert those totals to square feet, you need to check the elevations—drawings that show a side view, including the height of the wall. The trick is to account for variables such as cabinets and chair rails that may not be included on the blueprint. You may catch a few extras by checking the written job specifications for details you may not find on the floor plans or elevation drawings. Knowing the customer's plans is also essential.

Once you know the variables, you can use either the square-foot method or the count-strip method to calculate the number of rolls required. *(Note: To estimate using the count-strip method, you must also know the width of the wallpaper and the length of the packaged bolts.)*

Special note: Professional installers should always make a point of informing their clients about the amount of extra material that is required for large-pattern repeats and include this information on the estimate-contract form. Whatever the paper or pattern, don't figure the job so closely that you risk coming up short—an embarrassing and unprofessional situation, particularly if you made a special trip just to estimate the job.

Murals can fill a single wall or repeat to wrap around an entire room. When installing a mural, place the focal point at eye level.

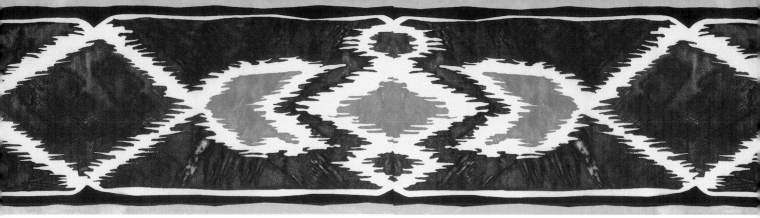

Chapter 4

Preparing Walls

On anything but a brand-new house with nearly perfect walls, professional painters and paperhangers will tell you that preparation is half the job. On older homes with crumbling cracks, popped drywall nails, and layers of peeling paint, prep work can seem to be a lot more than half. By the time you're done scraping, finishing with joint compound, and sanding, actually hanging the wallpaper may seem like the easy part—icing on the cake.

In case you haven't experienced the thrill of an endless drywall repair job, here's what happens after you pick out patterns and colors and finally set down to work. First comes the moving: couches to the center of the room, books off shelves, stereo equipment and TV cable lines disconnected, electronic equipment moved out, and everything draped in dropcloths, including doorways so clouds of fine joint-compound dust won't spread throughout the house.

Ready to hang the first sheet of paper? Probably not, because the walls have some oily hand prints, and maybe a few crayon streaks, and could use a good washing to improve adhesion. But as you scrub, you get more than dirt. Little flecks of old paint peel away and a few chunks of old joint compound. When you're done the wall looks better because it's cleaner, but it also looks worse because you can see all the cracks so clearly.

Out come the drywall knives. You could smooth on a coat here and there, and do a little bit of touch-up sanding when it dries. But the patch would probably shrink, and then you'd see a gully under the new wallpaper. If a problem popped up under a layer of fresh paint, you could make the repair, then feather more paint over the area—even match the stipple pattern of a roller to help the area blend in with the rest of the wall. But with wallpaper it's difficult to patch without calling attention to the fix. That means you need to get the wall smooth and flat with repairs that won't give way later on. You have to dig out cracked joint compound from past patches and fill voids in stages. Apply at least two coats with adequate drying time in between to avoid shrinkage and cracking.

Then there's the sanding, and the vacuuming, and the priming—a crucial step even if you're papering instead of painting. You need to seal all the dry and porous joint-compound patches so they won't suck moisture out of the wallpaper adhesive and create dry spots that turn into wrinkles and bubbles. But the amount of prep work you need to do depends a lot on the kind of wallcovering you plan to hang. If you want wafer-thin foil that highlights every imperfection, each crack should get a finishing coat of soupy joint compound and a fine finish sanding. But you don't need to be

nearly this finicky with a wall that supports a heavyweight, textured vinyl.

Whatever paper you use, its adhesive must go through a drying period, usually 24 to 48 hours, although some conditions such as high humidity and extra paper thickness can extend the process. A lot of potentially damaging stress occurs between the paper and the wall during this drying period. If layers of paint have not bonded properly, the wallpaper will adhere to the paint and pull large patches of it off the wall.

The first link of the adhesive chain is the wall surface. This may be the face paper of gypsum drywall or the first layer of paint on a plaster or cinderblock wall. The second link is the primer-sealer, or sizing, which must be compatible with the first layer to form and maintain a strong bond. The third link is the adhesive itself. The fourth link is the substrate, or backing, of the wallpaper, which is bonded to the final link, the decorative surface of the wallpaper. If any link fails, the wallpaper will not stay on the wall.

This problem has other implications you'll discover when you decide to remodel at some point in the future and want to remove the paper. Then you'll be trying to pull the paper off the wall in one big sheet instead of a thousand little strips. That's when the weakest link in the adhesive chain will give way. It may be the substrate separating from the decorative surface, the adhesive leaving the substrate, the primer-sealer peeling from the adhesive, or the worst case, drywall surface paper ripping off the wall and taking some chunks of gypsum along with it.

Preparation Products

Products designed to prepare a wall for wallpaper have two purposes that

One of the most important steps to successful wallpapering is proper preparation, including the application of a wallpaper primer-sealer.

seem to be contradictory: to improve adhesion, and to make it easier to remove wallpaper when you decide to redecorate. If you don't prepare a wall properly, you may get one but not the other. Adhesion may be so good that half the drywall comes off when you strip the paper. But if you use these products correctly, you can get both.

There are many varieties of these products on the market, each designed for a specific purpose. For example, some primer-sealers are made specifically for painting applications, while others are made to work specifically with wallcoverings. Here's a look at the selection, starting with primer-sealers.

Two notes for do-it-yourselfers. First, some primer-sealers are designed to protect the surface of drywall during wallpaper removal. Don't confuse

them with primers designed to go under paint. Second, specialized primers and sealers may be available only in commercial supply houses where professionals shop. For typical residential work, you'll do fine using one of the "universal" coatings—modern products that are formulated to work on many surfaces. When you see the word "universal" on the can, chances are there's a pigmented acrylic sealer inside.

Pigmented acrylic primer-sealers.

This type—sometimes referred to as a universal primer-sealer—can be used over all surfaces including existing wallpaper, vinyl, and even plastic laminate. The nice thing about acrylic products is that they clean up with water. These primer-sealers do a good job of protecting drywall from excessive

surface damage during future wallpaper removal. Pigmented acrylic primer-sealers can be tinted slightly with the wallpaper background color to enhance their ability to hide show-through. They can also be used to seal poor-quality latex paints.

Fast-drying alkyd primer-sealers. This type can be used under all types of wallcoverings and over all surfaces except existing wallpaper and vinyl, because their inks may bleed through. The clear types will not hide existing colors, but the pigmented types will. Fast-drying alkyds dry within 2 to 4 hours and provide excellent protection against damage to the drywall during future wallpaper removal. If the primer-sealer is thinned down with paint thinner (one to two pints of thinner per gallon of sealer), it will soak into and help bond poor-quality latex paint to the wall surface. The slow-drying variety requires 10 to 24 hours of drying time.

Clear acrylic primer-sealers. This type dries clear, so it won't hide colored stains under a semitransparent wallpaper. It can be used under most wallcoverings and on most wall surfaces including existing wallpaper and vinyl. It does not bond poor-quality latex paint and will not protect new drywall when wallpaper is later removed.

Heavy-duty acrylic primer-sealers. This type clear but tacky. It is designed to promote the adhesion of wallpaper. It won't bond poor-quality latex paint or protect new drywall during stripping because the acrylic soaks into the drywall and becomes part of the wall. Heavy commercial wallpaper will bond well to acrylics, but it creates a weak link of adhesion in the drywall paper facing.

Stain killers. This type of primer-sealer is used exclusively for hiding stains, including ink, lipstick, water damage, grease, crayon marks, smoke, and food stains—just about everything. Without at least one coat of stain killer, these stains can be easily visible through the wallpaper. Because stain-killing primer-sealers are not wallpaper primer-sealers, they require an acrylic primer-sealer topcoat to make the wallpaper bond. To test whether or not you will need to apply a stain killer over an existing wallpaper, rub a pattern section of the wallpaper using a cloth moistened with ammonia and

Testing for Stains

Test existing wallpaper for bleeding inks by rubbing with a cloth moistened with ammonia and water.

Alkyd Primer-Sealer

An alkyd wallpaper primer-sealer helps bond poor-quality latex paint to the wall and protects the wall surface during wallpaper removal.

water. If the inks are colorfast, they will not change color; if they are bleeding inks, they will turn a shade of greenish blue, and you will need a stain killer.

Sizing. Although people rarely use these anymore, the traditional approach involves a combination starch and cornflower sizing, in which the starch holds together the cornflower once it is mixed with water. It should only be used over a good-quality latex- or oil-based paint, and never underneath a nonbreathing type of wall-covering, because it does not contain chemical agents that will prevent the buildup of mildew. Starch sizing will not protect new drywall during the removal of wallpaper and will not guard against the poor qualities of latex paint. There is also cellulose and pine flower sizing, in which the cellulose holds the pine flower together after it is mixed with water and applied to the wall surface. This product sometimes comes packaged premixed in a container and has the approximate viscosity of milk. Cellulose sizing will not cause a mildew problem, but it won't protect walls covered with a poor grade of latex paint or protect drywall during future stripping.

You can also make a homemade sizing from wallpaper adhesive thinned down to the viscosity of paint. The idea is to provide extra holding power as moisture from the adhesive reactivates the diluted adhesive sizing.

Clearing and Cleaning

The amount of time you spend on preparation depends on the condition of wall surfaces, of course, but also on the kind of paper you plan to hang. For thin, smooth, reflective papers

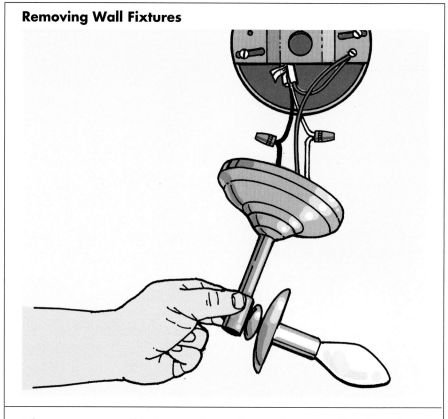

Removing Wall Fixtures

Before you remove wall fixtures, make sure to turn the power off at the main panel. Draw a wiring diagram if necessary to aid reinstallation.

such as foil, you need a dead flat wall with no nicks. Small imperfections are better concealed by a duller, rougher paper with a textured or embossed surface that scatters light.

The size and location of the wall also is a factor. Minor flaws are difficult to spot on short lengths of architecturally detailed wall—for example, a wall broken up by a row of windows with complicated trim. But the same type of flaws will be more obvious on the long, unbroken stretch of wall above a staircase. Bear these factors in mind as you fill flaws and sand them—a difficult process on an old wall surface that you may never be able to smooth out completely.

Removing wall fixtures. Preparing the wall surface and installing wallpaper

will be much easier if all obstacles are removed. You'll get better results, too.

Remove small light fixtures, picture hangers, mirrors, and the cover plates of electrical switches and outlets. (Always trip breakers and remove fuses in the appropriate electrical circuits before working on fixtures and wiring. Use a circuit tester to confirm that wires are not live.) If a mirror is too large to move safely, consider it a permanent fixture and paper around it.

Many bathroom and kitchen accessories, such as towel racks and soap holders, are held in place by a small setscrew you can remove with a screwdriver. On some fixtures, you'll find a hollow-headed fastener that has to be removed with a hex wrench. It's a good idea to collect all fasteners and small parts in a plastic bag.

To remove light fixtures you have to undo electrical connections.

You'll generally find a black wire, a white wire, and a green (or bare copper) ground wire. Some fixtures may contain other wires—for example, stairway fixtures that turn on and off from two switches, will have a red wire, as well. You don't have to remove electrical outlets and switches. Just remove the cover plates.

The connections between the fixture wires and the circuit wires in the wall may be taped together or, more commonly, screwed into a plastic cap called a wire connector. To undo the connections, simply unscrew the cap and unbraid the wires. It's a good idea to draw yourself a wiring diagram to make sure you wire the fixture back together correctly.

Cleaning dirty or greasy walls. Wash dirty or greasy walls with a solution of equal parts of warm water and ammonia, and let them dry several hours before applying a primer-sealer. Don't use a detergent containing phosphorus, which can prevent coatings from bonding and may give them a spongy texture.

Spot-patching and sanding. Start by sanding walls with a coarse (80-grit) sandpaper to remove little bumps. Then spot-patch cracks, holes, and indentations using a lightweight water-based nonshrinking joint compound. Don't use an oil-based product because it may bleed through the primer-sealer and stain the new wallpaper.

Remove flaking paint or dried adhesive with a broad knife or putty knife. Apply a light skim coat of thinned-down joint compound over the scraped areas. Allow it to dry, and then sand it until smooth.

Concealing shadows. To deal with dingy areas such as shadows from drywall patches and seams, apply a coat of white-pigmented wallpaper acrylic primer-sealer. This is particularly important for walls under semitransparent papers.

To test the transparency of a wallpaper, make a dark pencil line on a piece of white paper, and move the

Spot-Sanding

Spot-sand rough or raised areas with 80-grit sandpaper.

Spot-Patching

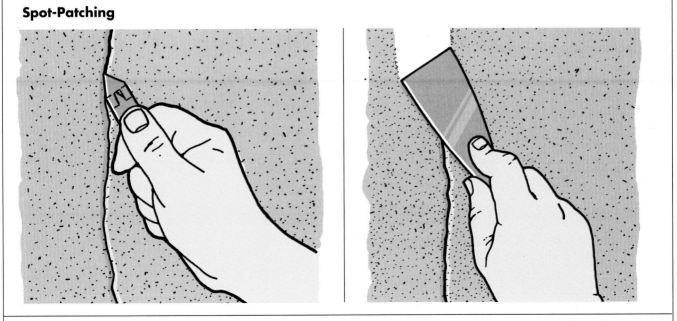

Some professionals find a can opener the perfect tool to remove loose material from cracks in plaster walls. After cleaning, fill cracks with a non-shrinking water-based joint compound. Allow it to dry, and then sand the areas smooth.

Concealing Stains

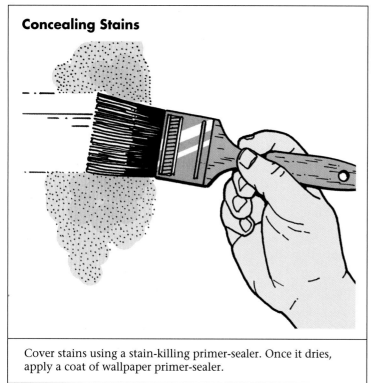

Cover stains using a stain-killing primer-sealer. Once it dries, apply a coat of wallpaper primer-sealer.

Diagnosing Moisture Problems

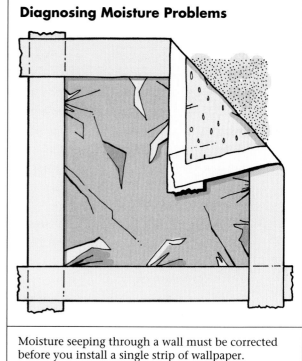

Moisture seeping through a wall must be corrected before you install a single strip of wallpaper.

paper behind a sample of the wallcovering. If you can detect the line, you've got a semitransparent paper and even minor discolorations are likely to show through.

Concealing stains. Spot-prime stained areas such as lipstick, grease spots, ink or pencil marks, graffiti, crayon, nicotine, and food stains with a stain-killing primer-sealer. Apply a pigmented wallpaper primer-sealer over the entire wall surface before installing new wallpaper.

Diagnosing moisture problems. Moisture can loosen new wallpaper and create mildew. Both conditions can ruin an otherwise perfect job. To solve moisture problems, the first step is to find out where the excess moisture is coming from. Here's a simple test that will tell you.

Tape a piece of aluminum foil about 12x12 inches to the problem wall. Use duct tape to seal all edges, and

leave the foil in place for a few days before removing it. If there is moisture under the foil, it comes from the wall; for example, from a pipe leak or a roof leak. You may have to check flashing, window trim, and other possible sources of a leak. If the moisture is on the outside of the foil, the problem is interior condensation, not a leak, and a dehumidifier will help.

Treating mildew. Mildew fungus grows in dark, moist environments such as bathrooms, shower stalls, basements, and closets, as well as behind nonbreathing wallcoverings. To eliminate mildew, wash with a 1:3 solution of household bleach and warm water, and rinse with clean water. When the area dries, spray it with a germicidal disinfectant.

Before hanging the wallcovering, apply a pigmented wallpaper primer-sealer. When hanging the paper, you may also wish to use an adhesive that

has an anti-mildew agent, or add one tablespoon of a strong mildewcide to each gallon of standard adhesive.

Repairing rusted corner guard. Occasionally, a metal corner guard used in drywall construction will rust. The rust can bleed through the primer-sealer and discolor the wallpaper. To prevent this problem, sand the rusted area with 120-grit sandpaper, prime with a rust-resistant primer, and allow it to dry. Then reprime the surface with a water-based pigmented primer-sealer.

Repairing damaged drywall. Drywall that survives a soaking with wallpaper-removing solution and then the subsequent scraping may have some minor blisters or sections where the surface paper has come loose. Here's how to repair this problem.

Wet damaged sections with a mist of warm water to make blisters and delaminated areas swell and become

more visible. Cut out damaged areas of paper with a razor blade, and remove any loose drywall face paper. Allow the areas to completely dry, and then apply an oil-based enamel undercoat thinned down with paint thinner, or a proprietary primer-sealer. When dry, lightly sand the affected areas with 120-grit sandpaper, and repair with a nonshrinking, lightweight joint compound. Finally, sand and reprime these areas with the primer-sealer used on other parts of the wall.

Painted Wall Surfaces

When damaged areas are repaired and primed, it may be tempting to start hanging paper. Before you do, investigate the undamaged surfaces to be sure your primer-sealer and new wallpaper

will stick. The choice of primer-sealer depends on the type of paint on the wall and the type of wallpaper. Here are some general recommendations for different paint finishes.

Flat oil-based. Etch the surface with coarse sandpaper, such as a 50-grit sand-paper. An acrylic wallpaper primer-sealer serves as a good surface for the wallcovering.

Flat latex. Test latex wall paint by rubbing the surface vigorously with a cloth moistened in warm water. If the cloth doesn't pick up any color, use a clear or pigmented wallpaper acrylic primer-sealer. If some paint transfers, apply one coat of pigmented wallpaper acrylic primer-sealer.

Latex enamel. Latex enamel paint provides a good foundation for wallcovering, provided it has dried for at least 14 to 21 days. Nonetheless, it's a good idea to apply an acrylic wallpaper primer-sealer before beginning the installation.

Glossy enamel. Sand glossy enamel paint with 50- to 80-grit sandpaper to etch the surface. This helps the wallpaper primer-sealer bond. Then apply an acrylic primer-sealer (either clear or pigmented), and allow it to dry a minimum of 6 hours before papering. If you install a nonbreathing wallpaper —for example, a fabric-backed vinyl— over glossy paint, you may want to add an absorbing liner paper to pick up moisture from the adhesive.

Repairing Damaged Drywall

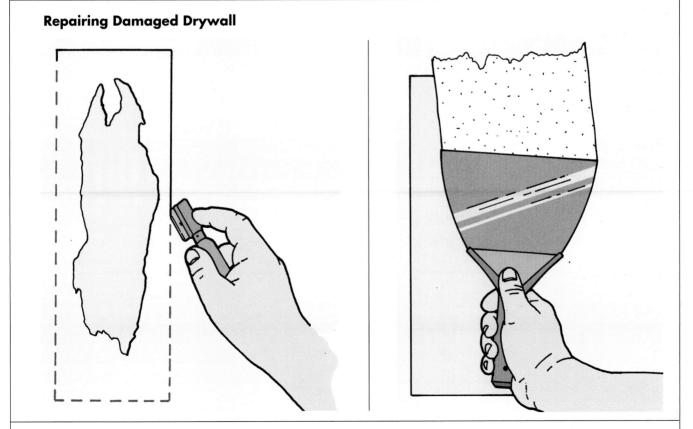

Moisten damaged areas of a drywall panel, and then cut out damaged sections using a razor blade. Repair damaged drywall with an enamel undercoat followed by a water-based non-shrinking joint compound.

HOW TO REPAIR A HOLE IN DRYWALL

1 Cut a new piece of drywall into a square or rectangle slightly larger than the hole. Use a patch piece that's the same thickness as the gypsum on the wall. Place the scrap piece over the hole, trace the outline with a pencil, and use a keyhole saw or utility knife to cut through the lines. Once you remove the damaged edges, the trimmed hole should match the repair piece.

2 Cut one or two pieces (depending on the size of the hole) of ³/₄-inch-thick wood to fasten inside the hole and support the patch piece. The wood should be long enough to extend several inches past the hole. Insert the wood support. Hold on to keep it from dropping into the wall cavity and secure it by driving a drywall screw into each end from the face of the gypsum panel.

3 With a small drywall knife, butter the edges of the hole with joint compound (adding a few dabs to the wood supports). Then nestle the patch piece in place, and secure it to the wood supports with a couple of drywall screws.

4 Place fiber-mesh tape over the seams to reduce cracking, and cover them with joint compound. Extend it several inches past the seams to feather out the repair. When it's dry, sand the compound with 120-grit sandpaper. Sand lightly in a circular motion, and try to stay clear of the drywall paper surface next to the patch. Excessive sanding will scuff the paper into a furry surface that pulls moisture out of wallpaper adhesive, which could lead to bubbling. Remember to seal the fresh joint compound with a wallpaper acrylic primer-sealer.

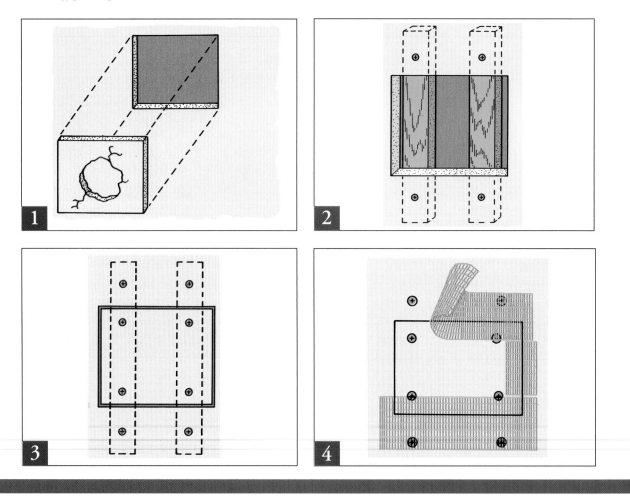

Preparing Special Surfaces

Metal. Clean dirt and grease off metal surfaces with a solution of equal parts of ammonia and water. Apply an oil-based rustproof paint, and allow it to dry. Then apply a pigmented acrylic primer-sealer, and allow to dry 24 hours.

New drywall. Seal the surface paper of drywall before installing wallpaper to prevent the paper from drying out the adhesive prematurely—and so you can easily strip the paper in the future. Use an oil-based enamel undercoat or sanding sealer thinned with paint thinner (one quart of thinner per gallon of sealer). If you're going to install semitransparent wallpaper, use a pigmented primer-sealer to hide the contrasting color between the drywall and the drywall mud on seams.

Plaster. Unpainted plaster must be at least 90 to 120 days old and washed with a strong solution of vinegar to neutralize any alkaline areas. Scrape out large cracks to remove loose material, and reinforce the plaster repair with mesh tape. Use patching plaster that contains a latex bonding agent. (In some cases you may need to apply a liner paper or fabric-backed vinyl over plaster walls that have a history of cracking.) Before papering, apply a wallpaper acrylic primer-sealer, and allow it to dry.

Prefinished paneling. After nailing down any loose seams, wash the surface with a solution of equal parts of ammonia and water, sand lightly with 80-grit paper, and apply an acrylic primer-sealer.

After at least 24 hours of drying time, install a medium-weight liner paper horizontally to bridge the vertical grooves.

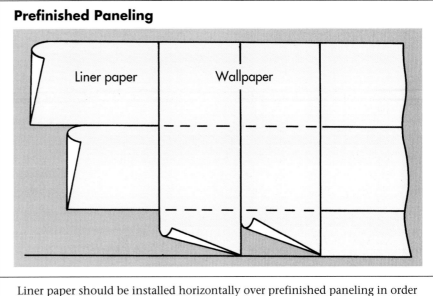

Prefinished Paneling

Liner paper   Wallpaper

Liner paper should be installed horizontally over prefinished paneling in order to bridge the grooves.

Some installers fill these voids with joint compound, but that can't take the place of liner paper, which you need to keep the wet adhesive from bonding to the compound and causing it to shrink. Check the surface for places where the liner paper may have sunk into the grooves, and fill them as necessary with lightweight joint compound.

If you're using prepasted paper, apply acrylic primer-sealer on the liner to keep it from soaking excessive moisture from the adhesive.

Block and brick. These materials are difficult to cover because their surfaces are rough, gritty, and often subject to moisture problems. Over new block or brick, apply a block sealer to fill crevices and mortar joints, and then use an acrylic primer-sealer. Allow at least 12 hours of drying time—much more in damp conditions. Finally, install a heavy liner paper to help bridge the joints before installing the finished paper.

Ceramic tile. To install wallpaper over ceramic tile, follow the recommenda-

tions for concrete block and brick walls. Make sure to clean the tile completely of dirt, grease, or soap film before applying the sealer.

Contact paper. If you want to install wallpaper over self-sticking contact paper, apply a layer of wallpaper pigmented acrylic primer-sealer, and allow it to dry. Apply joint compound to any overlapped edges of existing paper, and then sand smooth and reprime it with the same primer-sealer. Without this coating, joint compound may not bond to the slick surface.

To remove contact paper, wash it with a solution of paint thinner or lacquer thinner. *Caution:* Use these products only according to the manufacturer's directions with adequate ventilation, and avoid any type of open flame. Once the walls have dried, apply acrylic wallpaper primer-sealer.

Tongue-and-groove boards. Wall surfaces made from individual boards expand and contract in response to changing temperature and humidity.

This motion makes them an unsuitable base for wallpaper. You have to remove the boards or bury them under drywall.

Plywood walls. Apply a pigmented acrylic primer-sealer before papering over unfinished plywood. If the sealer raises the wood grain, sand it smooth with an 80-grit sandpaper.

Sand-painted walls. Wallpaper will not bond to a sand-painted finish—at least not for long. Either recover the surface with drywall, or sand down the gritty surface and apply an acrylic primer-sealer. Even then, it's wise to use a heavily embossed wallpaper with a matte finish to camouflage remaining roughness.

Laminate. Sand plastic laminates with a 50- to 80-grit sandpaper to engrave the surface so that a primer-sealer will bond. Then apply clear acrylic wallpaper primer-sealer, and allow it to dry at least 24 hours before papering.

Paint over paper. Sometimes it's better to paint over wallpaper rather than remove it. This is especially true if wallpaper removal will damage the wall.

If you want to paint over grasscloth, stringcloth, or flock, prime the wallpaper with an oil-based stain-killing primer-sealer to prevent any bleeding dye or ink on the existing wallpaper from penetrating the final paint application. The finish layer of paint should be a good latex or enamel paint.

Removing Wallpapers

If you're interested in hanging new wallpaper, it's likely that you have some old paper on the wall already that needs to be removed. (If it's in good condition, you may be able to leave it; read Chapter 7, starting on page 94, for tips on how to hang paper over paper.) But before you take out a scraper or rent a wallpaper steamer, see if you can avoid a lot of the mess and simply peel the paper.

Use a scraper or putty knife, and lift a small corner of the existing paper away from the wall. Pull the paper away at a shallow angle. Avoid pulling directly away from the wall, which can tear the wall surface. If the wallpaper strips off without causing excessive damage to the wall surface, continue peeling.

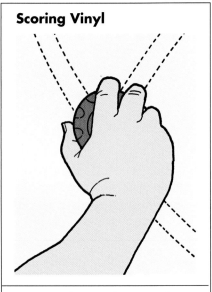

Scoring Vinyl

Use a scarifying tool to score the surface of non-breathing wallpaper.

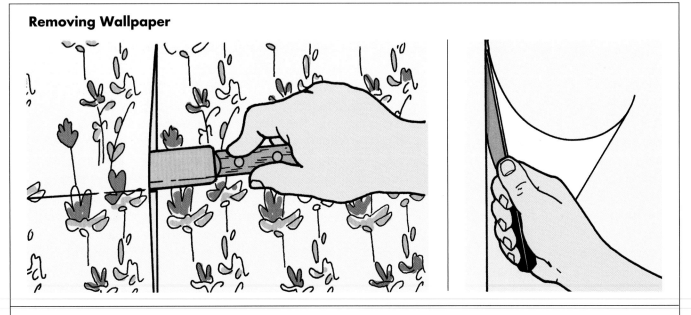

Removing Wallpaper

To remove the old wallpaper, work a putty knife underneath the seams, and lift the edges off the wall as much as possible. Use a scraper to remove wallpaper soaked with remover solution.

If the wallpaper does not completely dry-strip, use a spray bottle to saturate a test area (about 4 square feet), with hot water and wallpaper-removing solution. (You can also use a gel remover, which minimizes mess as well as potential water damage to woodwork and floors.) Allow the solution to soak in for about 15 minutes. If the wallpaper is porous, the solution will immediately soak in and dissolve the old adhesive. If the surface isn't porous, the solution will not soak in, and you will need to score the surface before applying the wallpaper remover. (Specialized tools that do this job are called scarifiers.) You can use coarse floor-sanding paper, a scarifying tool with teeth that cut into the paper, or even the toothed edge of a handsaw. Finally, remove the wallpaper using a scraper or broad knife.

Note that the decorative surface of some wallpaper is designed to separate from the paper backing during removal. In this case, you simply dry-strip the decorative surface and then use the wallpaper-removing solution and a broad knife to strip the backing from the wall. Of course, if the wall surface was not prepared properly, it may be impossible to remove the wallpaper without causing excessive damage to the wall surface no matter how carefully you work. If this is the case, it's generally better to install new wallpaper right over the existing paper. But if you follow the same stripping sequence for the existing wallpaper, the surface revealed underneath may need only a few touch-ups.

Whatever type of covering you encounter, bear in mind these general rules: First, don't oversoak an existing wallpaper with a remover solution

Commercially available scrapers speed wallpaper removal.

This palm-sized scarifying tool has cutter wheels underneath.

Removing Strippable Wallpaper

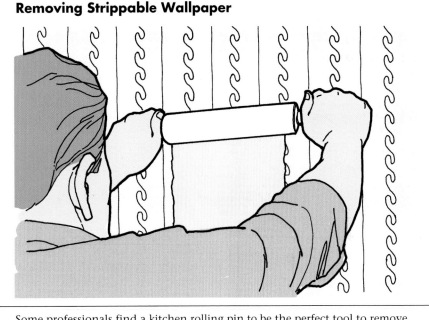
Some professionals find a kitchen rolling pin to be the perfect tool to remove dry-strippable wallpaper.

because it can penetrate the drywall and cause significant damage. Typically, about 15 to 20 minutes is enough soaking time. Second, don't try to pull the paper straight away from the wall. Instead, pull at a shallow angle. Here are some other tips on removing different types of wallcoverings.

Commercial vinyl. Most commercial wallcoverings easily dry-strip from sound walls. The job is even easier if you pull the wallcovering off the wall at about a 10-degree angle, and in narrow widths, such as 4- or 6-inch-wide pieces.

Cork veneer, felt, and suede. Cork veneer is shaved from cork planks and then laminated to a substrate paper. Felt and suede wallcoverings have a leather-like finish with a napped surface resembling the leather made from the skin of a goat. Generally, you remove

these kinds of wallcoverings by first stripping the decorative surface from the backing. If necessary, score the remaining substrate paper with coarse floor-sanding paper, and then soak it with full-strength wallpaper-removing solution. Once the solution soaks in, remove the backing by scraping with a broad knife. If the substrate is completely secure on the wall surface, you could install new wallpaper over it, although it's preferable to remove both layers.

Flocked. These wallcoverings are made from very fine cotton, silk, or nylon fibers. If the substrate is paper, use a wallpaper-removing solution or a steamer. If the paper won't budge and you have to score the surface, moisten the flock fibers to keep them from flying; then saturate the scored surface with remover for about 15 minutes, and remove the paper with a broad knife. If the flocked paper has a fabric backing, it should peel away like a commercial wallcovering.

Foil. Foils have a thin sheet of aluminum laminated onto a substrate of paper or scrim, and sometimes sandwich the material around a polyester sheet to prevent water in the adhesive from contacting the foil. Whatever the configuration, you should score foil paper with rough sandpaper and wet it with a wallpaper-removing solution.

Grasscloth, hemp, jute weave, paper weave, reedcloth, stringcloth, and rushcloth. These handcrafted wallcoverings are made from various natural plant materials. Remove the decorative surface by saturating it with wallpaper-removing solution and scraping; then repeat the procedure to remove the paper backing. If the backing won't come off the wall, let it dry; then sand it and use it as a liner paper.

Expanded vinyl. This product has a raised effect, which is heat-embossed using a thermoplastic material such as vinyl. Normally, you can peel away the surface layer, but the paper backing remains on the wall. You can use this backing as a liner paper for the new wallcovering or remove it by soaking it with warm water and removing solution, then scraping.

Liner paper. This plain paper often is used as a backer that provides a smooth surface for a finished paper. You can install most papers over liner paper that is secure on the wall. If you need to remove a liner paper, try dry-stripping first, then the standard soaking and scraping sequence.

Moiré. Most moiré wallcovering has a paper backing and resembles solid sheet vinyl. The decorative surface will

Sanding Paper Backing

The paper backing left after wallpaper removal can be removed by scraping, or it can be used as a liner paper after it is lightly sanded with a drywall sander.

peel away from the backing, which requires the soak-and-scrape treatment.

Photo mural. You can usually delaminate the decorative surface from the backing. If that doesn't work, score, spray, and scrape it.

Mylar. The foil-like surface of this paper generally dry-strips from the backing, which responds to soaking and scraping.

Solid sheet vinyl, silkscreen prints, and wet look. The vinyl decorative surface of these wallcoverings can be removed by pulling the surface layer from the paper backing. The backing is then removed by soaking with removing solution and scraping.

Standard paper. This pulp paper with a thin vinyl coating can be scuffed with coarse sandpaper, sprayed with warm water mixed with removing solution, left to soak for about 15 minutes, then scraped off the wall.

Vinyl-coated. Most vinyl-coated papers (many are prepasted) can be dry-stripped off a wall. If necessary, score the surface with sandpaper or a scarifying tool, and then soak with removing solution and scrape.

MAINLY FOR CONTRACTORS

The number-one way to avoid call-backs is to do the best job possible. Bypass the most important steps, and you are likely to get a call from a frantic customer who has whole sheets of expensive wallpaper buckling and falling to the floor. A do-it-yourselfer has no one to blame but himself if he cuts a few corners. If you cut corners, he has you to blame.

There are some wall conditions that you have to be aware of if you want the wallpaper to stay on the wall. You will usually recognize these through experience. Knowing how to handle the situation can make or break the job. Moisture in the walls is a good example. If there is a cold-water pipe running next to the wallboard or if the wall lacks a vapor barrier, you might be setting up conditions favorable for mildew formation. Moisture in walls is a problem that you must correct before you can hang a single strip. Structural settling is another factor in a long-lasting wallpaper installation. It's a good idea to wait for a year or so before hanging wallpaper on large walls such as cathedral walls.

After soaking wallpaper with a removing solution, use a wide drywall knife or scraper to get it off the wall.

Using the proper preparation techniques and careful attention to detail results in a beautiful installation that will last for years.

Chapter 5

Patterns & Seams

Ever since 1688, when the Frenchman Jean Papillon invented wallpaper with repeating patterns, people have been taking up the challenge of installing it correctly. The trick, of course, is to align parts of the pattern so precisely that your eye sweeps across the wall without spotting a single seam. It's a straightforward job with plain-colored papers and random textures where there is no pattern. But with many of the intricate, highly detailed designs available today, even a minor mismatch can stand out on the wall like a glaring mistake.

There is so much variety in wallcoverings that pattern matching may seem too difficult for do-it-yourselfers. But there are only five basic pattern types to contend with, and once you know how to spot the differences, you can make any combination of repeating shapes and colors flow smoothly across seams. All it takes is a framing square and some simple calculations.

There are two other parts of the pattern-and-seam puzzle, and you have to tend to them while you're in the middle of aligning the pattern: using the right technique to join strips in a neat, flat seam, and using the right application of adhesive to make sure they stay where you put them. Naturally, there are many types of adhesives, and a number of different techniques for joining strips of wallpaper. You won't use all of them on every job, but knowing how they work allows you to select the most efficient method for any situation.

Whatever paper or pattern you settle on, the installation will look better if you plan the job so seams fall in the best possible locations. Once you get started, the width of the wallpaper will determine where each successive seam falls. But by adjusting the first strip, you may be able to avoid some problem areas where it's difficult to match patterns and create a seamless appearance—for instance, where narrow strips fall beside windows and doors.

If you're working with a patterned paper, it can pay to start in a location where the beginning of the first strip and the end of last strip never meet—-or at least where the seam won't be obvious. For instance, you might start the layout on one side of a built-in bookcase and finish on the other. In a room with four flat walls and no built-in hiding places, you might start in the least visible corner regardless of where the seams fall—for example, behind a door that's normally left open.

This kind of adjustment is important because the starting line usually is also the finishing line, and you won't know for sure how true the sheets are running until you get there. You might make several minor matching errors as you work your way around the room that are not noticeable one at a time.

But the combined effect could mushroom into an obvious mistake by the time it comes up against the first sheet.

Once you assemble the materials and reserve time for the project, it's tempting to plow ahead. But careful planning before the job starts is a good investment of your time on any home-improvement project. With wallcovering jobs, this kind of seam-and-pattern preview can uncover problems while you're measuring to see where seams might fall. That's a lot easier than peeling off crooked little strips stuck in a mess of adhesive.

Pattern Matches

There are thousands of wallpaper color combinations and at least as many patterns—enough to create an almost limitless number of possibilities where one strip meets another. But there are only five types of pattern matches: random match, random texture, straight across, half drop, and multiple drop. Once you can identify the type of pattern match required for the paper you're using, you can determine the best seam placement, or even change seam placement without altering the pattern sequence.

Random match. Vertical stripes are a good example of a random-match pattern—the term for any design that does not repeat vertically. The stripes themselves are vertical, of course, but the pattern they form in a row across the wall is horizontal. Because there is no vertical pattern, you can cut from the roll without having to worry about cutting extra for matching. Just make sure you leave 2 to 3 inches at the top and bottom of each strip for trimming.

This is one of the easiest matches to make, but there is a catch. If some stripes are thicker than others or different

colors, the paper will only work in one direction, and if you inadvertently flip a sheet end-for-end, the spacing and color sequence may be out of sync.

Random texture. Vinyl imprinted with a crinkled surface and woven fiber-

glass wallcoverings are good examples of a random-texture pattern—the term for any paper with a non-matching design or texture. You don't have to match this wallpaper vertically or horizontally because there is no right side up; it's the same everywhere.

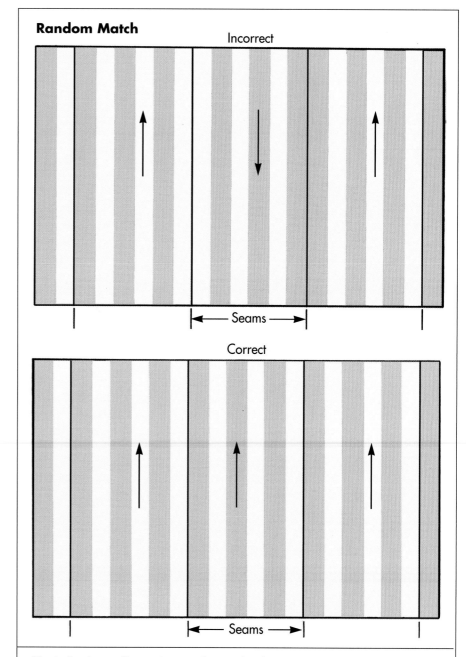

Vertical stripe wallpaper is a good example of a random matching pattern you can cut from the roll without having to worry about matching. The top illustration shows a common random-match mistake. Because vertical stripe paper repeats horizontally, it's important to orient all the strips properly.

Random Texture

Incorrect

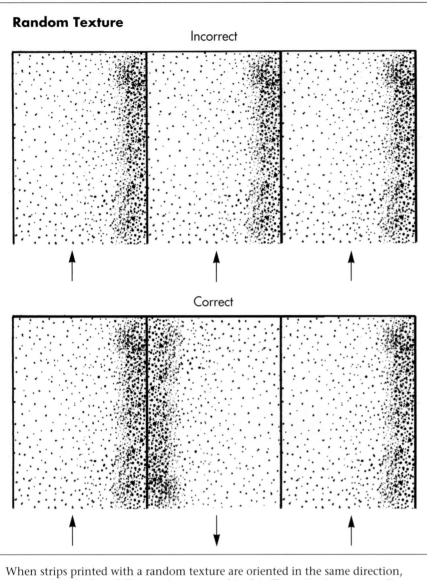

Correct

When strips printed with a random texture are oriented in the same direction, a noticeable shading difference (exaggerated in this illustration) can occur. By reversing the direction of every other strip, the effect can be minimized.

Matching the Top

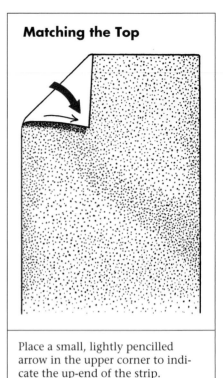

Place a small, lightly pencilled arrow in the upper corner to indicate the up-end of the strip.

But there is a potential troublesome area on wallpaper printed with a random texture. During the printing process, a misadjustment on the press may sometimes cause ink to be applied slightly more heavily on one side of the sheet than the other. The discrepancy generally is undetectable when you look at the roll. But you may notice the change in shading when you put two strips together, lighter edge against darker edge. The resulting undulating pattern may become very obvious when you stand back a few feet and view the strips on the wall.

Luckily, there's an easy way to avoid even a slight mismatch (and avoid a return trip to the home center), and it won't foul anything up even if the paper is perfectly printed. The solution is to just turn every other strip upside-down—a process called reversing—during the installation. That way, the lighter edges will meet, and the darker edges will

meet, and you usually won't see the contrast of one against the other. During installation, the best way to avoid potential confusion is to unroll each bolt in the same direction and cut all the strips from the same end of each bolt. As you cut each strip, mark a small "this-end-up" arrow on the backside in the trim area, or just notch the end of each piece to indicate the top. (This notch will be removed when you trim the allowance.)

When some wallpapers are wet with adhesive, the shading will not become evident until the wallpaper completely dries. At this point, of course, it's too late to correct the problem. Better safe than sorry!

When installing wallcoverings with a random texture, such as grasscloth and stringcloth, it's a good idea to try reversing each strip during installation unless it has a matching background pattern design. Because the weave of these handmade papers creates a

horizontal shading effect, grasscloth seams become a dominant feature on the wall and need to have a well-balanced layout.

Straight across. Horizontal stripes are a good example of a straight-across pattern—the name for any design that lines up horizontally across the seams.

Sometimes a straight-across match isn't as obvious as stripes. Here are two ways to identify straight-across matches.

■ Select a design element on one side of a strip, and then select a particular point on that element. Then, use a framing square to align that point with the corresponding point of the design on the opposite side of the paper. If the points of the design are parallel, the pattern is a straight-across match.

■ In some cases, a straight-across match is identified by a pattern sequence that repeats itself horizontally as well as vertically. This is shown by the star/square sequence in the illustration. Once you identify the sequence,

you have to be sure that every strip is the same at the ceiling line, or duplicate designs will appear together out of sequence.

Half drop. Any design that lines up in a diagonal sequence is called a half-drop match. As a rule, every other strip will have the same set of designs at the ceiling line.

You can identify a half drop with the same two-step process used to check a straight-across match—with one key difference. Instead of checking straight across the strip to see if two points of the pattern align, measure down the same side of the strip until you reach the design repeat. Then check across the strip to see how far the pattern

Maintaining Straight-Across Pattern

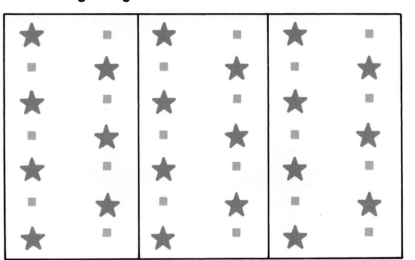

Correct Sequence

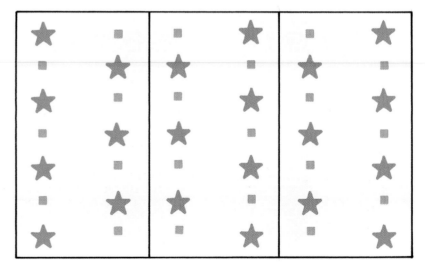

Incorrect Sequence

Make sure the pattern sequence is the same at the ceiling line for every strip, or duplicate designs will appear out of sequence.

Straight Across

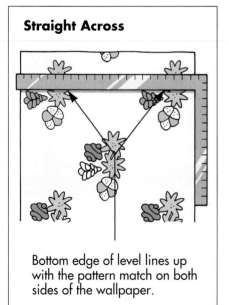

Bottom edge of level lines up with the pattern match on both sides of the wallpaper.

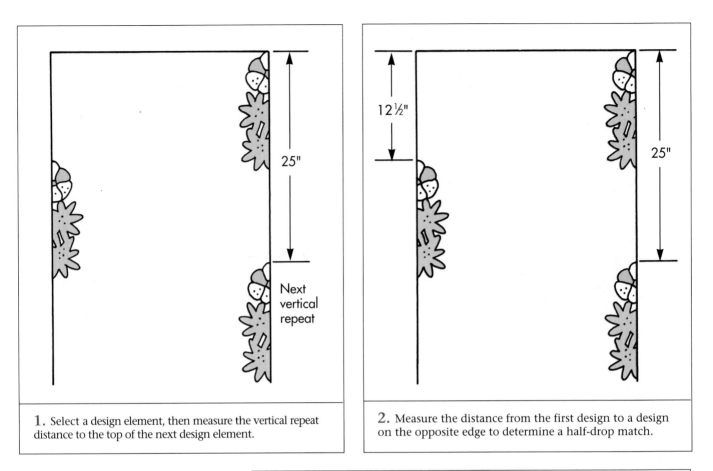

1. Select a design element, then measure the vertical repeat distance to the top of the next design element.

2. Measure the distance from the first design to a design on the opposite edge to determine a half-drop match.

drops before it repeats. (*Note: Every patterned paper except for random patterns and textures has a vertical repeat.*) Here are the steps.

1 Find a place where the design is cut off by the right or left edge of the strip. Look down the same side of the strip, and find the vertical repeat for this cutoff design. Measure and note the distance.

2 Measure the distance from your first cutoff design to the second cutoff design on the opposite edge of the wallpaper. If the distance is one-half the vertical repeat measurement, you have a half-drop match.

A half-drop match can exist even when there is no cutoff design in the pattern. Duplicated pattern segments may appear in single-double

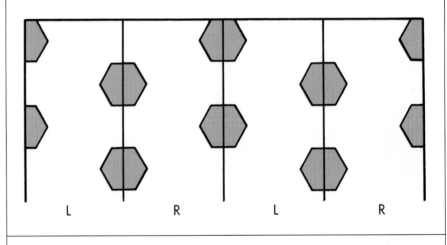

As a general rule, when you have a half-drop matching pattern, every other strip will have the same design at the ceiling line.

or double-triple form. In any case, the rule holds true: every other strip will show the same pattern of designs at the ceiling line.

To reduce the possibility of accidentally installing identical strips, take a

second when you mark the locations of the seams to indicate with letters which strip will be placed in each spot. For example, if the left edge of the matching design is at the ceiling line, label that strip "L." If the matching design on the

right side of the paper is at the ceiling line, label it "R." Make your marks very lightly in pencil on the wall and on the waste allowance of the wallpaper strip.

Multiple drop. This type of pattern match is the rare bird of the wallpaper world. However, it's important to identify a multiple-drop before the first strip is cut. One way to identify it is by process of elimination. It's likely that if your wallpaper does not conform to a straight-across or a half-drop match, it is a multiple-drop match. Multiple-drop patterns are most often found in series of three, four, or five sheets. However, in some multiple-drop matching patterns, the designs are so dense that they can drop in sequence up to 20 times before they reappear on the ceiling line. This can be an

advantage in an old house where the ceiling line isn't level, but it's important to understand the multiple-drop pattern to get the best results. Here's another way to identify a multiple-drop match before you start cutting.

1 Choose a cutoff design on one side of the wallpaper, and draw a horizontal line across the strip using a framing square.

2 Next, use a measuring tape to measure straight down from the cutoff design to find the vertical repeat distance in inches.

3 Measure the distance down from the horizontal line on the opposite side of the strip to where the other half of the design will

match. Divide the first measurement by the full vertical repeat distance to determine the multiple-drop match, which is expressed as a proportion or fraction. In the illustration, the design on the right side of the strip drops 8 inches from the ceiling line, one-third of the vertical repeat distance of 24 inches.

4 The design on each consecutive strip drops an additional 8 inches until the pattern finally repeats at the ceiling line; in this case, at every fourth strip. Because 24 inches divided by 8 inches equals 3 inches, this particular example is called a one-third multiple-drop match.

Figuring multiple-drop proportions. The math may seem a little much: it's

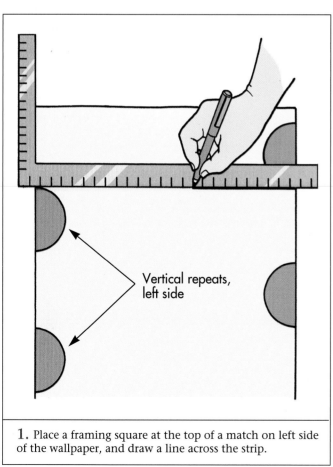

1. Place a framing square at the top of a match on left side of the wallpaper, and draw a line across the strip.

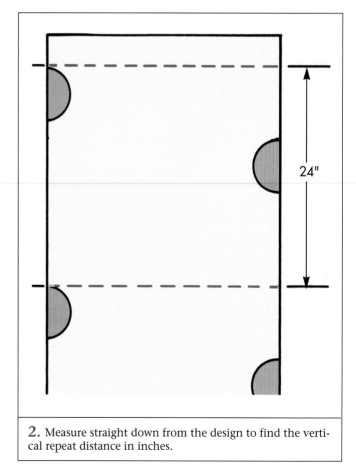

2. Measure straight down from the design to find the vertical repeat distance in inches.

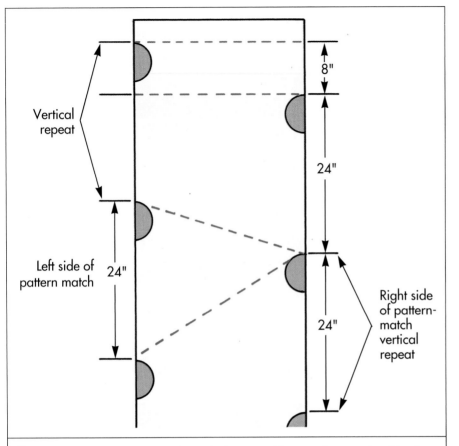

3. Measure the distance down from the horizontal line on the opposite side of the strip to where the other half of the design will match.

only wallpaper, after all, and a few extra dollars can buy enough extra wallpaper to increase your margin of error in estimating. On large projects (and for pros who can't afford to pay for paper they don't need on job after job), crunching numbers pays off. When the rate of drop changes, so does the proportion. Here are the calculations for a one-fourth multiple-drop match shown on page 60. The design has a 24-inch vertical repeat on the left edge of strip 1. The cutoff design on the right side of strip 1 drops 6 inches from the reference line. Because 24 divided by 6 equals 4, this is a one-fourth multiple-drop match. The design on consecutive strips will drop 6 inches, and will start over again every fifth strip.

Fractional drops. In some tricky multiple-drop matches, the pattern doesn't repeat in whole inches. In this case, you have to figure the exact multiple-drop match in fractions. For example,

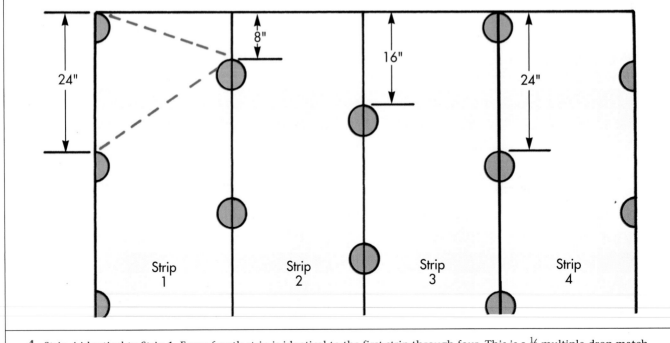

4. Strip 4 identical to Strip 1. Every fourth strip is identical to the first strip through four. This is a ⅓ multiple-drop match.

if the vertical repeat on one side of the strip is 3½ inches, and the matching design on the opposite side drops only ⅞ inch, you will have to convert 3½ inches into eighths in order to determine the multiple-drop. Expressed mathematically, 3½ inches = ²⁸⁄₈. Then, ²⁸⁄₈ ÷ ⅞ = 4 (one-quarter multiple drop).

Seams & Seaming Techniques

To make a neat, durable seam, a lot of things have to come together besides two pieces of wallpaper—most of them at the same time. It can get tricky (and sticky) because floor-to-ceiling sheets are cumbersome and covered with paste. Some will slide onto the wall just where you want them, and some will slide everywhere else. While you're getting all the pieces organized and positioned, some of the adhesive may dry out too soon, before you've aligned the seam, or too late, allowing the papers to separate.

Some of the things that can go wrong include improper application

Figuring Multiple-Drop Proportions

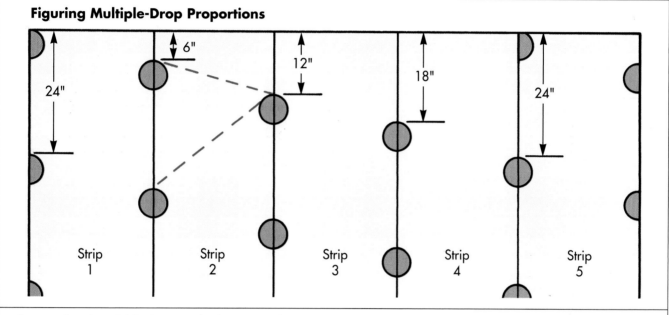

In a one-fourth multiple-drop match, the pattern element (at 6 in.) repeats at the ceiling line every fifth strip.

Fractional Drops

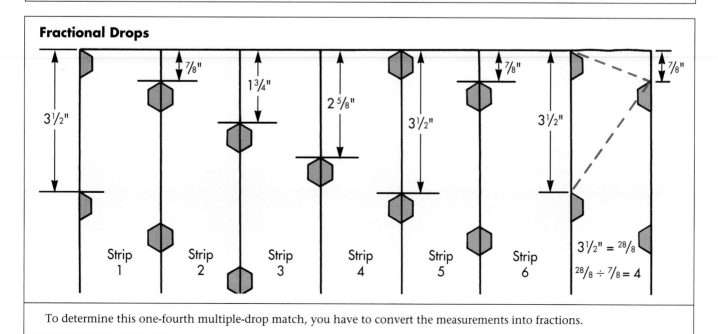

To determine this one-fourth multiple-drop match, you have to convert the measurements into fractions.

of the adhesive, resulting in bad adhesion, and excessive evaporation of adhesive, especially in hot weather on new construction. If you apply too much pressure on a strip during installation, you might stretch it beyond its limits, resulting in seams opening when the wallpaper dries and shrinks.

But it's not all bad news—with a little practice and a lot of planning, a do-it-yourselfer can make a good-looking, long-lasting installation. The key is to figure out where the seams will be before you hang the first strip. Here are four good reasons why.

■ Planning lets you balance a pattern on the wall between two corners of the room, the ceiling line and a chair rail, or a pair of windows. There are times when pattern placement is more important than seam placement.

■ In exceptional cases where seams will be evident, with grasscloth or stringcloth for instance, planning lets you balance a wall by adjusting the strips so that the pieces at each end are the same width.

■ Thorough measuring ahead of time reveals where the layout will create difficult seams, such as narrow strips next to windows and doors.

■ Even planning something as simple as which direction to work around a room can make the job easier to do. If you're right-handed, you'll be most comfortable hanging paper right to left so you can align each strip using your most nimble hand. A lefty will probably be happier heading in the other direction.

The best bet is to start your planning in the area of the room that presents the

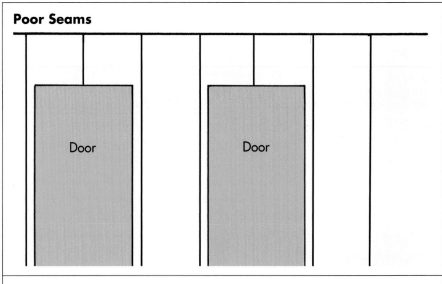

Poor Seams

Door   Door

Careful measuring can reveal where the layout will create problem areas, such as narrow strips near the doors.

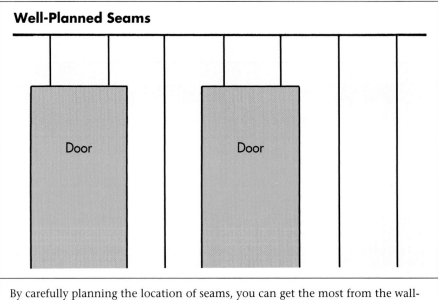

Well-Planned Seams

Door   Door

By carefully planning the location of seams, you can get the most from the wallpaper. The installation is not only easier but looks better too.

most difficulty. In some cases, you can work around the most troublesome spots, and establish your seams working in two directions back to a finish line. Overall, good planning will preview possible mistakes before you make them, ensure the maximum yield from materials, and save you time in the long run.

If you want to be precise about the job, you should also plan for seam

expansion—anywhere from $\frac{1}{4}$ inch to a full inch in width once the paper is pasted or submerged in water. That's more than enough to throw off your calculations.

To determine the expanded width of the wallpaper, apply the adhesive to the back of a small, full-width section, or submerge it in a water tray for about 10 seconds if it's prepasted.

Fold the pasted sides together with soft folds that don't leave creases, allow it to sit for 5 minutes, and then unfold and measure the expanded width.

Finally, you should decide what type of seam you want to use. Here are a look at the different types and a few tips on how to get good results.

Types of Seams

Butt seam. This is the most common type of seam used in wallpapering, and the most basic: two strips, edge to edge. Where the papers come together, gently roll the seam with a seam roller. Avoid overworking the edges, and recheck the seam after approximately 10 minutes. Never roll a heavily embossed or woven fiberglass wallpaper, because it may flatten or burnish the seam.

Wire seam. Although considered outmoded by some pros, the wire seam (also called a ridge seam) is sometimes useful when the wallpaper has scalloped edges or when the wall surface is uneven. You create the seam by overlapping the edge of one strip on an adjoining strip. Wire seams are undesirable in rooms with high ambient lighting, but if this method is necessary, try to make the majority of overlaps face away from the dominant entrance of the room. That makes them less noticeable.

After a wire seam has set up for about 3 to 5 minutes, gently pull papers apart with the palms of your hands, allow the edges to spring together, and gently secure the seam with a roller. This spring-loaded version of a wire seam is useful when installing sheet vinyl or wallpapers with slightly scalloped edges. (Note: The wire-seam overlap should never be more than about $1/64$ inch, or the tensioned seam may pucker.)

Double-cut seam. With this nearly foolproof technique, you start out with an overlap and wind up with a perfectly matched butt seam. Perfection is inevitable because you make a single cut through both layers at the same time with a razor blade. Then you remove the cut end of each strip and join the two new edges.

There are two variations: the padded double-cut and the masked-slipsheet cut. To create a padded double-cut seam, place wax paper or scrap wallpaper beneath the cutting area to prevent the

Butt Seam

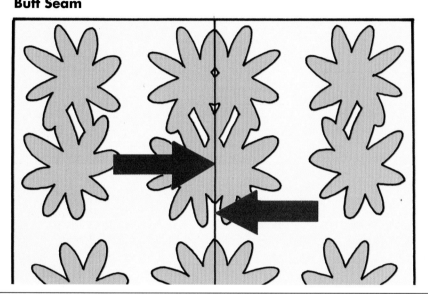

To form a butt seam, the ends simply join edge-on.

Wire Seam

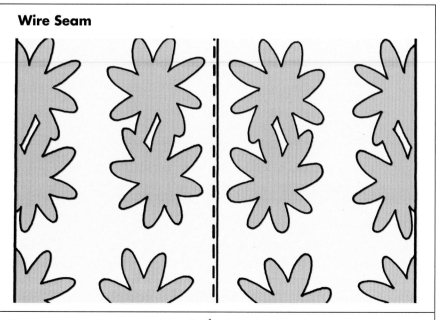

A wire seam should not exceed about a $1/64$-in. overlap.

Double-Cut Seam

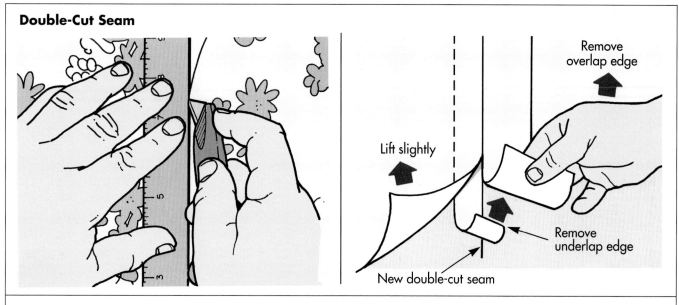

To form a double-cut seam, overlap the strips, and then cut using a straightedge and razor blade. After making the cut, lift away the top piece, and then lift the strip and remove the lower cut piece.

razor from damaging the wall surface. Remove the scrap after cutting. The masked-slipsheet seam uses wax paper or masking tape to protect the surface of the underlying strip from adhesive. This is useful when installing suede, stringcloth, or other heavily textured wallpaper. If you use masking tape, be careful not to pull off the decorative surface.

Wrap-and-overlap seam. This seam is useful to realign crooked outside corners. You make a vertical cut down the strip along the corner's edge, which separates the original panel into two sections. Peel the original section slightly away from the wall; then realign the new section so the pattern is level, and tuck its cut edge around the corner just under the original sheet. Finally, secure this small overlap with vinyl-to-vinyl adhesive.

Overlap seam. This technique, used for inside corners, provides a plumb sheet for each wall when a corner is out of plumb. It offers a slight safety

margin for errors because one sheet covers the edge of another. Secure this seam with vinyl-to-vinyl adhesive when needed.

Mitered seam. When you work with borders, it's sometimes handy to miter the corners with the same type of 45-degree woodworking cuts used at corners of picture frames. For an accurate seam, use the double-cut technique to slice at an angle through overlapped border papers that meet at 90 degrees. Here are some tips you can use no matter what type of seams you employ.

■ Prepare the wall surface properly to avoid poor adhesion and curling.

■ Always allow the wallpaper to relax (remain in booked form), until it has fully expanded—usually 5 to 10 minutes.

■ Always join the seam first, and then smooth out the remainder of the strip without pulling the seam apart.

Wrap-and-Overlap

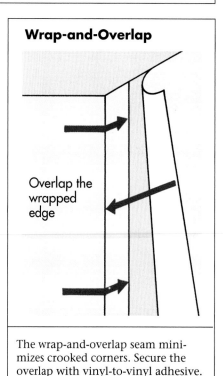

The wrap-and-overlap seam minimizes crooked corners. Secure the overlap with vinyl-to-vinyl adhesive.

■ Don't overwork the wallpaper. It stretches the paper and is probably the biggest cause of seam problems. If you are a little off when you hang a strip and there is a gap in the seam between the strips, remove the strip and reinstall it.

Seam Placement

In some cases it can be useful to change the placement of the seams without altering the pattern sequence— for example, to eliminate seams near windows and doors. Instead of matching along the edge of the last strip, you overlap the previous strip, pick up an-

other pattern match, and then double-cut through the overlap. Here are some examples with different patterns.

Straight-across match. In this straight-across match, the pattern appears three times across the strip of wallpaper. You can add either a 7-inch

or 14-inch segment over a door or window by overlapping one design on top of the other and cutting through the two layers.

As shown in the illustration at bottom left, normal seam placement (shown at the bottom of the illustrations) results in narrow strips that are difficult to cut and paste, as well as an unsightly seam that falls between the doors. If you add a 7-inch segment over each door, you can improve the seam placement without changing the pattern.

In a pattern with a straight-across match, such as that shown in the illustration on page 65, the design elements repeat themselves twice across the strip. This permits you to add a 10½-inch segment over a door or window by overlapping and cutting through the two layers. Compare the original seam placement with the new one at the top. If you add a 10½-inch segment over the

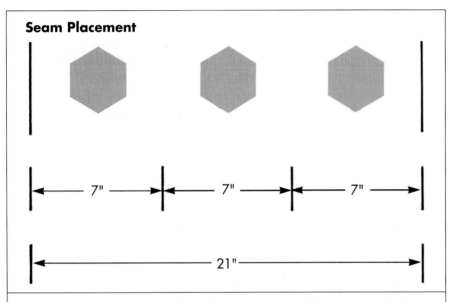

Seam Placement

In this straight-across match, the pattern appears every 7 in. across the 21-in. width of wallpaper.

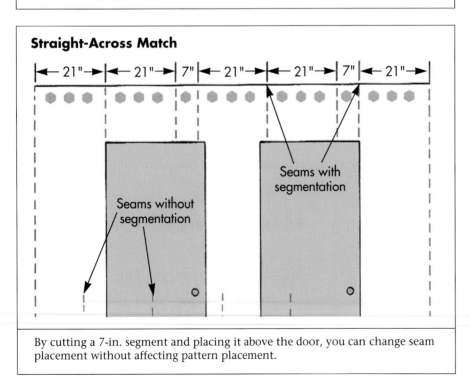

Straight-Across Match

Seams with segmentation

Seams without segmentation

By cutting a 7-in. segment and placing it above the door, you can change seam placement without affecting pattern placement.

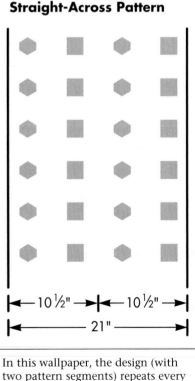

Straight-Across Pattern

In this wallpaper, the design (with two pattern segments) repeats every 10½ in., twice across a 21-in. strip.

door, you can eliminate the small vertical strip. The smallest section of wallpaper you can use in this situation is 10½ inches; you can't cut it to the width of just one or three of the pattern elements, because it will result in a mismatch.

Half-drop match. In the half-drop match shown below, you can change the seam placement by overlapping and double-cutting through two consecutive doubles or two consecutive singles. You also can over-

lap and double-cut a double with a single, to produce a smaller segment.

In the illustration, the normal seam placement (bottom) results in narrow strips and unnecessary seams. If you compare it with the change in seam placement (also called pattern segmentation) at the top, you can see how careful planning minimizes the number of seams and narrow vertical strips.

Once you determine where every seam will be, you should indicate the pattern sequence at the ceiling line for each strip. Make these indications on the wall using a very light pencil mark.

Prepasted Wallpaper

Prepasted wallpaper has a factory-applied adhesive on the back. It is the easiest material for do-it-yourselfers by far, and needs only water for application. Sometimes wallpaper contracts during this application, which may cause it to curl

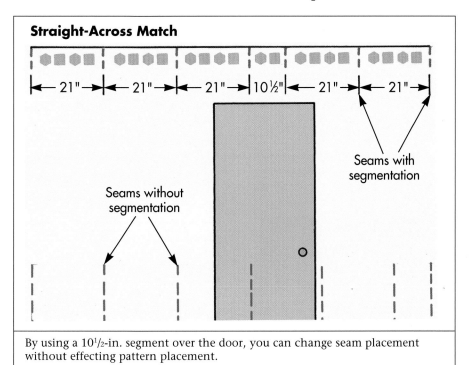

Straight-Across Match

Seams without segmentation

Seams with segmentation

By using a 10½-in. segment over the door, you can change seam placement without effecting pattern placement.

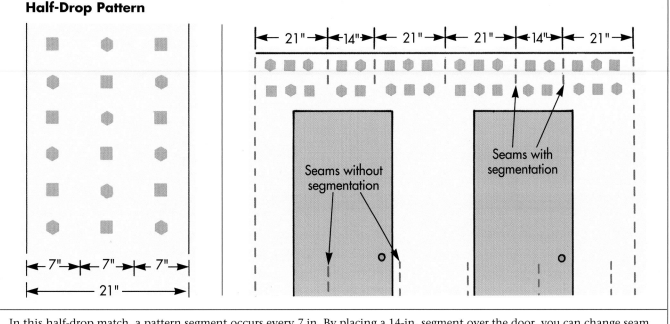

Half-Drop Pattern

Seams without segmentation

Seams with segmentation

In this half-drop match, a pattern segment occurs every 7 in. By placing a 14-in. segment over the door, you can change seam placement without effecting pattern placement.

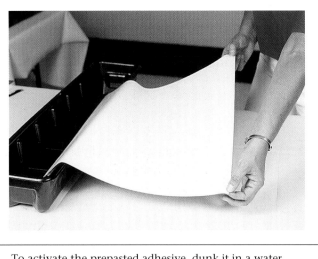

To activate the prepasted adhesive, dunk it in a water trough, then pull it out onto the worktable.

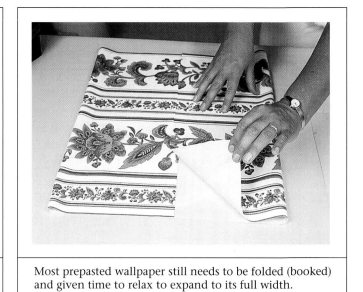

Most prepasted wallpaper still needs to be folded (booked) and given time to relax to expand to its full width.

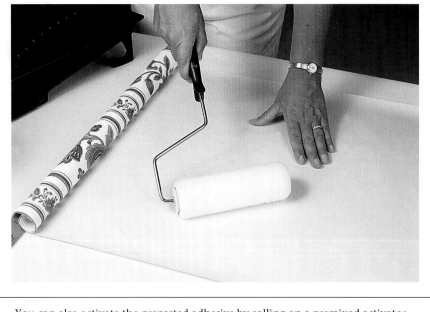

You can also activate the prepasted adhesive by rolling on a premixed activator solution, or adhesive diluted with 50 percent more water than normally required.

Prepasted paper is relatively stable, expanding only 1 to 2 percent after it's wet. But it is important to book the paper and allow it to relax for 5 to 10 minutes before hanging it on the wall. If you install it too soon, expansion can produce vertical blisters. If this happens, remove the wallpaper and allow it to relax for a longer period of time. To contain the moisture and prevent excessive drying during this wait, place the booked strips in a plastic trash bag until you're ready to install them. This tip is especially useful when the evaporation rate is high—for instance, during new construction in hot summer months.

Sometimes, prepasted papers don't contain enough adhesive to adhere properly to the wall, particularly a dry, porous wall. In a pinch, you can activate the adhesive by applying additional adhesive to the wallpaper backing with a brush or roller. Most manufacturers do not recommend applying an additional adhesive, however, because the adhesives may not be compatible. The trick is to dilute the additional adhesive with

during installation. But you can eliminate this problem by reverse-rolling or by pulling the strip across a tabletop at a 45-degree angle, a process known as drawing the wallpaper. This breaks the dried adhesive into tiny squares and allows the wallpaper to lie flat on the worktable.

Factory application is generally uniform, but sometimes the adhesive contains too much of an activating chemical, causing the adhesive coating to wash off when you dunk the paper. If this happens, add about one tablespoon of vinegar to the water tray. If too little of the chemical is present and the adhesive will not properly activate, add one tablespoon of ammonia to the water tray to help the adhesive dissolve.

50 percent more water than normally required. Don't apply the extra adhesive too heavily, or it will slow down the drying process, which in turn may cause a shrinkage problem. It's also important to make sure that you cover the entire backing; otherwise, the prepasted adhesive will not properly activate and the wallpaper may never fully expand.

Alternatively, you could submerge the wallpaper in the water tray, book it, and while the paper is relaxing, apply the watered-down adhesive directly to the wall surface using a brush or roller. Remember not to hang a dry strip of prepasted wallpaper on a wall covered with wet adhesive. The paper will expand on the wall and leave a mess of expansion wrinkles. DIYers should not try to use a clay-based adhesive for reactivating prepasted wallpapers. The solids in the adhesive may clog the pores in the backing of the wallpaper.

Adhesives

This is one subject where do-it-yourselfers and professionals part company—at least that percentage of pros who hang exotic materials and don't use prepasted products. For most do-it-yourselfers, prepasted paper takes the mystery out of the subject of adhesives, and most of the risk from the application.

If you want to try mixing adhesive on the job instead of dunking paper in a water trough, here are some of the things to consider, including the type of wallpaper and its breathability, the porosity of the wall surface, the ambient air temperature, the type of adhesive, and its consistency.

Improper mixing and application can cause many problems. For instance, if you apply too much adhesive, drying time increases significantly and may cause the paper to shrink excessively.

It can also result in a mildew problem, especially when you're applying a nonbreathing wallpaper over a nonbreathable wall surface.

If you apply too much adhesive to delicate wallpapers, such as linen, suede, grasscloth, stringcloth, textile, or fabric, the adhesive can penetrate the substrate and stain the decorative surface. On the other hand, if you apply the adhesive too thinly, the paper may dry too quickly, resulting in poor adhesion or edge curling. If this happens and you attempt to compensate by applying too much pressure to the wallpaper, you can stretch it or, worse yet, rip it.

Whatever adhesive you use, strive to keep the decorative surface of the wallcovering clean during installation so you won't create smears. It is especially important to protect wallcoverings such as stringcloth, grasscloth, linen, fabric, and textiles from adhesive to prevent permanent stain damage. Some wall-

coverings, such as foil, require drying with a soft cloth immediately after rinsing with a sponge and clean water to prevent the decorative surface from spotting. In some cases, even clean water can leave a stain.

Starch-based. These adhesives usually contain wheat starch, although some are made from potato, tapioca, and corn starches. Most premixed products on the market today consist of wheat starches. The nice thing about starches is that they dissolve easily in water and are fairly easy to clean. They provide good adhesion with cotton and paper-backed wallpaper. Manufacturers sometimes add special preservatives to prevent mildew growth.

Glue and paste. Animal glue is a protein gelatin made from collagen, a component of animal hooves and tissues. Glue-type adhesives, popular before the advent of modern adhe-

Adhesive consistency varies with the type of adhesive, the temperature, and the condition of the walls. Be sure to follow package directions carefully.

sives, provide a very strong bond in a short time. Also rarely seen today is paste consisting of starch, dextrin, and borax. Dextrin is a gummy substance that acts as a binder. Borax modifies the thickness and tackiness.

Cellulose. These adhesives consist of structural elements from cotton, wood pulp, or other plant fibers. Most cellulose pastes are nonstaining, have good slip (movement on the wall), will remain moist longer, and will not turn bad as fast as starches under the same conditions. Compared with starch adhesives, cellulose adhesives make it easier to strip wallpaper off the wall.

Clay-based premixes. These are starches with a clay additive that provide more tack during the installation by absorbing moisture within the adhesive. Clay-based adhesives also provide greater viscosity and make drying and setup time faster. Some professionals mix vinyl-to-vinyl clear primer into a clay-based adhesive, thin the mixture to a paint consistency, and apply it to the wall surface as a presizing. This clay sizing causes the adhesive on the

Some adhesives adhere to the wall so completely that your only recourse in removing them is soaking them with wallpaper remover.

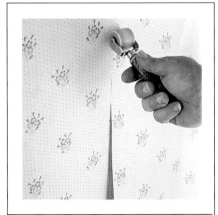

If you find that your seams are coming apart, chances are that you have either chosen the wrong adhesive or mixed it incorrectly.

wallpaper to set up even faster, while acrylic resins in the vinyl adhesive add an extra amount of adhesion, which reduces shrinkage problems. This is especially useful when installing wallpaper around small outside-corner returns, such as recessed windows, door frames, or soffit corners.

Clay-based adhesives should be used whenever a nonbreathing wallpaper is applied to a totally nonbreathable wall surface. Other adhesives may require a longer drying time in this situation and may sour or mildew before they dry. Some installers use an absorbent liner paper in place of the clay-based adhesive to serve the same purpose as the drying agent, because clay does have drawbacks. It's messy to work with and hard to clean up, and if adhesive wrinkles are not completely smoothed out during installation, they may never totally dry out.

Clear premixed. This adhesive is made from a wheat paste cooked with steam or acid. Because wheat

starch is a good adhesive and cleans up fairly easily with water, it has taken the place of clay-based adhesive for most applications. Unfortunately, these adhesives, which look clear during the installation, invariably dry to a haze. They are not nearly as messy as clay-based adhesives, and they are much easier to clean, but you will still see some staining.

If you apply a clear premixed adhesive too heavily, the material still dries and stretches the paper tightly to the wall surface. This is another advantage to using it as opposed to the clay-based type. You should not use a clear premixed adhesive when you install nonbreathing wallpaper over an oil-based primer-sealer. It will generally require twice as much time to set up and dry as a clay-based adhesive, and it may shrink in the process.

Vinyl-on-vinyl. Vinyl adhesives contain an acrylic resin that will bond to just about any surface. They contain very little moisture, which reduces

mildew problems, and are used mainly to bond vinyl wallcovering over vinyl wallcovering without the use of a special primer-sealer. Use vinyl-to-vinyl adhesives to install borders directly over existing wallcovering. Always check first to see if the wallpaper pattern shows through the border before installing it over the wallpaper. If the wallpaper is even slightly visible through the border, you can inlay it or apply a pigmented acrylic primer-sealer to the existing wallpaper. Allow the primer-sealer to dry thoroughly before applying the border.

MAINLY FOR CONTRACTORS

Seam sizing. To construct very tight seams, some professionals use this technique: Dilute clay-based adhesive with 50 percent more water than normal, then apply a very thin layer to the wall along all seams and edges. The adhesive is allowed to dry completely before installing the wallpaper. The dried adhesive acts as a blotter, which will in turn force the wet adhesive on the wallpaper edges to dry first. Once the adhesive at the seams dries, they will not separate. Be careful if you use a roller to apply the adhesive, however, because it may cause a textured effect that will show through.

Another technique, still sometimes used by professionals, is that of pulling a plastic wallpaper smoother down the seam. This forces the adhesive away from the seam and allows it to dry faster than the adhesive at the center of the strip.

Coloring seams. Sometimes a white gap appears in the seam of wallpaper that was fitted tightly together. This can be caused by excessive shrinkage before the adhesive has a chance to dry, but generally it is due to a manufacturing defect in trimming that leaves a slanted cut on the backing. (Some manufacturers provide a felt marker tinted in the background color to help hide gaps in seams.)

Another way to disguise the defect is to apply artist's watercolors that you have mixed to the color of the wallpaper's background. Mix the color thinly, and apply it into the seam with a small brush. Wipe the excess color off after about 5 to 10 seconds using a damp sponge. Dry the seam area with a soft cloth after wiping. You should try this technique on a scrap piece of wallcovering first because some colorants can stain a decorative surface.

Custom-mixed adhesive. In unusual circumstances, you can adjust an adhesive's viscosity to suit the wallcovering, the wall surface, and the weather using a measurement of ounces-per-traverse-inch. That's the gauge manufacturers use to establish the strength of an adhesive. To obtain the measurement, manufacturers apply an adhesive to a 1-inch strip of wallpaper, apply the strip to a particular surface, and allow it to dry. Then they record the force in ounces required to pull the strip away from the wall.

The average amount of force will determine the adhesive's final ounce-per-traverse-inch score. Generally, a force of 16 ounces per traverse inch or more destroys either the wall surface or the wallpaper, while a minimum of 6 ounces is needed for satisfactory adhesion.

Always apply adhesive carefully and consistently along the length of the wallpaper using a figure-eight motion.

Chapter 6

Basic Installation

As you finish up the prep work and get ready to hang paper, it's wise to back away from the project for a few moments and consider for the last time what you're covering up and how the wallpaper installation should progress. Here are some of the last-minute issues worth considering—to start with, the condition of the wall surface.

In some houses, thorough prep work can make an old wall look brand new, but only until forces you have temporarily hidden under the surface break through. Those chronic cracks often stem from fundamental problems in the building frame that can be corrected only by tearing off the wall surface and strengthening the frame from the inside out. If that's more than you bargained for, here are some ways you can work on problem walls from the outside in.

Choose a paper with a busy, random pattern—maybe a design with some dark lines about the size of the cracks to offer camouflage. The crack may open again but will be lost in the wallpaper design. A strong surface pattern also can disguise problems in a wall that is structurally sound but slightly bowed or wavy. Another option is to cover a crack with molding—a wide, vertical strip that matches other molding in the house—and create a frame design, or panels, across the entire wall. If the chronic cracking is along the joint between ceiling and wall, use horizontal molding. Even extensive cracking can be covered by wide cornice molding.

If you have trouble with cracks on ceilings (whether or not you plan to paper them), consider a highly decorative cover-up using old-fashioned tin ceiling tiles, available in a variety of patterns. To cover damaged areas around a ceiling-hung light fixture, try a decorative medallion, available in several paintable styles that resemble fancy plaster work.

If you anticipate problems in a wall, first make the strongest possible repairs, and then cover them with the strongest possible paper. If standard drywall compound or a combination of paper tape and compound hasn't held in the past, try one or more of these tips: First, scrape down the edges of the crack to remove all loose material, and undercut the edges so the patch material will get more of a bite. There are several possible trick fixes, such as filling narrow cracks with epoxy cement. But the most reliable heavy-duty repair for drywall is to replace conventional paper tape with fiberglass mesh tape. It's used by roofers to close flashing seams and can absorb a lot more stress than paper.

Even over a heavy-duty repair, you may want to use a strong wallcovering on a wall with potential problems. Instead of a wafer-thin reflective foil that would show even

The more complex your project is, the more important it is to take the time to create perfect seams.

Papering Walls

Because one piece of wallpaper is always linked to another, the location of the first strip on a wall has a ripple effect that flows past cabinets and windows and doors, completely around the room.

Planning the First Strip

Before you pick the starting point, make sure that all your rolls have the same dye-lot and pattern numbers, and check each roll for defects. Pattern colors should be in register, inks should be flat, and the vinyl surface coatings should be consistent. Save yourself some trouble in the process by reverse-rolling the paper after you inspect it. This will help straighten the wallcovering and eliminate the curling, window-shade effect that can be bothersome during installation.

Before you settle on a location for the first strip, remember to check how the most dominant part of the pattern will fall around windows and doors and along the ceiling. Planning seam placement takes extra time because you have to do at least a rough layout to see where the edges of strips will fall, but this dry run is about the best way to be sure that you will wind up with the most eye-pleasing installation.

Start the job at a vertical plumb line approximately 1/8 inch to the left or right of the edge of the first strip. Make the line using a carpenter's level and pencil or a chalk-line box. Remember to keep your marks at least 1/8 inch away from the seam to prevent the graphite or chalk from discoloring the joint. Also select the end point (sometimes called the kill point) for the last strip, which can be any inconspicuous area—say, behind a door or book-

case where you can hide a pattern mismatch. Remember, you can also start in the middle of a room and work in both directions to the end point.

You can save time if you rough-cut all the strips before you start pasting. Spread out an entire roll at your work-table so the wallcovering flops over on itself in an accordion pattern. Feed the top end of the roll design-side-up to the top of the worktable for measuring. Any ruler will do, but measuring is easy if you use a yardstick. If a strip is 62 inches long, measure it as 1 yard, 26 inches with the yardstick. Remember, a yardstick reads in reverse direction when you turn it over, so you don't have to flip it end for end as you measure.

Cut the first strip according to the wall measurement. Be sure to leave a couple of inches for trimming (the allowance) at the top and bottom of each strip, and measure the length of the strip from the pattern design, not from the allowance cut. After you cut the strip, roll it up, starting at the bottom and rolling toward the top. If you're installing a drop-match pattern, be sure to keep cut strips organized in separate stacks. After you cut all the strips, you're ready to begin pasting. (Instructions for prepasted wallpaper begin on page 88.)

Applying Adhesive

There is more than one way to apply adhesive to wallpaper. In fact, there are many little twists and turns that work for one person but seem awkward to another. Until you get the feel of it, try this sequence. If you're right-handed, place the top of the strip (face down, of course) at the right-hand end of the table. Lefties should place

slight cracking, consider using an embossed vinyl. Some wallcoverings are strong enough to bridge cracks—for instance, Lincrusta, a dense, linoleum-like compound, or Anaglypta, a heavy, embossed paper. There is also a heavier version called Supaglypta, made from cotton fiber and pulp and formed into stiff sheets.

For more modern settings, there are fiberglass weaves that have the strength of heavy-duty patching materials but the surface texture and patterns of finished wallpaper. And in any situation you can reduce the chance of old problems resurfacing in new paper by installing liner paper, even though applying this buffer adds a step to the installation.

the top of the strip at the left-hand end. For convenience, place the adhesive bucket on a stand at the same end of the table as the top of the strip.

1 Dip the brush or roller into the adhesive. (Tap a brush lightly from side to side to fill the bristles.) Apply the adhesive to the back of the wallpaper with a smooth and continuous motion (a figure-eight if using a brush) that leaves an even coating. Along the edges, use slightly lighter, one-way strokes that go off the paper. A back-and-forth motion can curl or even rip the edge.

2 Fold the top section of the wall-paper paste-side to paste-side (a procedure called booking), and then roll it up in a large, loose fold so that the paper won't crease at the folds.

3 Pull the remainder of the strip onto the table, apply paste, book the

1. Use a figure-eight motion when applying paste to wallpaper. Use light one-way strokes along the edges that take the brush off the paper.

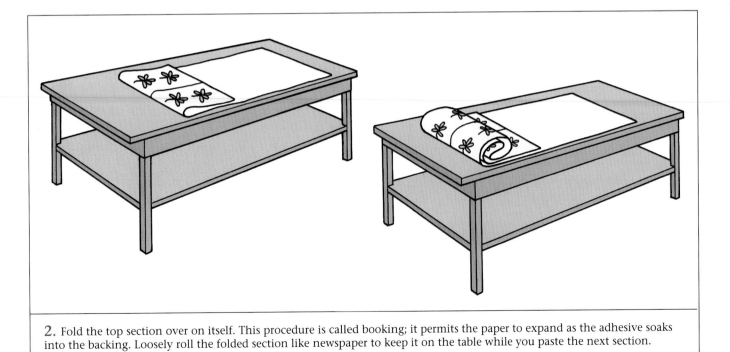

2. Fold the top section over on itself. This procedure is called booking; it permits the paper to expand as the adhesive soaks into the backing. Loosely roll the folded section like newspaper to keep it on the table while you paste the next section.

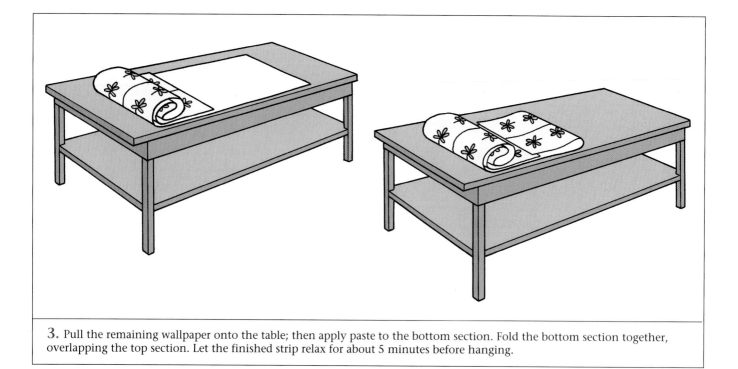

3. Pull the remaining wallpaper onto the table; then apply paste to the bottom section. Fold the bottom section together, overlapping the top section. Let the finished strip relax for about 5 minutes before hanging.

bottom half paste-to-paste, overlap the top half by about 1/2 inch, and roll the strip as above. If you prefer, you can make large folds instead of rolling the paper up in newspaper fashion — with a slightly larger top fold to help distinguish the top from the bottom. But rolling helps to reduce curling along the edges as the wallpaper expands and helps prevent it from drying out too soon. Let the wallpaper relax in the booked and rolled position for 5 to 10 minutes. This allows the paper to expand and the adhesive to penetrate the backing, and it is a crucial step in preventing wrinkling once the paper is on the wall.

Paste additional strips as the first ones relax. To keep track of things, place strips in order so that the first piece pasted is the first piece installed. You must install some types of grass-cloth and stringcloth immediately after pasting, however. If you let them relax, the wallpaper backing may delami-

nate, or the folds may stick together.

It helps to keep the work area well organized and neat — to avoid accidents, of course, and to avoid confusion about measuring and cutting. In particular, keep the work-table clean and free of adhesive, clean all tools often, dispose of scrap wallpaper while you work, and dispose of used razor blades safely.

Installing the First Strip

After you've pasted several strips and allowed them to expand, it's time to install the first strip. Once you get going, you'll find that it's nice to have a supply of strips waiting — and you'll learn to judge in advance how big the supply should be. For example, you might paste enough strips to work yourself to the edge of a bay window, where you'll need to do some special measuring and cutting. Here's how to get started with the first strip.

1 First, set a ladder or stool in position against the wall. Pick up and unroll the booked-and-rolled strip toward you.

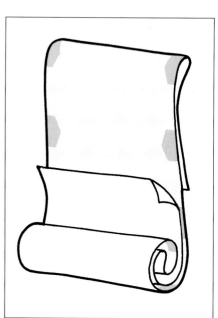

1. Once the strip has expanded, it's time to hang it on the wall. Position your ladder or stool next to the wall, and then pick up the first strip.

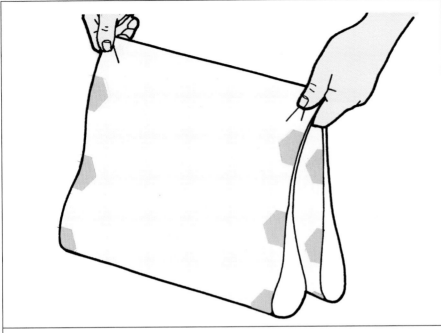

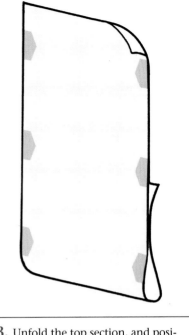

2. With the top of the strip facing you at the fold, gently grasp the strip at the areas where the bottom and top meet.

3. Unfold the top section, and position it on the wall.

2 With the top of the strip facing you at the fold, gently grasp the strip at the areas where the bottom and top meet.

3 Unfold the top section, and position it on the wall. To prevent stretching, leave the bottom of the strip folded until the top section is in position.

4 Align the edge of the wallpaper to the guideline, and check the pattern placement at the ceiling line. To keep the chalk or pencil guideline from discoloring the seam, position the strip approximately 1/8 inch away from the line. Smooth the guideline edge of the wallpaper with a brush or plastic wallpaper smoother. Gently pull the opposite side of the strip away from the wall, and smooth out the paper working from the center of the guideline edge. This technique allows you to smooth the paper without trapping air bubbles underneath.

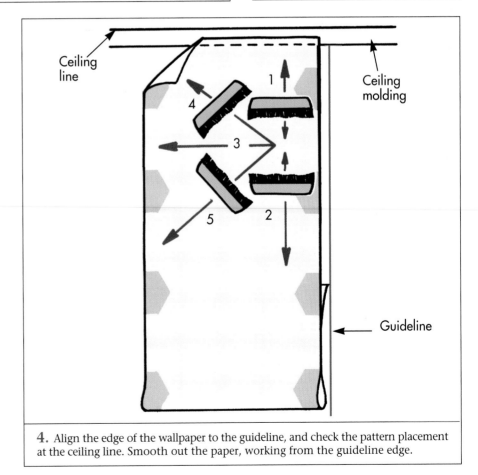

4. Align the edge of the wallpaper to the guideline, and check the pattern placement at the ceiling line. Smooth out the paper, working from the guideline edge.

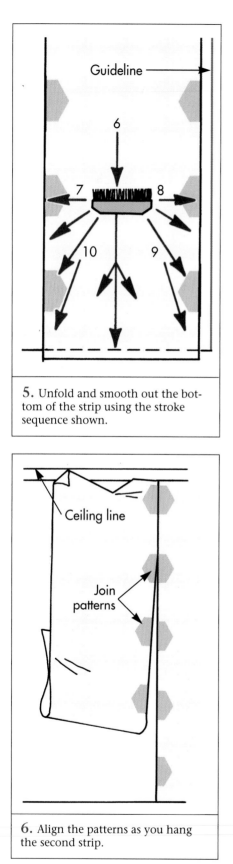

5. Unfold and smooth out the bottom of the strip using the stroke sequence shown.

6. Align the patterns as you hang the second strip.

5 Unfold and smooth out the bottom of the strip using a similar stroke sequence. (Follow the numbers in the illustration at left). Work gradually with gentle pressure from the brush.

6 Once you've installed the first strip and aligned it properly, continue with the second strip. Match the pattern as you join the seams of the two strips, aligning the seams with one hand while holding the opposite edge off the wall with the other hand. If the strip sticks to the wall in the wrong place, don't try to force a seam into position by sliding the strip. Instead, gently remove the entire strip and start over.

7 After you form the seam, use the same smoothing sequence for the top half of the strip as for the first strip. The bottom half requires a slightly different sequence—brushing and smoothing away from the joined seam to eliminate the possibility of forcing air back into the previously installed strip. Continue to install additional strips using the same installation and smoothing sequence.

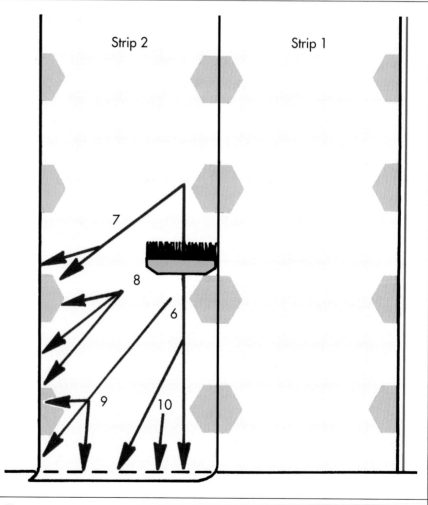

7. Hang the second strip, and smooth the top using the same sequence as before. Smooth the bottom as shown.

Trimming Allowance Edges

The secret to neatly trimmed edges is an ample supply of new razor blades. Change blades frequently, and you won't rip or tear the wallpaper when cutting it to size. On the most delicate and softest papers, you might find that it's necessary to change the blade after every few cuts.

The best procedure is to use a trim guide when you make a cut with a razor blade. You can use a broad knife or even a 3-inch slanted scraper to guide the shortest cuts. Whatever guide you use, try to position it on the wallpaper side of the cut, leaving the allowance edges exposed. This way if your blade should slip, you're likely to damage the excess instead of the fitted strip. Also, this is generally the safest way to cut: working away from your body instead of toward it.

You're bound to hit a few tight corners where it's next to impossible to maneuver a razor blade. In those cases, crease the wallpaper into the corner with the trim guide; then pull the paper away, and cut it with scissors along the crease. It doesn't hurt to leave a little extra (about $1/4$ inch) to wrap around the back side of a door or window frame.

Creasing also comes in handy when you're trimming the allowance edges away from the ceiling line. It reduces the chance of cutting through drywall tape. Crease along the ceiling line with the edge of the trim guide, pull the strip away from the ceiling, and use scissors to trim along the crease line. You may find that the crease is more visible and easier to follow if you cut from the back of the paper instead of the front.

Multiple-Mitered Relief Cuts

The trick to wallpapering around an odd-size window frame is to make the right relief cuts at the corners—the little snips and slices that help wallcovering change direction without buckling and wrinkling. Generally, the tighter the turn, the more relief cuts you need. Around windows, for example, most of the wallpaper inside the window frame is cut away, leaving approximately 2 to 3 inches for allowance. This prevents excess adhesive from getting on the window frame and removes excess paper so the final trim is easier and more accurate.

To reduce the chance of rips at corners, make the mitered relief cuts after the allowance cuts. When a relief cut leaves only a small piece attached, be careful that the weight of the remaining strip doesn't tear the relief cut. Some heavyweight papers need support until they are fixed on the wall.

Inside Corners

Most professional paperhangers precut corner strips, but do-it-yourselfers

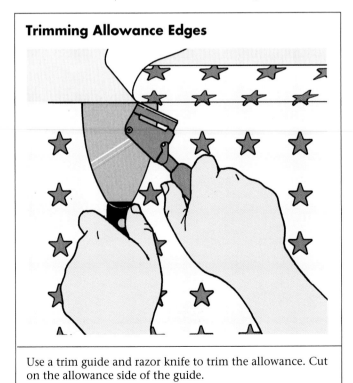

Trimming Allowance Edges

Use a trim guide and razor knife to trim the allowance. Cut on the allowance side of the guide.

Creasing

Crease wallpaper in hard-to-reach spaces; then pull the paper away from the wall and cut the allowance with scissors.

generally have better luck hanging a full strip, then cutting the corner on the wall, particularly if it isn't square and plumb. You should never hang a full strip that rounds an inside corner; as the strip dries, it will pull away from the wall and leave a void. Of course, you must make an exception when an obstacle keeps you from getting into the corner to make the cut—something substantial like a bathroom toilet that you can't move to make neat cuts. If a corner like this is out of square, a mismatch is likely to occur. But you can minimize errors by using the following procedure.

Testing for Squareness

The first thing you have to do is determine whether or not the corner is square. You can check by triangula-

tion: mark 3 feet from the corner on one wall and 4 feet on the other, and measure across the corner, mark to mark. This measurement, as the hypotenuse (the longest side) of a 3-4-5 right triangle, should be 5 feet. Of course, in some old houses you don't have to measure—one look is all it takes to know the corner is cockeyed.

Professional paperhangers have another way to test for squareness. They use short strips of wallpaper as spacers to check corners, as follows.

1 Cut three short lengths of paper (about 3 to 4 inches wide) across the width of the strip. Paste the strips, book them, allow them to expand, and then tack them horizontally from the edge of your last strip into and around the corner.

2 Hold a level or plumb line at the exposed ends of the spacer strips to determine which one is closest to the corner. In the illustration, the first spacer is 10 inches away, the second is 10½ inches, and the third is 11 inches from the inside corner. In this case, you need to establish a plumb line ¼ inch past the edge of the top spacer (10¼ inches from the corner). Make a small pencil mark at this point; then remove the spacers, and establish a plumb guideline.

3 Now hang the corner strip, aligning it to the guideline you created in step 2. Smooth the strip toward the corner, and tuck the paper into the corner as you would beside a door frame. Cut the entire

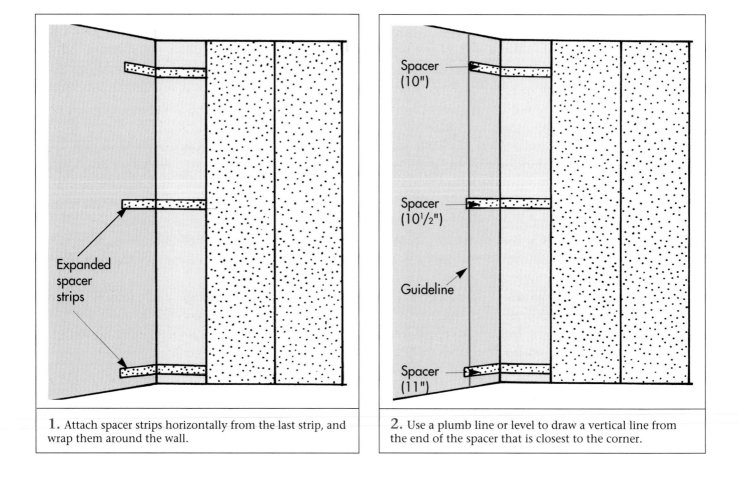

Expanded spacer strips

Spacer (10")

Spacer (10½")

Guideline

Spacer (11")

1. Attach spacer strips horizontally from the last strip, and wrap them around the wall.

2. Use a plumb line or level to draw a vertical line from the end of the spacer that is closest to the corner.

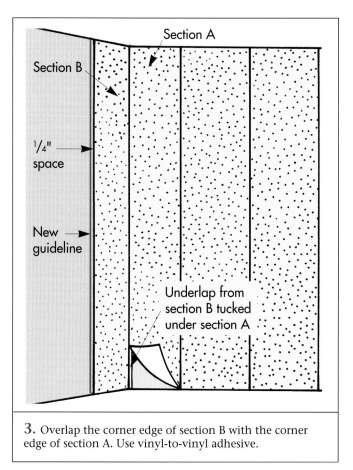

3. Overlap the corner edge of section B with the corner edge of section A. Use vinyl-to-vinyl adhesive.

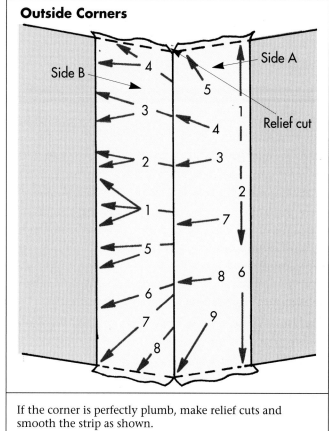

If the corner is perfectly plumb, make relief cuts and smooth the strip as shown.

strip from the top to the bottom in the corner, using a razor knife and a trim guide. If the corner structure is weak and likely to give way during cutting, make a crease with a trim guide; then remove the strip of paper from the wall, and make the cut with scissors.

Separate the strip into two sections, A and B, as shown. Align section B about ¼ inch from the guideline, and allow it to overlap section A at the narrowest place in the corner. Match the cut patterns of sections A and B as closely as possible where the overlap occurs. Lift the corner edge of section A away from the wall, and tuck the corner edge of section B underneath. Lastly, cut away any underlap on section B that is wider than ¼ inch. Spread vinyl-to-vinyl adhesive on the remaining underlap, and

glue section A down on top of section B. Wipe up any excess adhesive.

Outside Corners

Outside corners by their very nature often turn out to be the most visible parts of the job—focal points where a dominant pattern must line up with the corner. Patterns with stripes must appear parallel, and diagonal patterns must sweep into the corner the same way. It's such an important location that you should never cut a strip on an outside corner unless the corner is so far out of plumb that a wrap and overlap technique is the only possible way to correct the problem. Cutting directly on a corner not only exposes an edge that may be pulled away, it also causes a mismatch on the focal point.

If the corner is perfectly proportioned, just follow the smoothing sequence shown in the illustration above. Smooth side A, make the relief cuts precisely on the corners, and then smooth side B. Be sure to keep the corner edge tight and smooth to prevent puckers from forming as you install the strip around the corner. (*Note: If the corner is out of plumb, use one of the following techniques.*)

Shredding. This technique is suitable on corners that are out of plumb by ½ inch or less; it can actually make a leaning corner appear plumb. The trick is to cut the wallpaper into two vertical sections within the background—say, between a row of prominent pattern designs. Make the cut about 6 to 8 inches away from the corner.

Wrap-and-Overlap

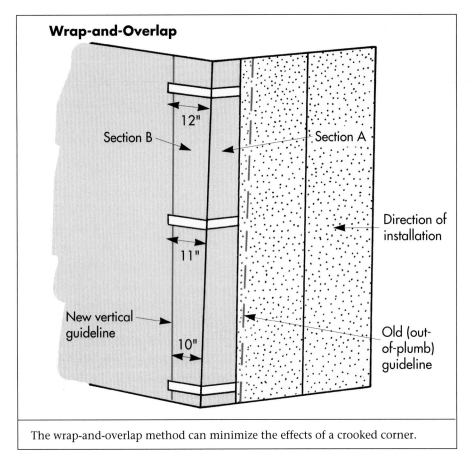

Section B

12"

Section A

Direction of installation

11"

New vertical guideline

10"

Old (out-of-plumb) guideline

The wrap-and-overlap method can minimize the effects of a crooked corner.

Then install the first section next to the previous strip, and shift the second section slightly so that the pattern appears parallel with the corner focal point. It's as if you folded over a small slice of the strip to make the end work out evenly. The adjustment will make the cut end overlap the first section, but you can double-cut through the two strips to create a butt seam.

Wrap-and-overlap. When an outside corner is more than an inch out of plumb, no sleight-of-hand wallpapering can straighten it. But you can minimize the effect with the wrap-and-overlap technique. Start by tacking three expanded spacers around the corner and determining a new plumb guideline—the same technique used on inside corners (page 78). In the

illustration above, the first spacer is 12 inches from the corner, the second is 11 inches, and the third is 10 inches. In this case, you need to establish a plumb line 1/2 inch in from the edge of the third (shortest) spacer to allow for overlap on the corner.

Install a strip next to the previous strip using the same smoothing strokes as a normal straight corner. Then use a new razor knife to cut the strip from top to bottom into two sections (A & B) directly over the outside corner, and align section B with the plumb line. On a corner fully 2 inches out of plumb, this will produce a 2-inch overlap at the top of the corner and a 1/2-inch overlap at the bottom. Lift the edge of section A, wrap the edge of section B around the corner and under section A, and then secure the overlap with

vinyl-to-vinyl adhesive. In extreme cases, consider using a protective outside-corner molding, either painted or stained, to eliminate an obvious mismatch.

Changing wallpaper at a corner. In the unusual circumstance where a companion paper is introduced on an outside corner, follow these steps. First, overlap the outside corner with the first wallpaper approximately 1 to 2 inches —enough to ensure that the corner does not lift or pucker after it has dried. Apply a lightweight, non-shrinking joint compound over the exposed edge of the strip, and sand it smooth using 100- to 120-grit sandpaper when dry.

The next step is to establish a new plumb guideline on the adjoining wall. For example, if the wallpaper is 21 inches wide, make the mark 21 3/8 inches from the corner. This places the plumb guideline 1/4 inch past the edge of the wallpaper to prevent chalk or pencil lead from penetrating the seam and adds a 1/8-inch allowance to prevent the corner of the new strip from falling directly on the outside corner.

Hang the new wallpaper on the adjoining wall, aligning the left edge of the strip with the guideline. If the outside corner isn't plumb, back up the strip to compensate for the problem, and cut the right-hand side so that it is 1/8 inch short of the corner. Finally, secure the overlap on the corner with a vinyl-to-vinyl seam adhesive.

Parallels and Guidelines

You can call it fudging or splitting the difference, but it's really the art of making slightly unbalanced spaces look balanced—even when they're surrounded by trim and walls and ceilings that aren't level or plumb. Professional installers use

a variety of guideline techniques to get the best results in less than the best circumstances. Parallel guidelines can make patterns appear even with an out-of-level ceiling, chair rail or counter-top, and vertical guidelines can accommodate oddball door frames and crooked cabinets and windows.

You can get the idea behind these techniques in the illustration below—how they rely on what your eye per-ceives instead of actual readings and measurements for plumb and level. A guideline snapped at true level will look crooked when compared with an off-kilter ceiling line or chair rail. A pattern with horizontal elements will look straighter if installed on a guideline parallel to the off-kilter line rather than truly level. (This isn't true for a wallpaper with a vertical pattern.)

Unlevel ceilings and chair rails. Before you begin, check the wallpaper pattern against the edge of the paper for square-ness. If it isn't square, the pattern will appear to run uphill or downhill—a flaw referred to as "printed on the bias."

Measure down an equal distance from the ceiling at both ends of the wall, and draw a horizontal guideline to connect the marks. Next, use a fram-ing square to draw a vertical guideline at a right angle to the horizontal guide-line. Then install the wallpaper accord-ing to the vertical guideline and not with a true vertical plumb line. Using a true vertical plumb line would not make the pattern parallel with the ceiling and chair rail.

The following tips will also prove useful:

■ If you're going to install a floral pat-tern with an all-over print, you will not need a guideline.

■ Always install plaids using a hori-zontal guideline.

■ When two borders such as a ceiling line and a chair rail are not equally out of plumb, try to install the paper with the truest line, or split the difference.

■ If there is no chair rail, install the wallpaper in line with the ceiling line.

■ Step back to see what the installa-tion looks like.

Vertical guidelines. These come in handy when you can't get a carpen-ter's level in tight places and when

Parallels and Guidelines

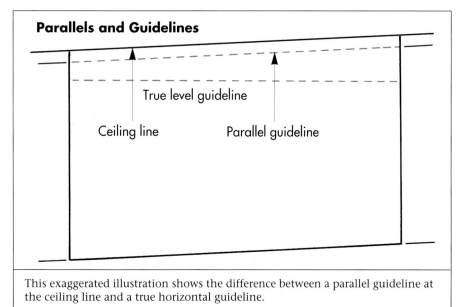

True level guideline

Ceiling line   Parallel guideline

This exaggerated illustration shows the difference between a parallel guideline at the ceiling line and a true horizontal guideline.

Vertical Guidelines

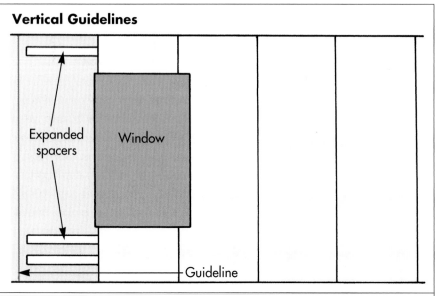

Expanded spacers

Window

Guideline

Around large windows, you can use an expanded spacer to establish a new plumb guideline past the opening.

you're trying to match strips of wallpaper around obstacles such as windows. Because it's difficult to draw an accurate plumb line across a window, move past the opening where it's easy, and then measure back from that plumb guideline to be sure that the wallpaper sections above and below the window line up. If the last strip is not plumb, you can use the expanded spacer technique to determine the position of the guideline. This way the vertical guideline will be exactly parallel with the strip. (Note: Remember to mark the guideline approximately 1/4 inch past the seam to prevent a pencil mark or chalk line from penetrating the seam.)

Around large windows. Use expanded spacers to determine the vertical guideline past the opening. With horizontal guidelines above and below the window, you could install and match several strips, and probably meet the next full-height strip right on. But some installers prefer to install the next full strip (hung to the guideline created with expanded spacers), then measure back to align the short strips above and below the opening. Don't trim the allowance edges on the next full strip until you have finished hanging all the strips.

When a strip isn't plumb where it meets a window or door frame, some installers try to correct the problem by slipping the strip to a plumb position following the obstacle. The trouble is that whatever you gain above the obstacle you lose below it—or vice versa—and one part inevitably winds up with either a gap or an overlap.

Concave and convex walls. When a job involves concave or convex walls, the guideline procedure can become a continuous process. You may need to establish a vertical guideline for every other strip to keep the vertical alignment as true as possible. This extreme measure may be the only way to compensate for a wall that doesn't have a uniform curve. If a curved wall is very uneven, consider using an overall pattern or heavily embossed wallpaper pattern to compensate for the problem—and use a wallpaper that stretches more than normal. (Note: Because most convex and concave walls are associated with stairways or other architectural features, safety can become an important consideration. Generally, special equipment is needed to establish a level work surface to ensure a safe installation. It doesn't pay to jury-rig a scaffold on a circular staircase or high arched wall—the savings can be wiped out by a trip to the emergency room. If you do not possess the equipment to install wallpaper in these situations, offer the job to someone who does.)

Working around Door Frames

Openings in the wall can interrupt the paper, but not the pattern, which should pick up across the doorway as though the opening didn't exist. There are two keys to creating this seamless appearance: making relief cuts at corners at the proper angles, and keeping the small section over the door from shifting out of plumb. Here is the basic, five-step sequence.

1 Cut the strip to remove excess material that overlaps the door,

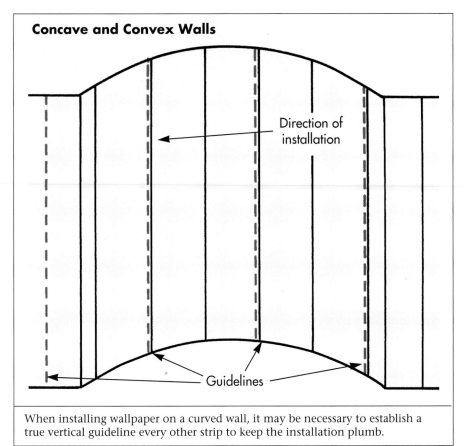

Concave and Convex Walls

Direction of installation

Guidelines

When installing wallpaper on a curved wall, it may be necessary to establish a true vertical guideline every other strip to keep the installation plumb.

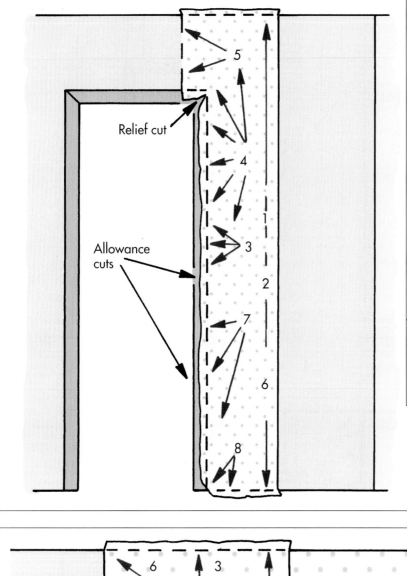

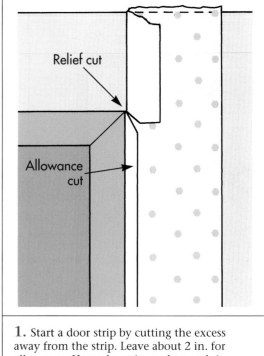

1. Start a door strip by cutting the excess away from the strip. Leave about 2 in. for allowance. Hang the strip, and smooth it using the sequence shown at left. Make a relief cut in the paper at the corner of the door.

leaving about a 2-inch allowance for trimming. Hang the strip on the wall, and smooth it out using the sequence shown. When you complete sequence 4, lift the left-hand side of the strip up and away from the door, and make a relief cut at a 45-degree angle. The cut should extend all the way to the back corner of the door frame next to the wall. Place a finger at the corner of the relief cut on the wall, and then position the small section of the strip over the door frame.

2 Hang the header section over the door, keeping the pattern level with the ceiling line. Smooth the header section using the sequence shown.

3 Establish a new plumb line so that it's easier for you to install the next over-door strip. Cut a full-width

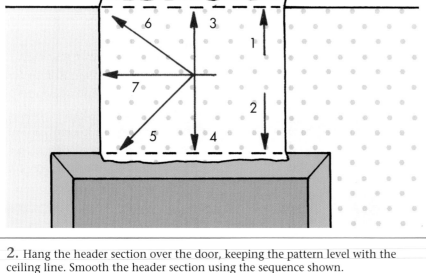

2. Hang the header section over the door, keeping the pattern level with the ceiling line. Smooth the header section using the sequence shown.

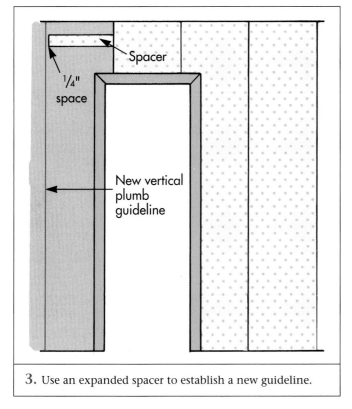

3. Use an expanded spacer to establish a new guideline.

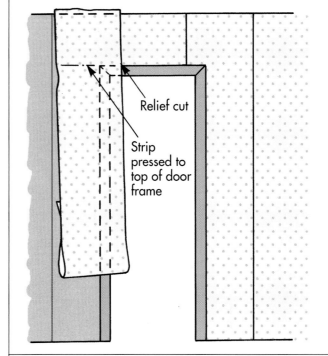

4. Carefully match the seam over the door.

piece of the strip to use as a spacer. Paste the spacer and allow it to expand; then use the expanded spacer, to determine the proper distance.

4 Hang the over-door strip by matching the seams, then pressing it gently in place at the top of the door frame. Use a razor knife to start the relief cut on top of the door frame, working back to the wall at the corner. Then use scissors to make a mitered relief cut away from the corner. Hold a finger at the corner of the relief cut to prevent a rip or tear. Gently unfold the remainder of the strip. If there is a lot of wallpaper overhanging the door frame, cut away all but 2 inches.

5 Align the left edge of the strip with the new vertical plumb line. Smooth out the strip using the sequence shown.

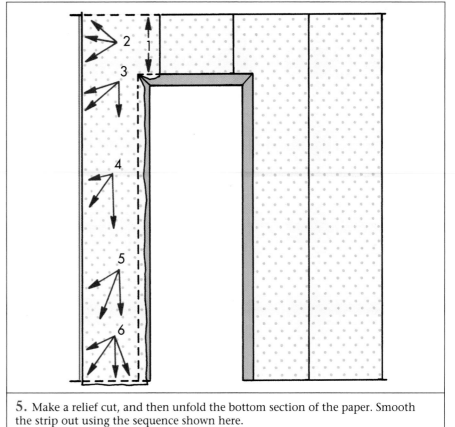

5. Make a relief cut, and then unfold the bottom section of the paper. Smooth the strip out using the sequence shown here.

Covering Electrical Plates

Covering wall switch plates with matching wallpaper is icing on the cake for any installation. It looks great and is easy to do.

1 Cut a scrap piece of wallpaper an inch or two larger than the cover plate so that it matches the surrounding pattern. Apply adhesive to the back side of the wallpaper scrap; then fold and book it, and allow it to set a few minutes. You can also use a vinyl-to-vinyl adhesive or contact spray adhesive to bond wallpaper to an electrical plate, even if the paper is prepasted.

2 Remove the screws from the electrical plate, but leave it in position, and apply the wallpaper to the top section of the plate. Align the pattern as closely as possible with the wall pattern. Use your fingernail to make a sharp crease on the wallpaper across the top edge of the plate.

3 Lift the plate away from the wall, and lay it face down onto a work surface with the underside of the plate facing upward. Make eight diagonal cuts (two at each corner).

4 Fold the exposed edges around the plate, and secure it to the back side. Start with the sides and do the top and bottom last. Allow the papered cover plate to dry in this position.

5 Hold the plate up to a bright light so that you can see the holes in the switch plate. Use a razor blade to cut out the bigger areas, and make small "X" cuts over the screw holes.

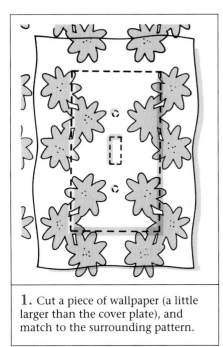

1. Cut a piece of wallpaper (a little larger than the cover plate), and match to the surrounding pattern.

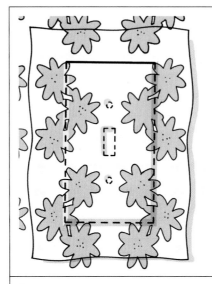

2. Align the patterns, and then use your fingernail to make a crease across the top edge of the plate.

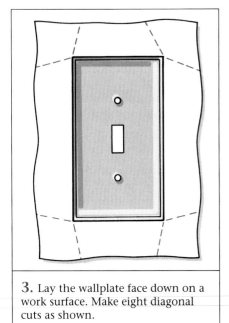

3. Lay the wallplate face down on a work surface. Make eight diagonal cuts as shown.

4. Fold the edges around the plate, and secure them. Allow the papered cover plate to dry in this position.

5. Use a razor blade to cut out the switch area, and make small "X" cuts over the screw holes.

6 Place the wallplate on the outlet box, and secure it with the screws. Do not tighten the screws all the way until the paper is completely dry.

6. Reinstall the switch plate. Do not tighten the screws all the way until the paper is completely dry.

Working around Fixtures

If you can't remove a wall-mounted fixture to paper behind it—or don't want to remove it—here are some tips on papering around it. First, plan the installation so that seams will fall on or close to the obstacle. Where the seam falls on the mounting of a towel bar, for example, you need to make only small cuts in the adjoining strips of paper. The farther the obstruction is from a seam, the more cutting you have to do. As a rule, place seams behind the obstacle where they are less visible. If you have to place seams midway to the obstacle, splice the wallpaper vertically to the bottom of the strip. A vertical splice is always easier to rejoin than a horizontal splice and is less likely to separate during the drying process. Always use new razor blades when cutting splices. On large fixtures such as a wall-hung sink, try to plan the seams to divide the fixture approximately in half. This allows for easier and more accurate relief cuts. If you remove the sink, let the wallpaper dry a full 24 hours before remounting it.

Papering Ceilings

It's called wallpaper, not "ceiling-paper," but there may be times when you want a pattern everywhere you look—even straight up. If there is a run to the pattern, generally it should be facing you when you face the focal wall. The trick, of course, is matching patterns where the papers meet at the ceiling line. In some cases, you can match distinctive patterns on one of the walls, but the chance of all four wall-to-ceiling joints working out is nil. A ceiling installation is much easier with a border or a textured paper that has no distinct pattern.

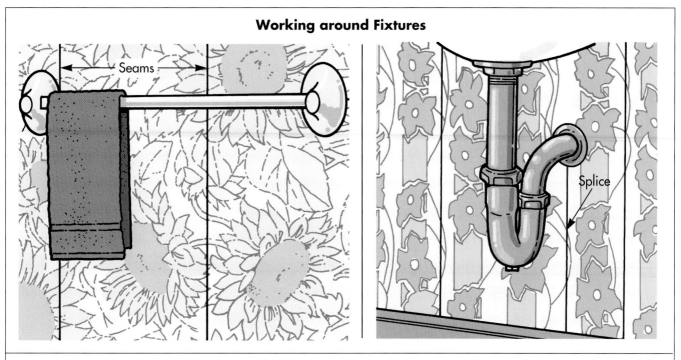

Working around Fixtures

Try to plan an installation so seams fall close to an obstacle. Place splices behind an obstacle if you have to cut the wallpaper (left). If you place seams midway to an obstacle, splice the wallpaper vertically to the bottom of the strip (right).

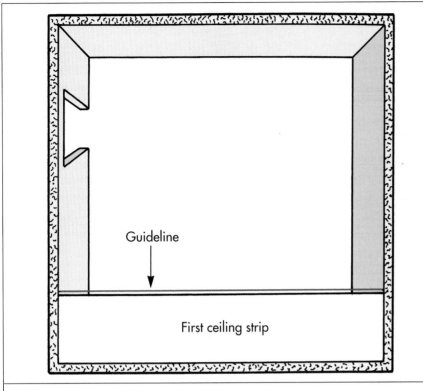

1. When hanging paper on a ceiling, a chalk guideline helps align the wallpaper.

2. An assistant feeds strips up to the ceiling across the top of the broom as you align the edge with the guideline. The assistant supports the wallpaper with the broom.

Installing Wallpaper on a Ceiling

1 To plan the seams, establish a guideline on the ceiling approximately 1/4 inch outside the first seam location at two points at opposite ends of the ceiling. Snap a chalk guideline between these two points.

2 When cutting strips for the ceiling, add 3 inches for the allowance cuts at both ends of the strip. If the strips are very long, book them after pasting, and fold accordion style. To install the strips, have a helper support the folded strip on one arm and hold a broom or some similar tool with the opposite hand. The assistant feeds the strips up, across the top of the broom, and you align the edge with the guideline. Then the assistant supports the wallpaper with the broom as you smooth it to the ceiling.

3 If you are planning to install wallpaper on adjoining walls, leave a 1/2-inch overlap onto the walls when trimming along the edges. Establish a vertical plumb line on the wall so that

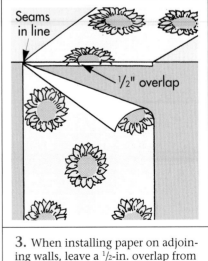

3. When installing paper on adjoining walls, leave a 1/2-in. overlap from the ceiling strip onto the walls.

the seams on the ceiling will be in line with the seams on the focal wall. Match the patterns on the wall strip with the ceiling strip, and allow a 1- or 2-inch overlap on the ceiling. Crease the overlap with the trim guide at the ceiling line; then pull the top of the wall strip away from the wall, and cut through the crease using scissors. If you are installing vinyl wallpaper, secure the overlap from the ceiling to the wall with a vinyl-to-vinyl adhesive.

Liner Papers

If you want to install wallpaper over prefinished paneling or concrete block walls, you will have to install a liner paper to achieve good results (unless you're installing a fiberglass wallcovering). You can also use a liner paper to smooth out a wall surface damaged during wallpaper removal or to provide sound and uniform support for an expensive designer wallpaper. Whatever the situation, the following tips will help you get the best results.

■ Repair and sand the wall as necessary, apply a wallpaper primer-sealer to the surface, and allow it to dry.

■ Cut the paper to length, and then apply the manufacturer's recommended adhesive on the back of the liner or on the surface of the wall.

■ Install the liner paper horizontally. Make the first smoothing strokes toward the beginning of the strip, and use long strokes toward the end of the strip.

■ Keep the liner tight during installation. This allows it to bridge hollow areas such as the grooves in paneling.

■ Install subsequent strips using butt seams. Overlap seams will show through the decorative wallpaper.

■ Do not round the corner. Instead, use a trim guide, and cut the liner paper directly in the corner.

■ Use a bright light to scan the wall surface after the liner has dried, to find imperfections. Fill these with non-shrinking joint compound, and sand it smooth after it dries.

Prepasted Wallpapers

Use prepasted paper, and you take a lot of the mystery and a lot of the hassles out of hanging wallcoverings. You don't have to worry about the right paste and the right proportions or brushing or rolling on a perfectly even coat that won't wrinkle or bubble. You just add water. And you don't have to be too delicate doing it, either. Manufacturers recommend that you activate a prepasted adhesive by submersing the wallpaper in a tray filled with water. But some professionals prefer to re-activate the adhesive by brushing or rolling on a diluted adhesive or a premixed activator that is compatible with prepasted wallcovering.

If you want to try activating it with adhesive, first you have to find out what kind of adhesive will be compatible. Here's a simple test that will tell you: Place a small drop of iodine on the adhesive surface. If the drop turns brown, the wallpaper is coated with a starch adhesive. If the drop turns purple, the wallpaper has a cellulose adhesive. If the drop turns purplish-brown, the wallpaper is coated with a mixture of both. It is important to dilute the additional

Prepasted wallpaper is a do-it-yourselfer's dream come true. To avoid making a mess, place water troughs on a folded towel.

adhesive with at least 50 percent more water than recommended for non-pasted wallpapers. If the adhesive is too thick, it may not contain enough moisture to fully activate the adhesive on the paper and could take so long to dry that the paper shrinks apart at the seams.

If you use the water-tray method and dunk the paper, bear in mind that most prepasted wallpapers expand when wet. To avoid expansion wrinkles on the wall, it is vital that you book the wallpaper and let it expand for 5 to 10 minutes after you activate the adhesive. Timing is another key factor. If you don't submerge the paper thoroughly or long enough, the adhesive may not fully activate, and the paper won't stick solidly to the wall. But if you submerge the wallpaper for too long, the adhesive may wash off.

Preparing Prepasted Paper

1 Precut each strip, and loosely roll it from the bottom to the top.

2 Fill the water tray about two-thirds full of lukewarm water, and place it at the end of a worktable on a large towel. Submerge the entire precut strip for no longer than 10 to 15 seconds.

3 Pull the strip out of the water tray slowly, allowing excess water to drain into the tray, and then put the wet strip pattern-side down on the top of the worktable.

4 Book the top half of the strip about midway, being sure to align the edges of the strip. Immediately roll the booked end up, starting from the folded end, just as if it were a loose newspaper roll. Don't crease the fold. Fold

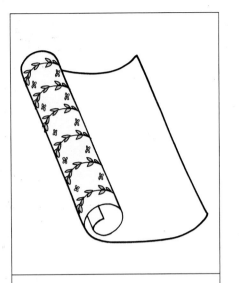

1. Each strip you will need should be precut. Roll them from the top, small enough to fit into the tray.

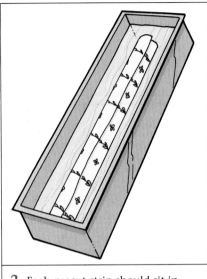

2. Each precut strip should sit in lukewarm water for about 10 to 15 sec., no longer.

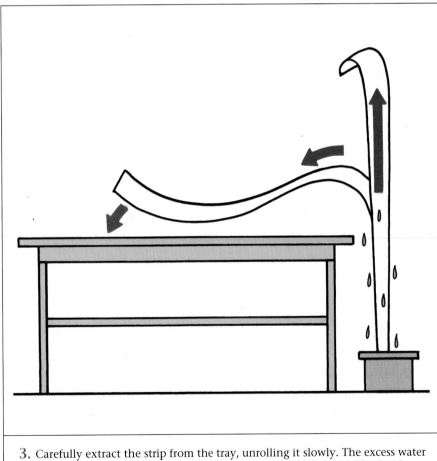

3. Carefully extract the strip from the tray, unrolling it slowly. The excess water will drip back into the tray. The soaked strip should then be placed back-side up on the worktable.

the bottom half of the strip, one paste side to another until it overlaps the end of the first fold approximately ½ inch. Continue to roll the strip from the top until it is completely rolled up. Let the booked-and-rolled strip relax and expand for a minimum of 5 to 10 minutes.

After the paper has fully expanded, unroll the relaxed strip, and unfold the top fold only. Position the top section of the strip on the wall, and then unfold the bottom section and finish installing the strip. If the prepasted adhesive does not reactivate, you can apply a thin layer of diluted wallpaper adhesive to the wall. But don't apply a dry strip of prepasted wallpaper onto a wet adhesive on the wall surface. The wallpaper will fully expand on the wall and become covered with expansion wrinkles.

Dry-Hanging Paper

With this unusual system, you apply paste to the wall instead of the paper. Dry-hanging works only with some wallpapers that do not shrink or expand, such as foils and some woven materials. It can save some mess and some time—pasting thin, delicate papers can be difficult—but the process is tricky; you might want to leave this one to a wallpapering professional.

If you want to try it, it is important to predetermine the seam placement of each strip. You also must be sure to apply the adhesive to the wall smoothly and evenly with a roller (using a ½-inch-nap roller cover). Another tip is to precut inside corner strips vertically before installing to prevent creasing it. You will also want to use a tapered seam roller to secure edges of the paper around door and window

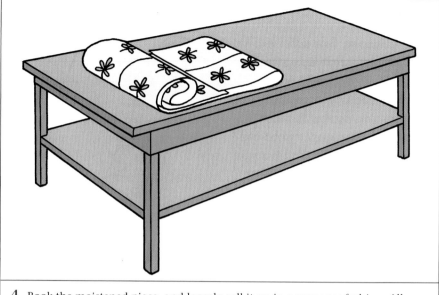

4. Book the moistened piece, and loosely roll it up in newspaper fashion. Allow the booked strip to relax for 5 to 10 min. before unfolding.

Dry-Hanging Paper

Wallpaper adhesive roller

For a dry-hanging application, you'll want to be sure that you apply the adhesive to the wall as evenly as possible.

When trimming wallpaper for a short, irregular line, it can be easier to cut it already installed, against the blade of a putty knife.

Dry-Trimming

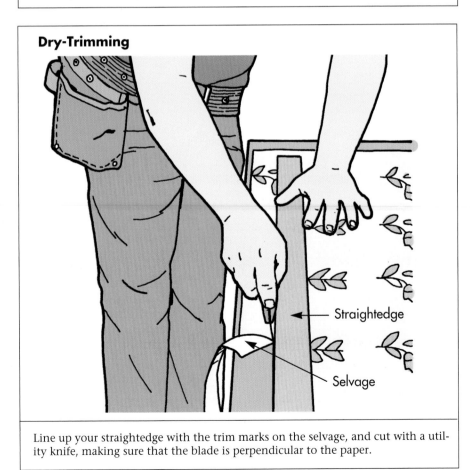

Line up your straightedge with the trim marks on the selvage, and cut with a utility knife, making sure that the blade is perpendicular to the paper.

frames. And whenever you overlap wallpaper, secure the overlap using a vinyl-to-vinyl adhesive.

If you double-cut to remove the selvage of untrimmed wallpaper (page 92), leave the exposed edge lifted away from the wall until you're ready to join the next strip. If you leave the edge down, it can dry prematurely and cause damage to the wallpaper or the wall surface. If these lifted edges dry out, re-wet them using a small brush and fresh adhesive — or you can use a household spray bottle with warm water to reactivate the dried adhesive.

Finally, use a soft bristle smoothing brush or soft rubber squeegee to remove air pockets when dry-hanging foil or Mylar wallpaper. If you use a squeegee, apply warm water with a household spray bottle to the decorative surface of the wallpaper to make the smoothing easier and to help prevent surface marring.

Untrimmed Wallpapers

Most wallpaper comes from the factory already trimmed. There are still a few styles, though, that come with the trim, or selvage, still attached. If you elect to install wallpapers of this type, you will absolutely need the proper equipment. There are three ways to trim the selvage: dry-trimming, wet-trimming, and double-cutting.

Dry-trimming. To dry-trim wallpaper selvage you'll need some new razor blades, a straightedge trim guide, and a stable worktable. Align the straightedge along the trim marks on the selvage, and hold it securely while you

Wet-Trimming

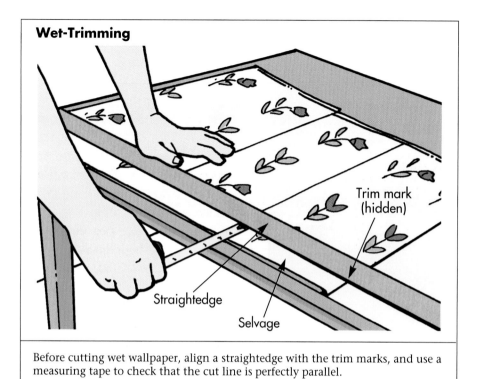

Before cutting wet wallpaper, align a straightedge with the trim marks, and use a measuring tape to check that the cut line is perfectly parallel.

trim the wallpaper on the worktable. First, establish a vertical guideline for the first strip. Then use a pair of scissors to remove most of the selvage to within $1/4$ to $1/2$ inch outside the trim marks on all rolls. Paste the first strip, book it, and allow it to relax and expand. Hang the first strip, but remember that a portion of the selvage still remains at this point. Trim the allowance cuts from both the top and bottom, and immediately lift the edges approximately 3 inches away from the wall. This will prevent them from drying on the wall. Cut the next strip, paste it, book it, and allow it to relax. While the second strip is relaxing, re-paste the edge of the first strip that the second strip will join. This will provide a freshly pasted edge for double-cutting once the second strip is

cut. It is important to use a razor blade holder that makes it comfortable to hold the blade at a 90-degree angle to the worktable. Any tilt of the blade may result in a bevel at the seam, causing a white edge to show from the substrate.

Wet-trimming. As the name implies, you wet-trim wallpaper after it's pasted. Precut the strip, paste it, and fold it before trimming. Align a straightedge with the trim marks, or if only one mark is visible, use a ruler to measure the exact distance from the edge in at least three places to ensure a cut parallel with the edge. Cut through the booked strip of wallpaper, and remove the selvage. Then reverse the strip on the table, and repeat for the other edge of the strip.

Double-cutting. This is the preferred method because it produces a perfect butt seam and eliminates the need to

Double-Cutting

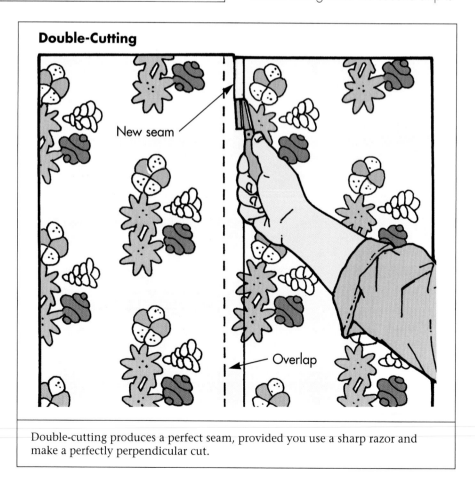

Double-cutting produces a perfect seam, provided you use a sharp razor and make a perfectly perpendicular cut.

Rolling Double-Cut Seams

Double-cut seams should be rolled lightly with a seam roller.

overlapped. In some situations, such as during hot weather, it may be necessary to reactivate the adhesive on the first strip by spraying it with warm water from a spray bottle. (It is not advisable to create an overabundance of adhesive along the edge of the wallpaper.) Hang the second strip, and match the designs by slightly overlapping the first strip. Perform the double-cut using a straightedge and a new razor blade. Repeat these steps to install the rest of the wallpaper.

Always be careful when double-cutting on drywall. If you cut the face paper of the drywall, it is likely to pull apart as the wallpaper dries. After making the cut, remove the cut edge strips, and lightly roll the seam with a seam roller. If you are installing a material like suede or silk and need to cut the selvage, it is important to keep the decorative surface clean of adhesives to avoid staining.

MAINLY FOR CONTRACTORS

Protecting seams. On heavy commercial wallpapers, which usually require a heavy-duty adhesive, keep the decorative surface clean. The seams are usually created using the overlap-and-double-cut technique. If the surface is relatively smooth, you can generally wash off any adhesive that gets on the front during double-cutting. If a vinyl wallcovering has a deep textured effect, use 1½- or 2-inch masking tape. For delicate materials, use the slip-sheeting technique. This technique also is valuable on stringcloth and rushcloth to prevent adhesive from damaging a previously installed strip.

To slipsheet, cut some 4-inch-wide strips of wax paper as long as the wallpaper strip. Install the first strip, and trim the allowance cuts. Then apply 4 to 6 inches of additional adhesive beside the strip where the second strip will be joined. Place a strip of wax paper so that it overlaps the first strip about 2 inches, while the remaining 2-inch area sticks to the adhesive. If you are pasting the wall surface, add about 2 inches of paste on the front of the slipsheet. This will secure the edge of the second strip to the slipsheet until it can be double-cut. Next, apply paste to the second strip and hang it, allowing the edge to overlap the slipsheet and the first strip about 1 inch. Then use a straightedge and new razor to double-cut through all layers. Lastly, remove all excess ends from the double-cutting step, including the entire slipsheet. Lightly secure the seam together, and wipe the seam area using a soft dry cloth or slightly damp sponge.

Material inspections. If you are doing work for hire and you find any imperfections in rolls during your initial inspection, be sure to point them out to your client before you hang any paper. If they want to go ahead with the project instead of waiting for replacement material, make sure they are aware of exactly what kinds of defects will be visible and how much more time it will take you to compensate for the manufacturing errors.

Chapter 7

Special Areas

I t's called wallpaper, but that doesn't stop people from putting it on the ceiling. In fact, some do-it-yourself decorators use it inside cabinets, to wrap shelves, and to line drawers—any place where they can catch a glimpse of the colors and patterns. Once you see the impact that new wallcoverings can have on a room, you may want to use it in some other locations, too.

The basic handling guidelines and installation steps still hold true in tight spaces with irregular shapes, such as stairwells and dormers, but there is generally more measuring and cutting in these locations than you'll encounter on regular flat walls. In stairwells, for instance, a combination of sloping borders and two-story openings can make material estimating and installation more challenging than they are on standard walls.

In this chapter, you'll find out how to meet the challenges of a wide variety of special areas and conditions. This includes the nooks and crannies of new houses and additions, plus some of the prime remodeling candidates in older homes. One of the most common is unfinished space—the best deal going in home improvement because you don't have to start from scratch with new foundations and framing. But before you get around to selecting wallpaper for that rough-framed attic or concrete-block basement, you

should give some thought to the characteristics of the space you're improving.

In many homes, areas that were not originally designed as living spaces have different, generally lighter-duty features than areas intended for people. There may be little or no insulation, no vapor barriers, inadequate ventilation, and not enough supporting lumber to keep $1/2$-inch gypsum drywall stable—all factors that can affect the appearance and durability of finished surfaces. You can generally spot the difference by comparing joists in the first floor with joists in the attic floor. Typically, first-floor joists are 2x8s, at least, and often 2x10s. If the attic joists are smaller, say 2x6s, they probably will need to be strengthened—and other parts of the framing, too. The smaller size might support what's called the dead load of building materials (only 10 to 20 pounds per square foot), but flex too much under the live load of people and furnishings that maybe twice as much per square foot.

Structural improvements are often needed when you convert an unfinished area, say, remodeling a garage or an attic to become usable living space. When you change the use of the space, you may be asking the structure to do more than it was designed to do—and more than local building codes allow. You'll need to run new heat-

This pantry alcove is made part of the room by using the same wallpaper on its walls and by wrapping the wide border paper into and out of the space.

ing pipes or ducts, water pipes, and electrical lines in unfinished spaces and prevent temperature variations from creating condensation that can cause problems on your new walls. In attics, ventilation is key. You have to leave room for air to circulate behind the new walls and under the roof framing. You will preserve wall surfaces (and save energy) by insulating water pipes, heating lines, and air-conditioning ducts. You can slip foam insulating tubes over pipes to prevent sweating. Heating or air-conditioning ducts can be wrapped with batts of insulation. Also insulate any vent lines from exhaust fans. That can prevent problems during the winter, when moisture in warm air coming from kitchens or bathrooms can condense on the inside of a cold duct before reaching an outlet.

New Paper over Old

You may need to repaper because the existing wallcovering is peeling and shredding. But maybe not. Maybe you want to change the appearance before the surface wears out. You could strip the wall and start from scratch, but it's okay to install paper over paper when the first layer is sound.

If any part of the existing wallpaper is loose and you don't make the necessary repairs, your new layer won't stick for long. Also, there are some wall-coverings that must be stripped: for example, heavily embossed wallpapers or natural wallpapers such as grass-cloth, reedcloth, stringcloth, and fabrics. With other coverings you can get good results papering over old paper by following a few basic guidelines.

The first step is to check the existing seams. Repair and sand every over-lapped seam, even if it is barely noticeable. If you don't, the overlap will show through new wallpaper just as the edge of old paint shows through a new coating. If seams are loose, resecure them with a seam adhesive, or cut them out with a razor blade and repair and sand the voids.

It's also important to check the inks on the existing wallpaper to see whether they are bleeding inks—if they are, they could show through the new sur-face. Moisten a cloth with a solution of ammonia and water, and rub the inked areas of the wallcovering. If the inks are colorfast, they will not change color. Bleeding inks, on the other hand, turn green-blue. If the inks bleed, prime the wallpaper with a stain-killing primer-sealer, and when it dries, apply an acrylic wallpaper primer-sealer. In any event, it's a good idea to apply a high-quality wallpaper acrylic primer-sealer over existing wallpaper. This will help the new wallpaper bond properly and prevent show-through if you are hanging semitransparent wallpaper.

If the existing wallpaper is a solid vinyl or nonbreathing material, install an absorbent liner paper first. The liner will soak up moisture and pre-vent a mildew problem. As an alter-native, you can use a vinyl-to-vinyl adhesive instead of a liner paper—or, of course, remove the paper completely, which is often the easiest route. One other point when installing a wallcovering over vinyl wallpaper: make sure the vinyl sur-face is completely clean. If the sur-face feels sticky or greasy or is obviously stained, wash it thoroughly with mineral spirits, and allow it to dry before applying the primer-sealer.

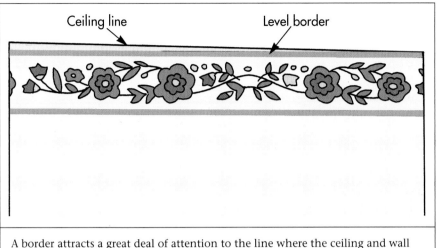

A border attracts a great deal of attention to the line where the ceiling and wall meet. An out-of-plumb wall or unlevel ceiling will be particularly conspicuous.

Borders

Strips of border paper can accent a wall along the ceiling line, chair rail, baseboard, doors, and window frames. Complex borders run along the top of high walls can visually scale down a large room, while a simple chair-rail border can make short walls seem taller. One thing you should keep in mind, though, is that a border attracts attention to itself as a focal point on the wall, so the wall and ceiling where the border will be installed have to be nearly perfectly level or plumb. Unlike wallpaper installed on a large wall, where small errors may be lost in continuing complex patterns, a narrow strip of border can accentuate slight imperfections. A ceiling line only a fraction of an inch out of level will suddenly appear quite obviously crooked when it interferes with the design of a border.

Conversely, sometimes you can use a border to draw attention away from a defect in the wall or ceiling. If you have a crooked ceiling line, for instance, install the border at chair-rail height. This will draw attention away from the imperfect ceiling line and focus it at a lower level.

Manufacturers usually package border material in spools 5 or 7 yards long or in longer rolls. To determine how much material you'll need, use a measuring tape or yardstick to measure the areas where you plan to install the border. If your border is on a spool, add 1 1/2 feet extra for every 15 feet measured to allow for pattern-matching between spools. If you buy a longer roll, add at least 2 yards to

compensate for crooked corners and possible damage to the ends of the roll. If you are going to install a border around windows and doors, allow at least 1 foot extra at each corner for miter cuts. (You should also make sure that the design of your border will allow you to turn corners around a window or door frame without creating a pattern mismatch.)

Double-Cutting Borders

The best way to form a seam between two pieces of border material is to use the padded, double-cut technique. To make a double cut, follow these basic steps.

1 First, place a small, thin scrap piece of wallpaper or wax paper on the wall surface underneath the overlapping sections of border material. This paper, called the pad, will protect the wall from the razor blade when you cut through the overlapped layers of border. The pad also prevents seam separation.

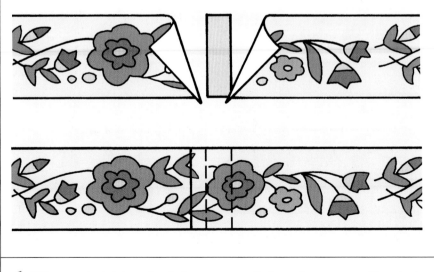

1. When you're joining a border's seam, a small piece of wax paper will protect the wall underneath where you will cut. Overlap the two pieces, being careful to match the pattern exactly.

2 Using a fresh razor blade, double-cut through both layers of the border, but be careful not to press too hard and cut through the wax-paper pad (and, as a result, the wall underneath). Also be careful to keep the razor cutter absolutely perpendicular or the seam will show white.

3 Remove the cut ends and the pad. Rejoin the new ends to form a seam, and use a seam roller to secure it. Wipe off the excess paste.

New seam

2. Cut through both layers of border with a sharp razor. Don't press too hard—remember that you don't want to mar the wall underneath. Keep the blade perpendicular so that the border material won't show.

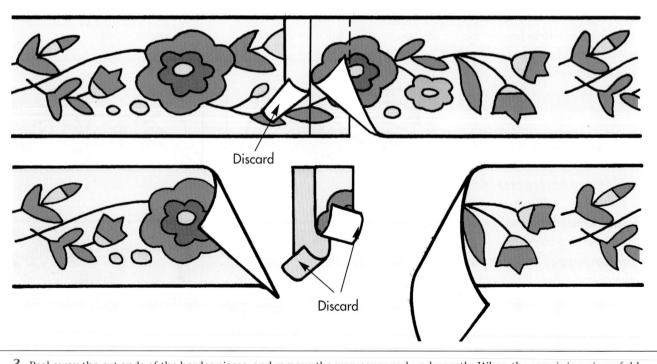

Discard

Discard

3. Peel away the cut ends of the border pieces, and remove the wax-paper pad underneath. When the remaining pieces fold back down in position, they should make a perfect seam.

1. To keep the border from curling on the wall, reverse-roll it. This is the time to inspect the roll for any flaws in the printing or any damage. Also, measure the roll to ensure that you have enough to complete your project.

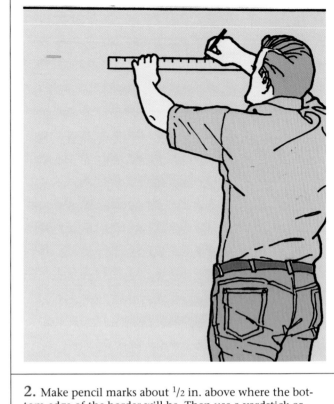

2. Make pencil marks about $1/2$ in. above where the bottom edge of the border will be. Then use a yardstick or other straightedge to connect these marks, giving you a guideline to install the border.

Installing Borders on Painted Walls

Proper preparation of the wall surface is essential before installing a border on a painted wall. Fill in any cracks with a non-shrinking joint compound and sand it smooth. After applying a good-quality latex paint, prime the wall with an acrylic wallpaper primer-sealer. When you are ready to install the border, follow these steps.

1 Reverse-roll the border to minimize curling, and inspect it for flaws. If there is a defect, now is the time to find it. It's also a good time to make sure you have purchased enough material. Cut a 3-inch-long piece, and apply paste to the backing (or submerge it in water, if it's prepasted). Fold the piece in half, and let it expand for about 5 minutes. Then measure the fully expanded piece edge to edge to determine its expanded width.

2 Make small pencil marks at 2- to 3-foot intervals at a distance below the ceiling line (or above the chair rail or baseboard) equal to $1/2$ inch less than the full expanded width of the border. For example, if the expanded border's width is 6 inches, place the pencil marks at $5\,1/2$ inches below the where you are installing the border.

Use a pencil and straightedge, such as a carpenter's square, to connect these marks to form a horizontal guideline. Use clean tools, and make the guideline as light as possible to prevent possible show-through.

A border can be an attractive addition around an opening, and take the place of wood trim.

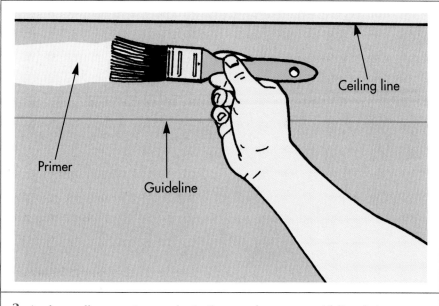

Primer

Ceiling line

Guideline

3. Apply a wallpaper primer-sealer to the area above your guideline, being careful not to allow any to go below the line.

3 Prime the area with an acrylic wallpaper primer-sealer, being careful to stay within the guidelines. The 1/2-inch allowance ensures that the primer-sealer does not extend past the border once it has been installed. The 1/2-inch area void of primer will not cause the border to come loose. Allow the proper drying time for the acrylic primer-sealer.

4 Paste the border, or submerge in water for about 10 seconds if it is prepasted. Book the border loosely in accordion folds. This prevents the adhesive from getting on the front of the border. Let the strip relax and expand for about 5 minutes.

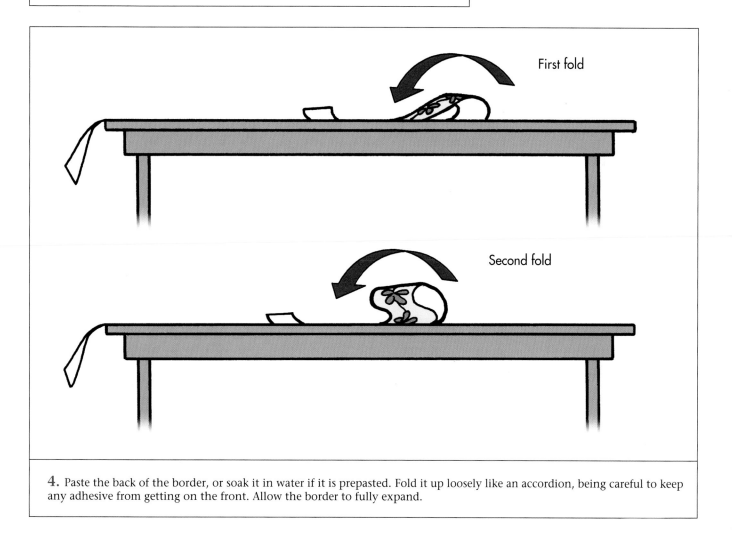

First fold

Second fold

4. Paste the back of the border, or soak it in water if it is prepasted. Fold it up loosely like an accordion, being careful to keep any adhesive from getting on the front. Allow the border to fully expand.

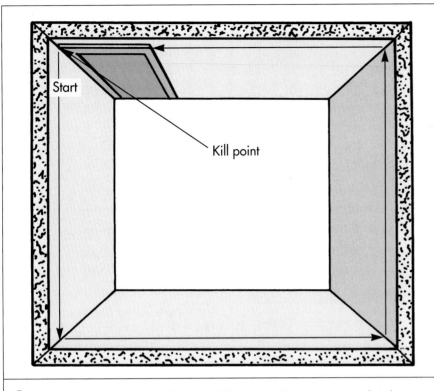

5. Pick an inconspicuous spot for your kill point so that any mismatch is less noticeable. Install the border around the room. When you start a new roll, be careful to match the pattern exactly before continuing.

Borders with Companion Wallpaper

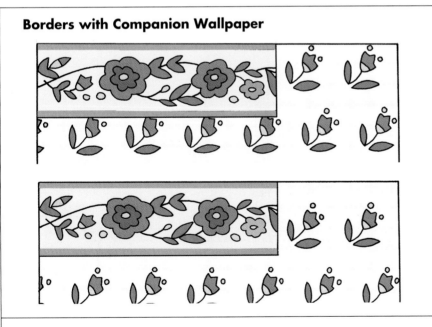

If your border is going to be installed over a patterned wallpaper, you need to make sure that the wallpaper's pattern is not going to be partially covered up or will otherwise clash with the border. If a border covers a small part of the wallpaper pattern (as in the upper illustration above), you should pick a border that is not quite as wide.

5 After about five minutes, the border is ready to install. Begin in an inconspicuous place (the kill point) so that any mismatch between the last border segment and the first will not be so noticeable.

Special Border Applications

With companion wallpaper. If you are going to install a border over a companion wallpaper, there are two things you will have to consider: how the border placement affects the pattern on the wallpaper, and the transparency of the border. You want to make sure that the border does not cover over half of a design element in the companion wallpaper, leaving the other half to peek out from underneath it. If this is the case, choose a wider or narrower border. If the designs on the wallpaper are visible beneath the border, you will need to use a white pigmented wallpaper primer-sealer over the companion piece to eliminate the show-through. And of course you will need to use a vinyl-to-vinyl adhesive to install the border on top of the companion paper.

Before installing a border over patterned wallpaper, set one against the other to test different arrangements—particularly when you're mixing different styles. All kinds of combinations are pos-

PRO TIP

First, when installing borders between doors or windows, be sure to balance the designs between the trim. Second, when joining two sections of border on the wall, overlap the ends of each spool so that the designs match perfectly.

Border as a Chair Rail

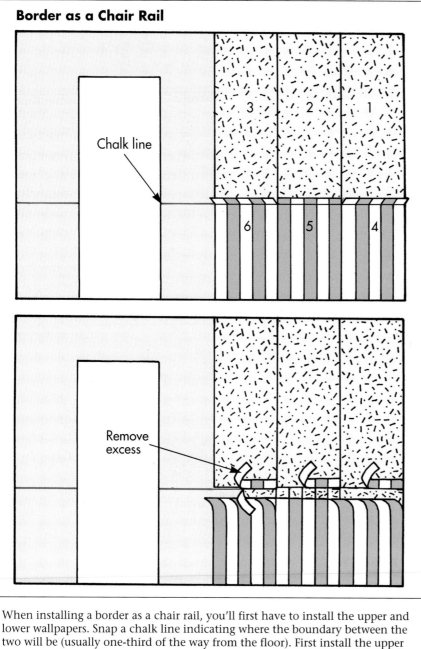

Chalk line

Remove excess

When installing a border as a chair rail, you'll first have to install the upper and lower wallpapers. Snap a chalk line indicating where the boundary between the two will be (usually one-third of the way from the floor). First install the upper wallpaper, overlapping the line slightly, then the lower paper, also overlapping. Double-cut along the boundary line for a perfect seam. If the wallpaper patterns are going to be visible through the border, you'll need to apply a white primer-sealer to that part of the wallpaper that will be covered, or inlay the border.

vide the wall into thirds and place the center of the border one-third of the way up from the floor. For example, on an 8-foot wall, you would center the border 32 inches up from the floor. On a 9-foot wall, center the border 36 inches from the floor.

There are two ways to install a border as a chair rail when using companion wallpapers both above and below the chair rail. The first method is to snap a horizontal chalk line on the wall to indicate the centerline of the border. You then install three strips on the upper part of the wall, making sure that their ends extend slightly past the center chalk line. Next, you install three strips on the lower part of the wall. Their ends should overlap the upper strips at the chalk centerline. Finally, make a double-cut through both strips on the centerline and remove the excess ends. It helps to secure the seam with an oval seam roller. This provides a smooth surface on which to apply the border. Continue around the room until the installation is finished, and then snap a new chalk line at the top of the chair-rail border to indicate border placement. Use a vinyl-to-vinyl adhesive when applying borders directly over the existing wallpaper. Cover the chalk line with the top edge of the border.

An alternative method is to hang the entire top portion of the room first, cutting the bottom of the upper strips at the bottom edge of the border using a 2- or 3-foot straightedge.

sible, but you'll find that you get the best results if you keep the edges of the border from overlapping a design. Ideally, the dominant pattern on the wallpaper should be 1 to 2 inches below the edge of the border so that they do not conflict. For example, if you are in-

stalling a 6-inch border at the ceiling line, snap a chalk line 7 inches from the ceiling. This will serve as a guideline for the wallpaper pattern.

As chair rail. When using a border as a chair rail, it's common practice to di-

Around door and window frames. If you want to install a border around a door or window frame, the first thing you have to consider is whether the border has a directional print. For example, a border with small pictures of sailboats would be considered a direc-

Border Height

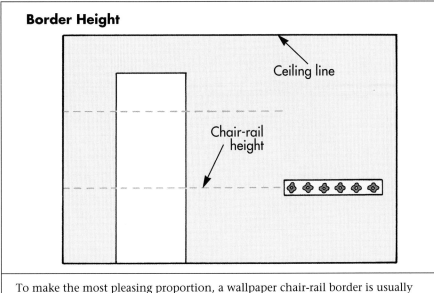

To make the most pleasing proportion, a wallpaper chair-rail border is usually installed one-third of the way up from the bottom of a wall.

mitered corner. To finish the joint, roll the seam lightly using an oval seam roller, and wipe the border clean with a sponge or cloth.

Along sloped ceilings. When you tackle wallpaper installation on a sloped ceiling, careful planning and creative methods will help you get the best results. When you come to an intersection where the ceiling angle changes, match the patterns as allowed by the design, and plan the double-cut so that it doesn't lop off a prominent feature or cut a dominant pattern in half. There are no hard and fast rules for making this kind of on-the-spot design decision,

tional print: unlike flowers, sailboats would look odd pointing up or upside-down. If your border has a directional print, you may wish to reconsider installing it around a door or window, because the sailboats (or other pattern) will appear in the wrong direction either vertically or horizontally.

When you install the border, be sure to measure enough so that you can extend the border past the end of the frame about 1 inch farther than the width of the border. This lets you overlap the following strip on the frame to achieve a balanced installation.

After you overlap the two strips, the best technique is to make a double cut at a 45-degree angle. If you have no choice but to make the double-cut near a pattern element, you should try to avoid cutting it in half. The patterns probably won't match up exactly, but on many designs they will be close. Use the padded double-cut technique if necessary.

Remove the excess border material (and the underlying pad if used), and join the strips together to form the

Around Window and Door Frames

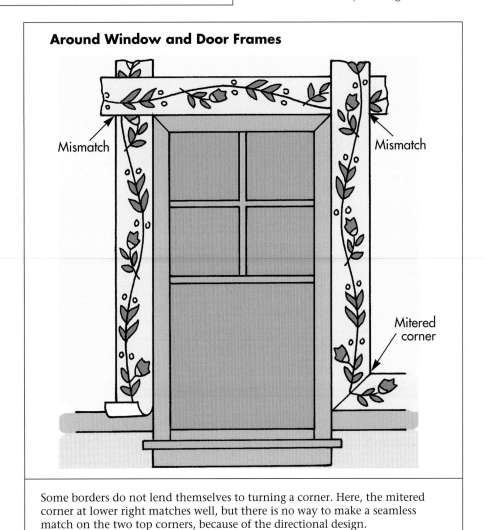

Some borders do not lend themselves to turning a corner. Here, the mitered corner at lower right matches well, but there is no way to make a seamless match on the two top corners, because of the directional design.

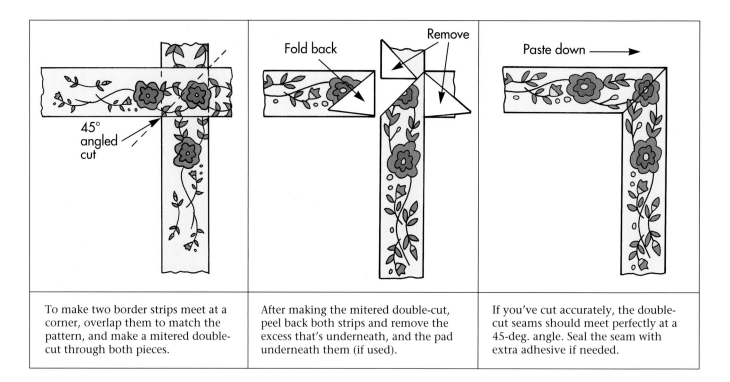

| To make two border strips meet at a corner, overlap them to match the pattern, and make a mitered double-cut through both pieces. | After making the mitered double-cut, peel back both strips and remove the excess that's underneath, and the pad underneath them (if used). | If you've cut accurately, the double-cut seams should meet perfectly at a 45-deg. angle. Seal the seam with extra adhesive if needed. |

just common sense and personal taste. Remember that the cuts do not have to be in the corner or at a 45-degree angle. You can double-cut around a pattern or even extend one section onto the adjacent wall to make a better match before making your cut.

Around corners. Nearly every border installation includes an inside corner or two. And border material, like wallpaper, can pull away from a corner after the adhesive dries or in response to settling or expansion and contraction of the structure. Use the following procedure to provide expansion joints that prevent the border from pulling away from the corner.

Begin the installation in a corner where the kill point will occur, with a 1/8-inch overlap on the wall where the final border strip will meet. This overlap hides the corner once you install the final strip. At each corner, tuck the border firmly into place, and cut it directly in the corner using a razor blade. Then lift

the cut end of the border from the wall, and start the next section, backing it up 1/8 inch onto the first wall. If the pattern is complex, you may have to trim the border to match the design in the corner. Secure the cut end so

that it meets perfectly in the corner and overlaps the 1/8-inch segment of the next strip. When you reach the kill point, crease the border in the final corner, lift it away from the wall, and then cut it with scissors. Secure

Corners at a Slanted Ceiling

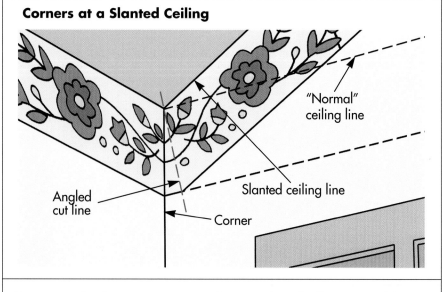

If you want a border to turn a corner and go up a slanted ceiling, some of the horizontal border will have to go out onto the adjacent wall. This extra piece will be used to match up with the angled piece as it comes down. Make a double-cut where the two pieces intersect, as shown in the illustration.

the cut end directly in the corner with vinyl-to-vinyl adhesive.

Cathedral Walls

Cathedral walls and vaulted ceilings can be challenging installations because you have to do everything you do on a flat wall, but on slanted surfaces while perched on high ladders and scaffolding. With this in mind, you should think twice before attempting this kind of installation. Unless you have the proper equipment to do it safely, this is definitely the kind of job you want to give to a professional.

Papering a Cathedral Wall

1 Once you get comfortable with the ladders and scaffolding, and before you start pasting, consider the pattern placement on the lowest wall. If the lowest wall is 8 feet high, the pattern placement on the taller walls should follow the ceiling line of this wall. Then, when a strip rounds the corner where the lower wall and cathedral wall meet, the pattern will automatically fall into place. Once you establish the pattern placement, snap a horizontal guideline across the cathedral wall at 8 feet.

Begin a cathedral wall installation with the longest strip, if possible. It's easier to align and install next to a strip that is higher than to join a strip next to one that is lower. (This is also true with stairways.) As you hang the strip, adjust the pattern to the proper height at the horizontal guideline.

2 Precut the strips on a cathedral wall (or vaulted ceiling), by first measuring the height over the horizontal guideline on each separate strip. This eliminates the need to measure from the floor to the highest point for each strip. Next, cut away the slant or pitch of the ceiling line on each strip as follows: Measure the expanded width of the wallpaper by pasting a small piece and allowing it to relax 5 to 10 minutes (27 inches in this example). (See drawing on page 106.) Establish a true vertical line with a spirit level or chalk-line box at any place along the cathedral-ceiling line (line 1). Establish another vertical line the exact width of the wallpaper strip away from the first line (line 2). Use a long spirit level to draw a horizontal line from the point where line 2 meets the ceiling to where it intersects line 1. Measure the distance from the intersections of line 1 and line 3 to the top of line 1. In the illustration on page 106, the distance is 15 inches.

This calculation tells you that the ceiling rises 15 inches vertically for

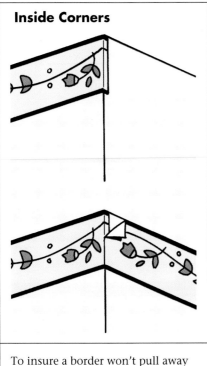

Inside Corners

To insure a border won't pull away at an inside corner, install it in two pieces as shown. The first piece overlaps the corner by 1/8 in., and the second piece is cut right over it.

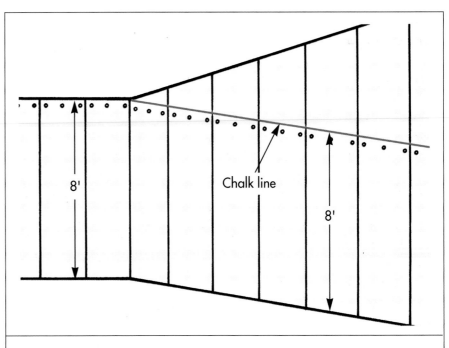

8'   Chalk line   8'

1. A horizontal guideline should be snapped across a cathedral wall at the height of the lower walls. This will aid you in pattern matching from the lower section of wall onto the cathedral wall. Hang the longest strips first.

First, determine the most difficult area or situation. Plan to start from that point, and work toward the easier areas. Give careful consideration to the direction of the installation and the location of scaffolding equipment for succeeding strips. This is important because you don't want to rest a ladder on any freshly installed wallpaper.

Upper stairway setup. The illustration below shows a typical setup for a standard stairway. You should start the installation with the longest well strip, then install the shorter strips toward the top of the stairs using the walk plank. Next, paste and install the two head wall strips from the plank. Leave the bottom of the head wall strips booked until you can rearrange the walk plank. You should only paste and install a couple of strips at a time because of the difficulty of doing this installation safely.

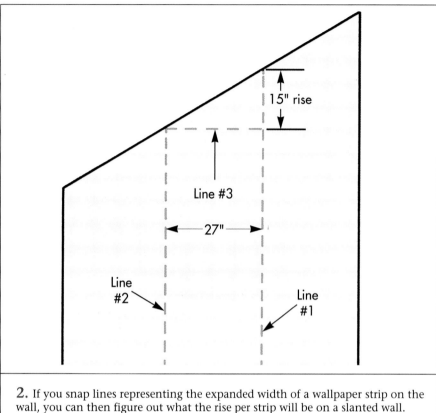

2. If you snap lines representing the expanded width of a wallpaper strip on the wall, you can then figure out what the rise per strip will be on a slanted wall.

every 27 inches horizontally—the width of the expanded wallpaper. When you cut the wallpaper strip, measure down 15 inches from the allowance cut on the left-hand edge of the strip. You have to cut the excess off the correct edge because you can't reverse the piece the way you can flop a piece of plywood.

Stairways

Stairway installations cover a wide spectrum of special areas, including spiral, multilevel, and single-flight stairways. Regardless of the type, be sure you have the proper equipment to do the job (ladders, scaffolding, and walk planks). If you don't, pass the work on to a professional who has the necessary equipment and experience to handle these jobs safely.

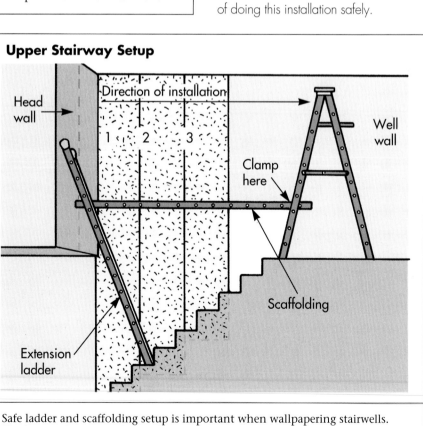

Safe ladder and scaffolding setup is important when wallpapering stairwells. Planks must be stamped as scaffold plank grade or should not be used.

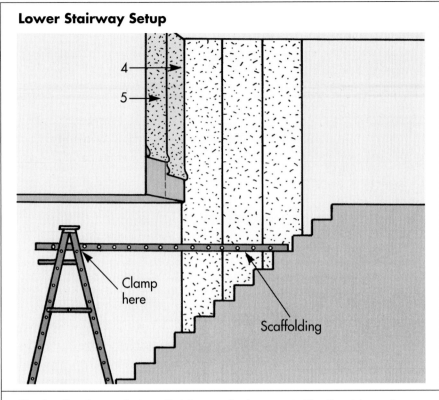

Lower Stairway Setup

4

5

Clamp here

Scaffolding

Head wall strips can be installed from a plank supported by the stairs and a single stepladder. Clamp the plank to the ladder to avoid slippage.

Lower stairway setup. Once you've installed the top portions of the head wall strips, you can now support the walk plank on the lower level with a stepladder (drawing above).

If the stairwell has two side walls and you are using the ladder and walk plank as a scaffold, install both side walls before installing the head wall. To ensure a pattern-match between the two side walls and the head wall, install expanded spacers at least one full vertical repeat in length. With the spacers in position, establish a vertical guideline for the first strip on the second side wall. Next, install a strip, and match the pattern to the spacer. Once the strip is in position on the side wall, remove the spacers. Cut the side wall strip so that it overlaps the head wall by 1/4 inch at the corner.

When you complete the installation on the side walls, paste and install the head wall strips, leaving the bottom half of the strips in the booked position. Then it is a simple matter to rearrange the scaffolding down to a lower level to complete the last few steps of the installation.

Murals

A wall mural forms a picture or scene from a sequence of numbered panels. Keep the numbers in order, and you get a completed picture, which can be combined with other wallpapers or left to stand on its own on a painted wall. Before you order a mural, consider these design and installation questions.

■ Is the picture on the mural paper large enough so that it will not look

lost on the wall but not so large that it will overwhelm the room?

■ Does the mural have extra background filler paper? If not, how much extra will need to be needed to fill out any excess wall space on each side of the picture?

■ Is the mural continuous (interlocking), meaning the first and last panel of the picture sequence will join? If so, how many extra panels will be required to complete the entire length of the wall?

■ Are there any particular details of your room, such as ceiling height or a chair rail, that could have an adverse effect on the mural itself? Will it be partially blocked by a lamp, furniture, or some permanent fixture?

Installing Partial Wall Murals

Generally, if the mural doesn't extend from floor to ceiling, you should install it so that the center of the mural is at eye level or a little higher. To do this, first measure the width of the wall and divide by two to find the center. Make a light pencil mark at eye level at the center of the wall. Use a long spirit level or a chalk-line box with a plumb bob to make a plumb line approximately 1/2 inch left of the center mark. This will establish a vertical guide for the first strip. Then install the first panel to the right of the center line, centered on the eye-level mark you made. Install the second panel to the left of the first panel. Install the remaining panels, being particularly careful to line them up correctly with the previous panels. If necessary, finish the wall with the background paper.

Murals aren't just pictures of tropical sunsets with silhouetted palm trees—a wide variety is available to suit all tastes and cover any size walls.

you start with the center lower panels first and then install the upper half of the mural second. This procedure works best when there are two installers working together. If you are working alone, install the panels in the sequence shown in the illustration at right.

Be careful to not over-soak or over-work photo mural panels. They become very tender, and will tear easily. Also, use caution and a gentle cleanser when wiping the seams or front surface of the photo mural; the ink may wipe off.

Because it is difficult to install panels perfectly square to each other, some manufacturers recommend that you overlap edges. If the bump caused by an overlap is undesirable, you can double-cut them during installation. If you choose to do this, lift the exposed edges of each strip away from the wall until you are ready to align the adjoining strip.

Manufacturers sometimes furnish a double or triple roll of background paper to cover the mural wall.

Sometimes, a mural may contain an odd number of panels. If this is the case, you should center the middle panel on the wall first. To make a vertical plumb guideline, measure the width of an expanded panel, and divide it by 2. Then offset the plumb line that distance plus 1/2 inch from the center of the wall to the left edge of the center panel.

Installing Photo Murals

Another option, photo murals, are the same as regular murals but are high-quality reproductions of photographs. Photo murals are installed the same way that regular murals are, except that they are sometimes divided into quarter panels. Most manufacturers suggest that

Installing Partial Wall Murals

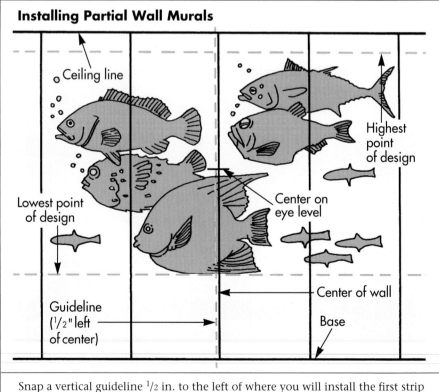

Snap a vertical guideline 1/2 in. to the left of where you will install the first strip of the mural—1/2 in. off-center if there's an even number of panels.

Installing Photo Wall Murals

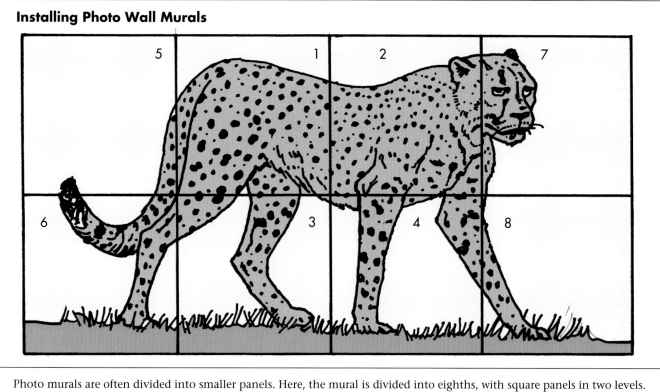

Photo murals are often divided into smaller panels. Here, the mural is divided into eighths, with square panels in two levels. Install these panels as they have been numbered, with the central lower panels first and the panels above them second, then moving to the outer panels.

This way, if the adhesive dries along the lifted edges, you can moisten it with a spray bottle filled with luke-warm water. Double-cut the panels immediately after joining the edges.

Soffits

Soffits are the undersides of built-up structures on a ceiling or high on a wall, whether it's the underside of a beam or duct that has been finished with drywall, or the underside of the dropped-down portion of ceiling on which kitchen cabinets are constructed. Applying wallpaper over soffits is not especially difficult, and it requires only a few basic techniques. The first step is to determine the pattern placement and to precut the strips that will be needed to the proper length. You'll have to measure all the surfaces where

Soffits

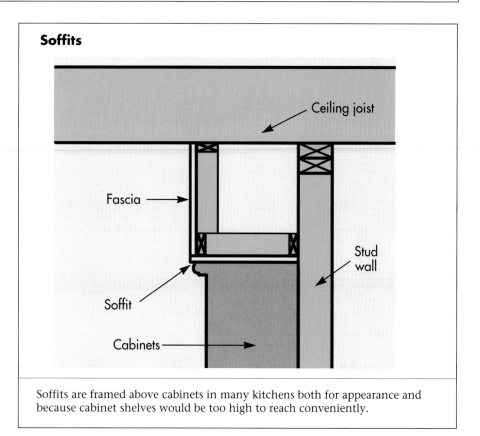

Soffits are framed above cabinets in many kitchens both for appearance and because cabinet shelves would be too high to reach conveniently.

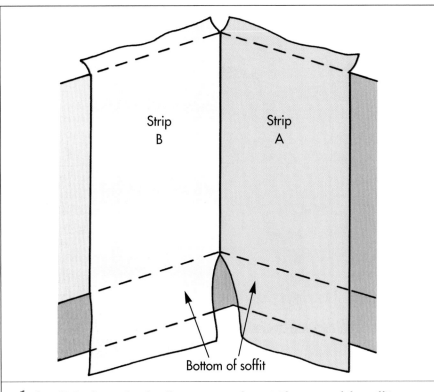

1. Install the first strip of wallpaper across the outside corner of the soffit, making relief cuts at the corners.

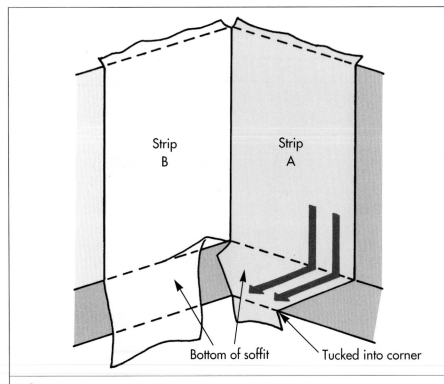

2. The bottom section of the first piece should be smoothed inward, and (using a putty knife) tucked into the back corner.

the paper will go, including the underside section of the soffit, leaving allowances for the top and bottom. Install the wallpaper using the standard techniques that you would use on any other wall. Align the pattern at the ceiling line, and then smooth the wallpaper down the vertical surface. Wrap the paper around the corner, and smooth the underside. When installing wallpaper on soffits, don't make any allowance cuts until you've installed at least three strips. Remember that you can't make any adjustments to a strip once you have trimmed it.

Papering Soffits

Here's the sequence for a typical installation, a box that includes a soffit with an outside corner.

1 Install the first strip, wrapping the edge around the corner approximately 1 inch. Use scissors, a fresh razor blade, or a utility knife to make a relief cut to the corner of the soffit. Install the second strip, bringing the edge of the paper right to the corner. You may need to secure the overlap with vinyl-to-vinyl adhesive.

2 Smooth the bottom section of the first strip (A) to the underside of the soffit, as shown in the illustration. Tuck the paper into the inside corner at the back of the soffit.

3 Smooth the second strip (B) to the underside of the soffit. This creates an overlap between the two corners on the underside, where you will make a mitered double-cut from corner to corner. Carefully trim off the allowances at the top and bottom of the box.

4 Use a straightedge and a razor blade to double-cut through both layers of paper at the overlap, being careful not to cut through to the surface underneath, or use a pad (if you have used one). This forms a 45-degree mitered cut on the underside of the soffit. Remove the excess from the double cut, and join the remaining ends together to form a perfectly fitted seam. Use a seam roller to secure the seam. Bear in mind that the mitered cut frequently results in a pattern mismatch, which is unavoidable because the paper is wrapped from two different directions.

Preparing Inside-Corner Soffits

There are two ways to install wallpaper on a soffit that turns an inside corner: using a single strip or using two strips. To hang a single piece of wallpaper, make a cut in the paper from the bot-

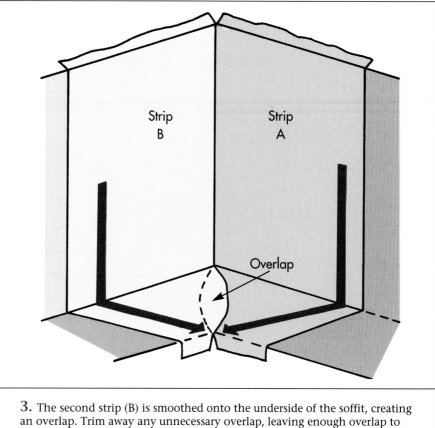

3. The second strip (B) is smoothed onto the underside of the soffit, creating an overlap. Trim away any unnecessary overlap, leaving enough overlap to double-cut a mitered seam at this point. Use a trim guide to tuck the excess into the back corner as tightly as possible.

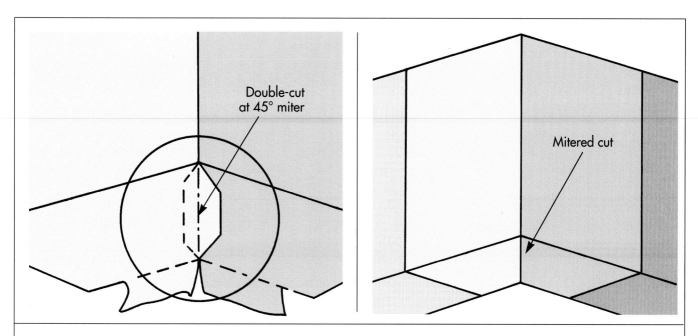

4. Double-cut the seam into the corner. Fold back the top pieces, and remove the excess underneath. When the top pieces fold back down, they should make a perfect mitered seam as shown at right. Press down on the seam with a seam roller. Most patterns will not result in a perfect match on a mitered cut; if this soffit is in a conspicuous spot, you might want to consider a random-patterned paper.

Inside Corner Soffits

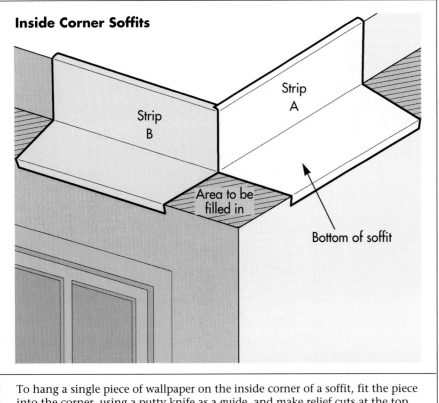

To hang a single piece of wallpaper on the inside corner of a soffit, fit the piece into the corner, using a putty knife as a guide, and make relief cuts at the top and bottom. The square left over will have to be filled with a scrap piece.

tom edge of the soffit down to the allowance. Smooth the wallpaper on the underside in two directions. Fill in the void with a scrap piece of wallpaper.

To hang using two strips, follow these steps.

1 Smooth strip A into the corner. Be sure to allow sufficient paper to go completely to the bottom edge of the soffit underside the adjoining wall. Cut away the excess and make a relief cut as shown.

2 Cut a strip that is identical (Strip B) to the one installed in the corner. Allow enough wallpaper to wrap around on the underside of the adjoining wall. Trim any allowances away.

3 Form a crease using a trim guide or broad knife in the inside corner where strip B intersects with strip A.

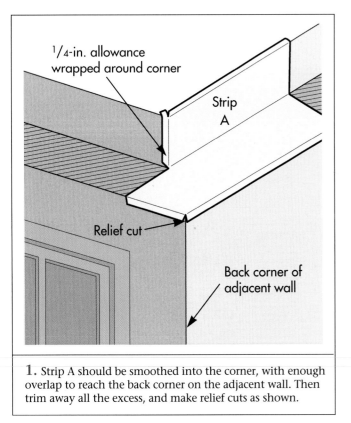

1. Strip A should be smoothed into the corner, with enough overlap to reach the back corner on the adjacent wall. Then trim away all the excess, and make relief cuts as shown.

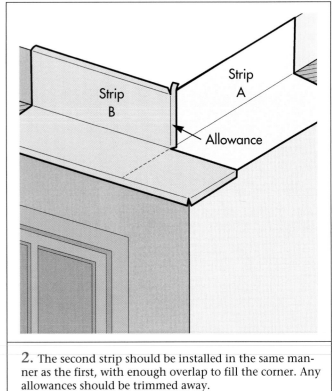

2. The second strip should be installed in the same manner as the first, with enough overlap to fill the corner. Any allowances should be trimmed away.

Use a pair of scissors and cut along the crease. Double-cut at a 45-degree angle from the inside of the corner of the underside of the soffit to the other corner, then remove the excess. Roll with a seam roller to secure the seam. This mitered cut will most likely result in a mismatch for most types of patterns, which are not designed to meet at an angle.

Matched seam. If the underside of the soffit is larger than the fascia, you can sometimes match the pattern at the mitered corner and have it form a mirror image at the seam. (See the illustration below). To achieve this, center the pattern directly on the inside corner.

Recessed Windows

Because of the additional inside corners and tricky pattern matches, recessed windows can be particularly difficult to decorate with wallpaper. However, with careful planning and attention to detail, incorporating a recessed window or door into your papering plan can result in an attractive addition to a wallpaper installation.

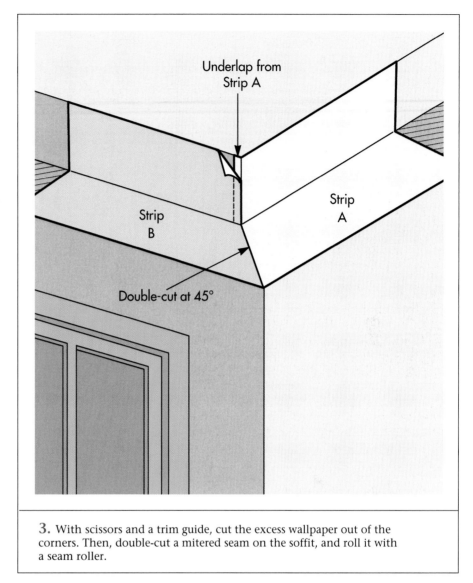

3. With scissors and a trim guide, cut the excess wallpaper out of the corners. Then, double-cut a mitered seam on the soffit, and roll it with a seam roller.

Matched Seam

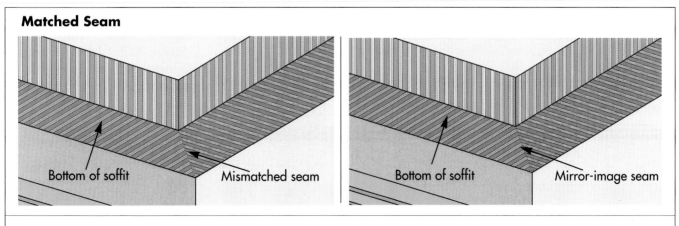

When the underside of the soffit is larger than profile, the mitered corner on the underside may possibly be matched to form a mirror image. The pattern motif must be centered directly into the inside corner of the profile to perform this technique, and therefore may require starting in this location in order to make the mitered soffit underside attractive.

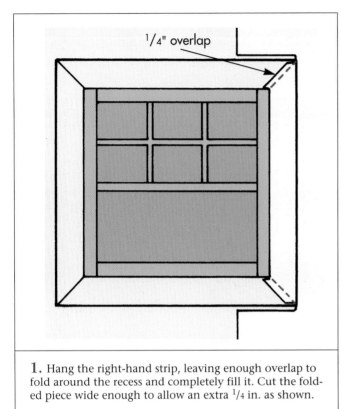

1. Hang the right-hand strip, leaving enough overlap to fold around the recess and completely fill it. Cut the folded piece wide enough to allow an extra 1/4 in. as shown.

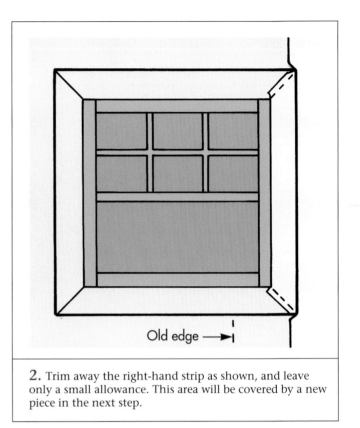

2. Trim away the right-hand strip as shown, and leave only a small allowance. This area will be covered by a new piece in the next step.

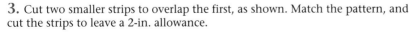

3. Cut two smaller strips to overlap the first, as shown. Match the pattern, and cut the strips to leave a 2-in. allowance.

Papering Recessed Windows

1 Hang a strip over the window opening, and make horizontal cuts about 1/4 inch above and below the window opening. Wrap the left edge of the strip into the recess, smoothing the extra 1/4 inch onto the top and bottom horizontal surfaces as shown in the illustration.

2 Using scissors, cut the remaining left-hand side of the strip away above and below the window. This will leave just a small allowance, as shown.

3 Cut two strips and hang them so that they overlap the first strip. (The left edges will be where the left edge of the first strip was before you cut it away in step 2.) Match the pattern and then cut the right-hand portion of the strips so that 2 inches remain. This will allow you to double-cut the seam.

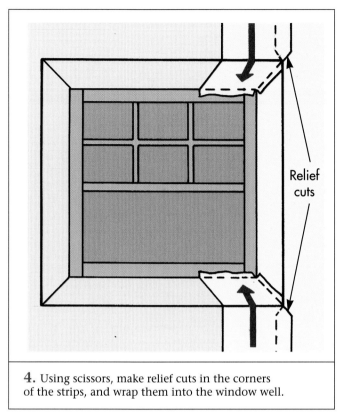

4. Using scissors, make relief cuts in the corners of the strips, and wrap them into the window well.

5. Trim the allowance near the window, and double-cut the overlap between the two strips.

4 Make relief cuts in the strips, and wrap and smooth them onto the top and bottom surfaces of the recess.

5 Trim the allowance cuts next to the window and in the inside corners of the recessed areas. Leave a 1/4-inch underlap around the inside corners when trimming the allowances for the first strip. Once you align the pattern, double-cut through the overlapped sections to form seams between the strips.

6 Cut, paste, and install the center strips, but do not trim the allowances. Cut two full-width strips of wallpaper to use as spacers. Paste or submerge them; then fold and allow them to expand for 5 minutes. Place the spacers at the points shown, and make a temporary guideline exactly in line with the spacers. Place the guideline 1/4 inch beyond the spacers to ensure that

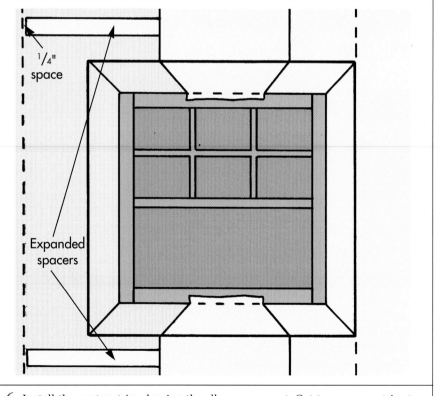

6. Install the center strips, leaving the allowance uncut. Cut two narrow strips to act as spacers, using them as a guide for the installation of the final strips.

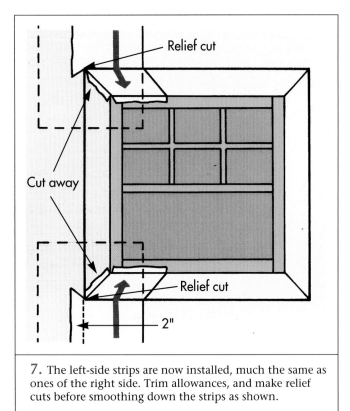

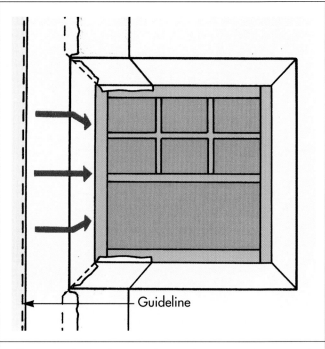

7. The left-side strips are now installed, much the same as ones of the right side. Trim allowances, and make relief cuts before smoothing down the strips as shown.

8. Install the final strip in line with the guideline created by the spacers. Cut away the excess, and wrap the piece around the recess as shown.

the chalk or pencil lead will not penetrate the seam. Remove the spacers.

7 Install the left-side strips. Cut away the left sides, leaving 2 inches for double-cutting. Make relief cuts as shown, and wrap and smooth the strips onto the horizontal part of the recess. Do not trim the allowances.

8 Install a strip in line with the guideline, and allow it to overlap the strips installed in step 7. Cut away the strip above and below the recess, and wrap the strip onto the vertical wall of the recess as shown.

9 To complete the installation, double-cut through the overlap on the strips to form seams. Remove the excess pieces, and trim all remaining allowance cuts.

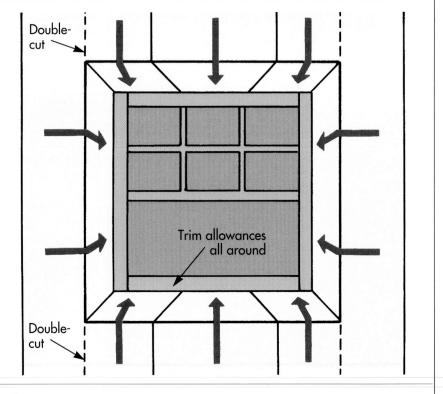

9. As you reach the end of the sequence, all seams should be double-cut to form perfect seams, and all allowances should be trimmed.

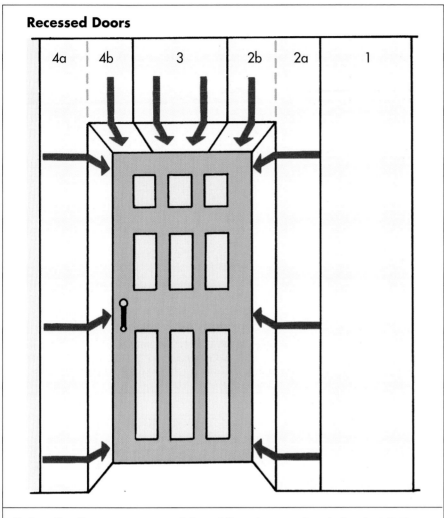

Recessed Doors

To install wallpaper on a recessed door, follow the steps for window installation; the strips should be installed as numbered in this illustration.

Recessed Doors. If you are installing wallpaper on a recessed door, use the basic techniques described for the recessed window, and follow the sequence shown in the illustration.

Archways

To get the best result on an archway, carefully plan the seam placement. If you position the seams to extend into the arch, each strip will completely wrap the inside of the arch. This prevents having a seam close to the corners of the arch, as well as within the archway itself.

Preparing an Archway

1 Hang the strips as shown. Make relief cuts in the side strips at the point where the arch begins its inward curve. Wrap and smooth the strip onto the recessed surface. If you are installing wallpaper on both sides of the arch, you can match the pattern in the recess up to the point where the arch begins curving. Trim the paper about 1/8 inch from the far opening, to prevent fraying.

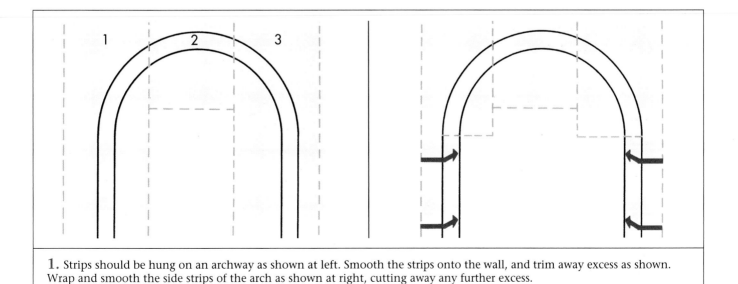

1. Strips should be hung on an archway as shown at left. Smooth the strips onto the wall, and trim away excess as shown. Wrap and smooth the side strips of the arch as shown at right, cutting away any further excess.

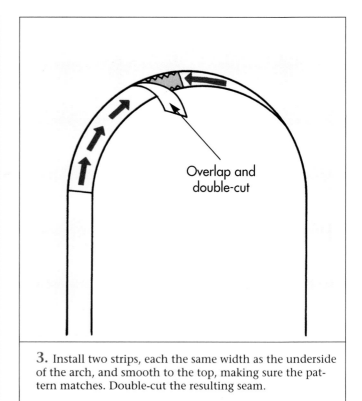

2. Trim the paper in an arch 1 in. larger than the wall arch, and then make a series of small relief cuts the entire length of the arch.

3. Install two strips, each the same width as the underside of the arch, and smooth to the top, making sure the pattern matches. Double-cut the resulting seam.

2 Trim the paper to within 1 inch of the arch wall, and then make a series of notch cuts. Wrap the allowance under the arch.

3 Cut two strips, each the thickness of the arch. Match and install each strip at the beginning of the arch, and smooth them to the top of the arch. The overlap where the two strips meet should be double-cut to provide a smooth butt seam.

Dormers

Dormers present unique challenges; in a way, they are like little houses unto themselves, complete with walls, trim, and sloping walls or ceilings—all coming together in a small space where room can be tight. Planning and attention to detail are the secrets to good results. The steps below show some of the special techniques involved.

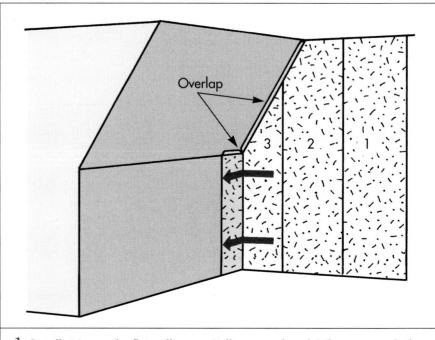

1. Install strips on the flat wall sequentially, as numbered. When you reach the eaves wall, overlap $1/2$ in. onto the sloped section.

1 Install the wallpaper on the vertical portion of the wall. Notice that strips 2 and 3 overlap the section of sloped wall approximately $1/2$ inch above where the flat and sloped walls intersect.

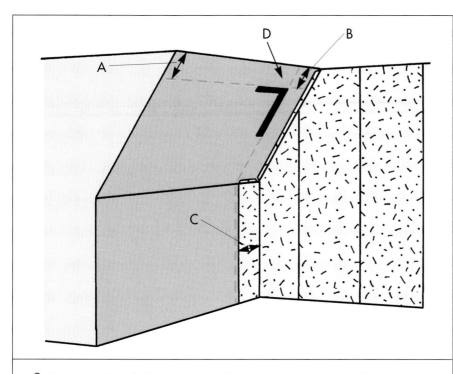

2. Snap a vertical chalk line for your first strip on the sloped wall. Measure down identical distances from the ceiling (A & B), and snap a horizontal line between them. Then measure $1/4$ in. past the inside corner strip (C), and use this line to draw your vertical guideline (D).

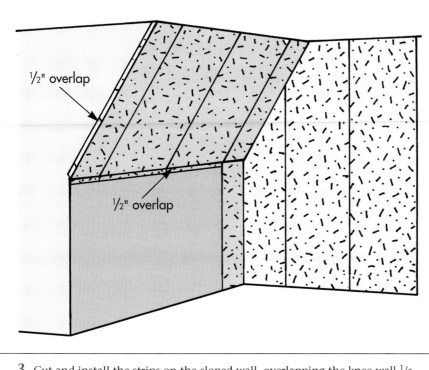

½" overlap

½" overlap

3. Cut and install the strips on the sloped wall, overlapping the knee wall $1/2$ in. The corner strip also overlaps the corner by $1/2$ in.

2 Establish guidelines for the first strip you will install on the sloped wall. Start by measuring down from the ceiling at points A and B. You can use any random measurement, just as long as you repeat it so that both marks fall on a line parallel with the ceiling. Snap a chalk line between these two points to create a horizontal guideline.

Next, measure $1/4$ inch past the edge of the inside corner strip at point C on the knee wall. Transfer this measurement to the sloped ceiling at point D on the horizontal chalk line. Use a framing square, and draw as much of the vertical guideline as you can. Extend it downward using a yardstick or other long straightedge. Remember that complex intersections such as these are likely to have dimensions and angles that are not exactly constant, particularly on older homes. There may be minor discrepancies where you need the lap for coverage—for instance, where walls do not form a right angle and where a rafter or two in the dormer or the ceiling may have settled a bit.

3 Cut and install the first sloped-wall strip, carefully following the guidelines. Secure the overlaps extending from the corner strips with a vinyl-to-vinyl adhesive to prevent peeling later on. Continue this section by installing the remaining sloped-wall strips until you reach the outside corner. Remember that you have two laps to deal with, and allow each strip to overlap the knee wall $1/2$ inch. The last strip should also overlap the outside corner $1/2$ inch where the corner of the dormer makes the transition from the sloping wall to a flat wall.

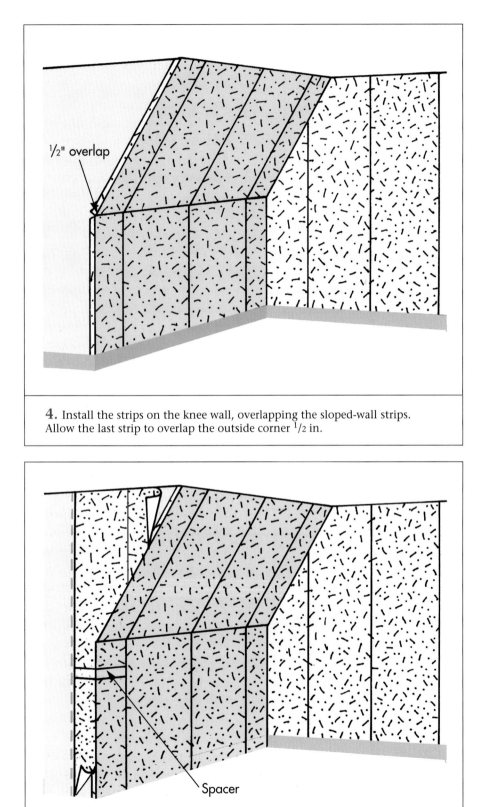

½" overlap

4. Install the strips on the knee wall, overlapping the sloped-wall strips. Allow the last strip to overlap the outside corner ¹/₂ in.

Spacer

5. Apply a spacer as shown, and then snap a chalk line ¹/₄ in. past the spacer. Install the full strip at the corner, matching the pattern if necessary.

4 Install the knee wall strips, allowing them to overlap the sloped wall strips in the horizontal corner. Secure overlaps using vinyl-to-vinyl adhesive. Allow the last knee wall strip (the outside corner strip) to wrap around the corner ¹/₂ inch.

5 Place an expanded spacer at the seam of the last full knee-wall strip installed, and wrap the outside corner. Make a mark ¹/₄ inch past the spacer, and then establish a plumb guideline at this point. Install a full-length strip as shown. If the wallpaper has a matching pattern, it should match the knee-wall strip exactly in the corner. Trim the full-length, strip and secure the overlaps using vinyl-to-vinyl adhesive.

To finish the installation, continue toward the other side of the dormer, and then reverse the procedure to install the strips on the walls of the opposite side.

Concrete Block or Brick Walls

One alternative to covering a concrete block or brick wall with drywall is to use wallpaper. Obviously, the uneven surfaces of these kinds of walls will still be visible through wallpaper. However, with proper planning and preparation, you can minimize this unevenness.

The first thing to consider is the type of wallpaper you will be installing. A floral pattern or other random design will hide unevenness better than a plain texture or stripe. A heavily embossed texture with a matte finish, such as a fiberglass wallcovering, will work best to obscure imperfections, much better than a smooth, shiny sur-

face. The second factor to consider is the ambient lighting. The more glare there is, the more the imperfections of the wall will be apparent. You will get the best results if the room has indirect lighting. As far as the wall preparation goes, the most important factor to consider is the presence of moisture on the inside of the structure. This moisture may cause a mildew problem or weaken the adhesive so that the wallpaper simply won't adhere properly to the walls.

To bridge over mortar joints and to camouflage the surface of the concrete or brick, you can install a heavyweight liner paper. You should first apply an acrylic wallpaper primer-sealer to the concrete or brick walls and allow it to dry for a minimum of 24 hours before installing the liner. If the walls are new, first seal them with a block sealer before applying the acrylic wallpaper primer-sealer. After installing the liner paper, repair any area that still looks bad using joint compound. If the walls still are too uneven to provide a satisfactory appearance, rethink the project. You may get better results if you frame out the wall with furring strips and install drywall.

Prefinished Paneling

If you want to install wallpaper over prefinished paneling, you will obtain the best results by using these techniques:

■ Check all the edges of the paneling, and renail or replace any panels wherever necessary.

■ Wash all paneling with a solution of equal parts of ammonia and water to remove any wax or dirt buildup that may be present. Allow this to dry before proceeding.

■ Lightly sand the entire surface of the paneling using 80-grit sandpaper so that the primer-sealer will properly bond to it.

■ Apply a wallpaper acrylic primer-sealer to the entire paneled surface. To be safe, allow it to dry a minimum of 24 hours.

■ Install a medium-weight liner paper. You should always install the paper horizontally on the paneling, to bridge over all the vertical grooves. Allow the liner paper to dry a minimum of 24 hours.

■ Using a 100-watt light and drop cord, check to see whether any liner paper has shrunk into the grooves of the paneling. If necessary, fill in sunken areas using a lightweight water-based joint compound. Do not use an oil-based product because it will penetrate the final layer of wallpaper and cause it to stain. Some installers recommend that you fill the grooves of prefinished paneling prior to installing the wallpaper or liner paper. In some cases, however, the adhesive can bond to the joint compound and cause it to shrink. The best result can be obtained by filling after the liner paper is installed.

■ Install the final layer of wallpaper onto the liner paper. If you're installing a prepasted wallpaper, apply another layer of wallpaper acrylic primer-sealer over the liner. This helps prevent the liner from soaking up the moisture from the adhesive.

Before installing wallpaper over new concrete or brick walls, apply a block sealer, allow it to dry, and then apply an acrylic wallpaper primer-sealer. In addition, you should hang a medium-weight liner on the wall before papering.

Chapter 8

Trouble-shooting

When a professional finishes hanging your wall-paper, chances are you won't notice any prob-lems. There may have been a few imperfections along the way—maybe a loose seam or a couple of air bubbles. But you probably never saw them because the pro resealed the seam and popped the bubbles without leaving a trace. That's one of the main differences between do-it-yourselfers and professionals: Both make mistakes, but pros make slicker repairs.

If you hang your own wallpaper, of course, you might wind up with a few imperfections you didn't expect. Even handy do-it-yourselfers have to expect their fair share. But there are three kinds of trouble you don't need, and all three are relatively easy to avoid: defects in the wallpaper due to manufacturing mistakes, defects in the supporting wall due to preparation mistakes, and defects that occur due to bad layout and planning.

The first thing you should do after you take delivery of materials is to make sure all rolls have the same dye-lot and pattern numbers. Remember, subtle color variations within the pattern may change the pattern number by only one digit. Check that multicolor patterns are not out of regis-ter, where one color pokes out behind another to create a blurred edge. The few minutes you spend checking the paper for flaws before it's on the wall can save hours of painstaking work stripping it off. (See "Material Problems," on page 125.)

The next step is to ensure proper wall preparation. This includes washing the walls thoroughly and sanding down any rough spots. If there is already wallpaper on the wall, you can remove it—or, if it won't come off easily, secure loose edges and seams with the appropriate adhesive, prime the entire surface, and wallpaper right over it. One of the most important points of wall preparation is to prime and seal with a good wallpaper primer-sealer. This helps bond poor-quality paint to the drywall surface and pre-pares the surface for adhesive. It's also important to seal any recently patched areas.

The final step is to plan carefully before you begin a pro-ject. Wallpapering can be tricky—and sticky— especially if the room has many windows and doors, or some unusual feature such as soffits or dormers. And once the wallpaper has dried, it's generally impossible to salvage a bad job. You can use seam adhesive to rescue loose edges and dab artist's watercolors (or markers provided by the manufacturer) in seams that have gapped. But your best bet is to antici-

pate problems that might crop up before it's too late to fix them.

Take your time, and make a careful layout, planning the location of every seam. It may help to cut a sample strip that you can try in different parts of the room to see where seams will fall. That will allow you to catch troublesome spots—for example, where a seam falls almost but not quite on a piece of trim. Checking your plan ahead of time with a piece of the wallpaper you'll be installing can also save you from making errors such as installing strong vertical patterns where the walls are noticeably out of plumb. Sometimes you can simplify the installation and save material by moving one seam just a few inches.

Patch Repairs

When it's more practical to repair existing wallpaper than to replace it, especially when the problem is limited to a small area, follow these steps to camouflage a repair: The overall plan is to create a patch piece larger than the damaged area and position it so you can make a double cut.

Spot Patching

1 Cut a circle around the damaged area using a razor blade.

2 Remove the damaged paper to the cut line. If the wallpaper is paper-backed, you might have to sand the area and use warm soapy water to soften the old adhesive. Work carefully with your scraper when you remove the paper so that you don't gouge the wall and complicate matters with a new repair on top of the original problem.

1. Small ripped areas of wallpaper are easily repaired with a patch. To make a patch repair to a damaged piece of wallpaper, first cut a circle around the damaged area with a razor, just a few inches larger than the tear. Be careful not to mar the wall beneath the paper.

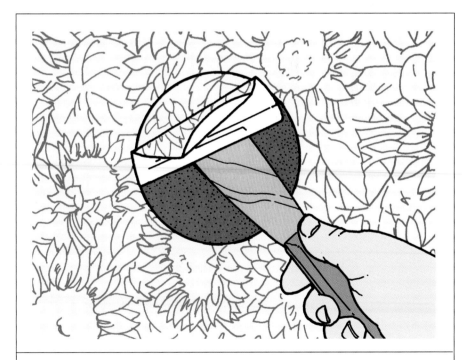

2. Using a scraper or a small drywall knife, remove the area you have cut out, being careful not to damage any wallpaper outside of the circle. You may need to remove any adhesive still stuck on the wall, and sand down the area that will be patched.

3 Cut a clean repair piece of wall-paper, at least 1 inch larger in diameter than the circle. Paste it, and allow it to relax in a booked position for about 5 minutes. Then position the repair piece, and match up the pattern as best you can. On papers with intricate patterns you will probably find that it pays to try several alignments before pasting.

4 With the patch in place, use a new razor blade to double-cut through the overlapped area of the repair. Make sure to hold the blade perfectly perpendicular to the wall; otherwise, a white seam may show. To further conceal the new piece, follow a pattern outline wherever possible. If you take the time to cut around the outline of a flower, for instance, no one will notice the seam. Lastly, remove the cut ends from the wall, and clean up excess paste.

Material Problems

Some manufacturing flaws you should watch out for include printing on the bias and flaking ink. You can't repair these conditions in the field and should return the rolls for credit. Check the edges of the wallpaper, too. Sometimes a dirty roller used in manufacturing causes black marks on the edges of the roll. If you can't clean these marks off, return the roll. Also check the edges to make sure they are smooth. A wobbly trim wheel can result in rough or scalloped edges and unsightly gaps in the seams when you hang the paper on the wall.

Black edges. Black edges are due to using dirty trimming devices to remove the selvage from the edges of the wall-

3. Cut a repair piece larger than the circle. If your wallpaper pattern has a large-scale design, cut a piece that will enable you to match the pattern. Paste or soak the patch piece, and allow it to expand for about 5 min. Then position it over the circle, matching the pattern as closely as possible.

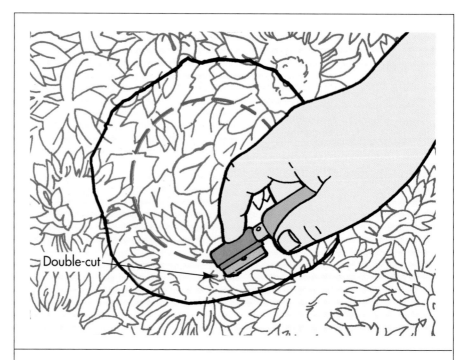

4. Make a double cut through the overlapped part of the top piece, following a pattern outline if possible to conceal the seam that will result. Remove the excess pieces from the patch. This should result in a perfectly matched, nearly invisible seam.

paper at the factory. You can usually eliminate them by using a wire seam (page 62) to lap a clean edge over the dirty edge or by using a double-cut seam (pages 62–63). If these techniques are not practical, don't install the wallpaper —return it to the supplier for credit.

Delamination. This is the separation of a wallpaper substrate from the decorative surface or intermediate layer of vinyl. The usual cause is excessive soaking before installation on the wall. Grasscloth, stringcloth, rushcloth, and jute are examples of wallpapers that delaminate easily.

Fabric fraying. Some fabric-type wallpapers (particularly the unbacked ones) are prone to fraying during installation. One major cause is inadequate pressure on the trim guide when trimming the allowance edges. A second cause is using the wrong adhesive. Use a small (3-inch) putty knife as a trim guide to help prevent fraying. File or sand the edge of the putty knife so it is fairly sharp, to help secure the fabric tightly when trimming. If the seams still fray, install several strips at a time, and do not secure the seams. Then use a small brush to apply a thinned clay-based adhesive to the wall surface under the seam areas. Let the adhesive set up for 3 to 5 minutes to establish tack; then secure the seams carefully with a cloth seam roller or light pressure with the palms of the hands. Before you use this technique, test the fabric for any show-through of the tan-colored adhesive. If the adhesive does show, consider painting the wall surface a light tan color to camouflage the adhesive.

Black Edges

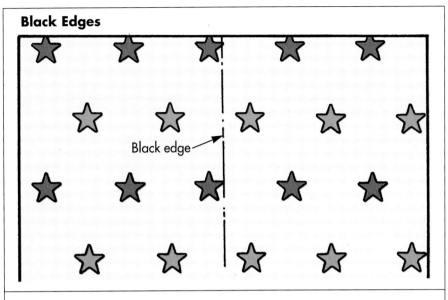

Black edges will result if the device used to trim the selvage at the factory is dirty—you might only see the blackened edges when you install the wallpaper. You can hide this by using the wire-seam method, but it's best to return the wallpaper.

Delamination

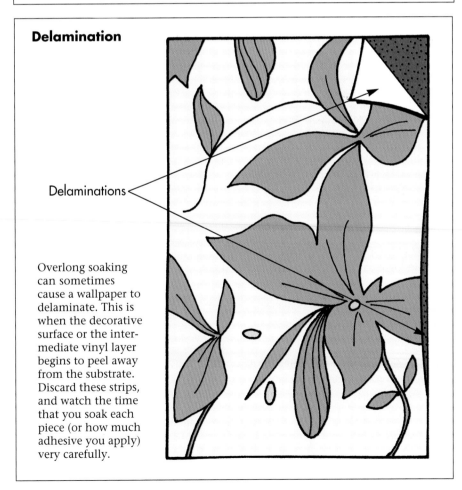

Overlong soaking can sometimes cause a wallpaper to delaminate. This is when the decorative surface or the intermediate vinyl layer begins to peel away from the substrate. Discard these strips, and watch the time that you soak each piece (or how much adhesive you apply) very carefully.

Grease and oil stains. You can usually wipe off grease and oil stains on washable vinyl wallcovering but not on paper-based wallpaper, where even small amounts of body oil from your hands can leave a mark. Normal cleaning can do more harm than good because you can't use abrasives or scrub vigorously without damaging the paper surface. A slightly unorthodox but practical solution is to cover the spot with blotter paper and press down gently with a warm iron. The heat loosens and thins the grease, which the blotter paper then absorbs. It's difficult to get out every trace of a stain in one shot. But if you have the patience for repeated treatments using a fresh section of blotter paper, eventually the spot will be unnoticeable.

Ink flaking. There are several factors that can cause ink to flake off a wallpaper surface. Creasing the wallpaper during installation can break the ink away from the wallpaper surface. Abrasive detergents, contamination from adhesive, and excessive adhesive moisture also cause ink flaking. Sometimes an adhesive (especially a premixed type) contains solvents or chemicals that can cause wallpaper inks to flake. Avoid contamination by cleaning the adhesive from the decorative surface as you install the wallpaper. A natural sea sponge works best, but be sure to keep the rinse water clean. Immediately dry the wallpaper surface after using the sponge to completely remove any adhesive residue from the decorative surface.

Over-worked paper. This is the result of reapplying a strip of wallpaper several times in an attempt to successfully install it. The strip will be stretched beyond its natural limits, thereby causing it to shrink excessively as the adhesive dries, possibly creating a pattern mismatch. Never force a strip of wallpaper into position with another strip. Instead, immediately and gently remove and realign it—beginning at the seaming edge.

Pattern-repeat inconsistency. This may result when the tension on the manufacturer's printing machine is not consistent all the way through the roll. This is a condition you can't do much about except return the paper and try another roll from a different production run. But this same visual inconsistency also can occur when the wall surface is not perfectly even. Whatever the cause, this problem causes the vertical pattern repeats to mismatch from the top to the bottom of the strip. A pattern may match at eye level, for example, but will not match at a higher or lower level on the wall. Some do-it-yourselfers are misled by this condition and assume that the mismatch must be due to their own mistakes in applying the paper. The trouble only gets worse when they start to work on the paper to align the pattern and stretch it out of shape. Generally, the industry standard for an acceptable pattern mismatch is 1/8 inch per 8 feet. If the match is off more than 1/8 inch, the wallpaper should be returned to the supplier.

Printing on the bias (out-of-square). One of the most important steps during wallpaper inspection is checking the squareness of the wallpaper pattern with the edge of the wallpaper. Make sure that the pattern design is printed

Pattern-Repeat Inconsistency

A pattern-repeat inconsistency will occur when a pattern is perfectly matched at one part of the seam but has drifted slightly out of alignment on another part of the wall. This is caused either by a varying of tension on the manufacturer's machine or by an uneven wall surface.

METHOD 1

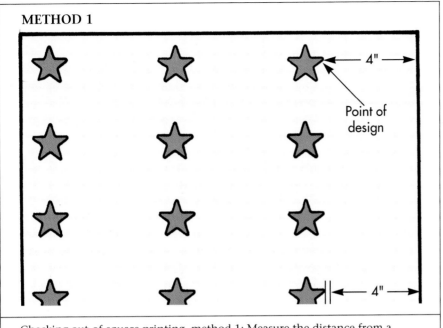

Point of design

4"

4"

Checking out-of-square printing, method 1: Measure the distance from a particular point on the design to the edge of the paper in a number of places up and down the strip; any discrepancy shows printing on the bias.

square on the wallpaper and not at an angle with the edge. If it is at an angle, then the pattern will run either uphill or downhill after the wallpaper is installed. This flaw is referred to as being printed on the bias or out of square. There are three methods for checking the bias of wallpaper:

METHOD 1: Measure the distance from a point of design on the wallpaper to the edge of the wallpaper. Then, using the same point of design, compare that distance with several identical vertical repeats for a distance of 10 to 15 linear feet. The distance should be constant. If it is not, the print cannot be square with the wallpaper and won't look right even when the paper is straight.

METHOD 2: Align one edge of a carpenter's framing square with the edge of the wallpaper and compare

either the horizontal pattern repeats (motifs) or a divided pattern design on a straight-across match with the squareness of the edge. They should align perfectly along the straightedge. If they do not, the print is out of square, or on the bias, with the edge.

METHOD 3: Fold the wallpaper strip, and align the edges. While holding the wallpaper securely in this position, flatten the paper to form a sharp crease at the fold. This crease will represent a perfect 90-degree angle with the edge of the wallpaper; therefore, any horizontal pattern repeats (motifs) should align perfectly with the crease, or the adjoining details of a straight across pattern should line up with the crease.

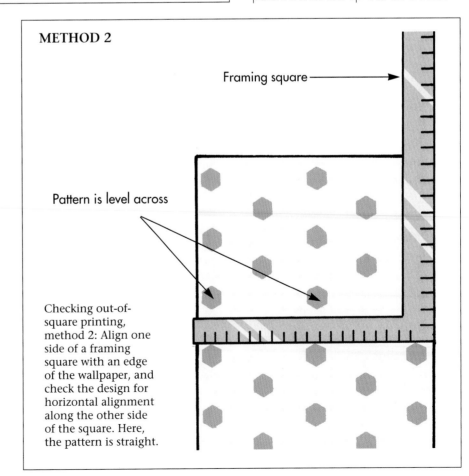

METHOD 2

Framing square

Pattern is level across

Checking out-of-square printing, method 2: Align one side of a framing square with an edge of the wallpaper, and check the design for horizontal alignment along the other side of the square. Here, the pattern is straight.

METHOD 2, *continued*

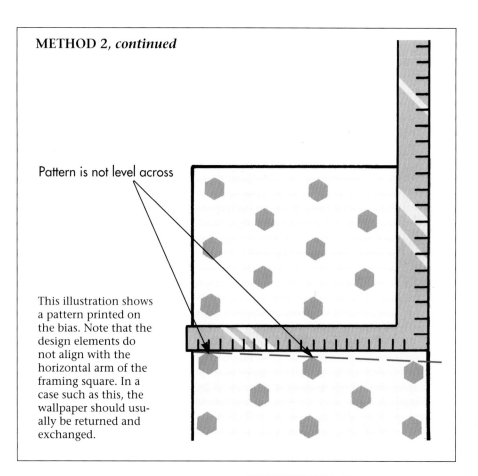

Pattern is not level across

This illustration shows a pattern printed on the bias. Note that the design elements do not align with the horizontal arm of the framing square. In a case such as this, the wallpaper should usually be returned and exchanged.

Always check pattern squareness before beginning the installation.

Scalloped edges. Scalloped edges result from the selvage being unevenly trimmed at the factory, thus leaving a wavy effect on the edges. You can compensate by using the seam-coloring technique. (See Chapter 5, "Patterns & Seams," page 69.) A slight over lapping wire seam is effective, but only about half the time. If standard butt seams are used with scalloped edges, then gaps will appear where the edges are not trimmed properly. If the seams cannot be joined satisfactorily, then don't install the wallpaper.

Screen marks. Screen marks are ink smears or smudges on the decorative surface of the wallpaper. They are caused when the screen printing device is either picked up or put down during the print-

If a one-half drop match is being checked, simply fold the wallpaper exactly from one vertical repeat to that identical vertical repeat. The crease will be exactly half the distance of the vertical repeats; therefore, you can examine the one-half drop pattern for squareness.

When dominant patterns such as plaids and checks are on the bias, the wallpaper should not be installed. If the pattern design is a floral print, the wallpaper strips may be tilted slightly off plumb to compensate for out-of-squareness. But remember, if a wallpaper pattern is 1/8 inch out of square across a single strip, the design will fall away 1/8 inch from a level horizontal ceiling line or chair rail, and that will equal one full inch every eight strips.

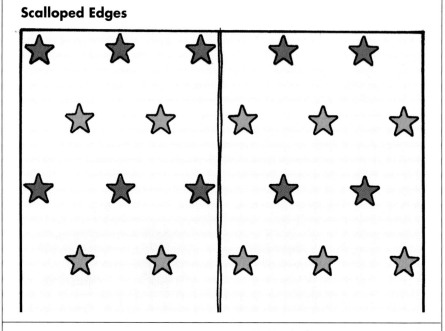

Scalloped Edges

Scalloped edges occur due to uneven selvage trimming at the factory, which results in this wavy effect on the seams. If the seams are too wide to hide by coloring the gaps or using wire seams, then you should return the paper.

Screen Marks

Screen marks such as these are a result of errors in the screen-printing process. If they are obvious, the paper should be returned and exchanged.

Selvage, Overtrimmed

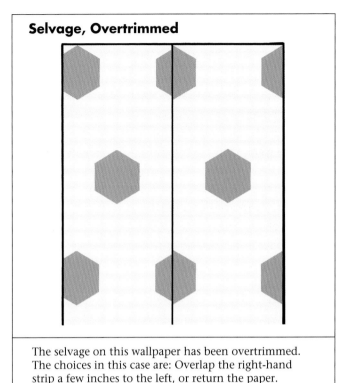

The selvage on this wallpaper has been overtrimmed. The choices in this case are: Overlap the right-hand strip a few inches to the left, or return the paper.

ing process. The marks may appear in screen-printed materials printed by machine or by hand. The imprint effect can vary widely depending on printing conditions. You may barely see the marks under the bright lights of a new installation in a bare room, and you could lose sight of them altogether under more typical conditions. But if the marks are noticeable even in normal lighting, don't install the paper.

Selvage, under- and overtrimmed. This problem occurs when a wallpaper's selvage has not been trimmed at the proper place on the edge. Under-trimmed selvage will result in too much background showing at the edge, or cause a double image to appear at the joined seams. Sometimes allowing a slight overlap and using the double-cutting technique can correct the problem. Overtrimmed selvage, because there is a noticeable sliver missing from

the design, is almost impossible to fix. If a pattern repeats many times horizontally, you can overlap the seam by enough to match the pattern toward the center of the paper.

Uneven embossment. In addition to potential mistakes in two dimensions—the length and width alignment of decorative surface patterns—some wallpaper has its pattern built into the third dimension of thickness. Embossed papers are like low-relief sculptures, typically with a raised pattern and a recessed background. The relief itself may form the pattern the way it does on reproduction papers such as Anaglypta, or be used with a color pattern. Problems with embossing will cause shiny streaks to appear once two strips of wallpaper are joined at the seam. If the embossment is raised or textured more on one side of the paper than the other, it will create an uneven surface once the

wallpaper is installed. If the wallpaper is embossed using the hot-embossed method, an uneven application of heat that warms one side of the paper more than the other will create a shiny or slick appearance at the seams. Uneven embossment (whether hot or cold) is a manufacturer's defect and the wallpaper should not be installed.

Problems with Wall Preparation

If the walls have cracks, you should determine whether the surfaces are still cracking and make repairs before you try to install wallpaper. For new houses, some pros suggest that to be on the safe side you should wait a year after constructing a house before you install wallpaper—enough time for the structure to settle. Usually you can fill cracks by first cleaning out loose wall material, then by filling with patching plaster or joint

compound and sanding the surface smooth. Once you repair the cracks, remember to prime the walls with wallpaper primer-sealer before installing wallpaper. If you forget this step, the dry, unsealed repair areas will suck moisture from the wallpaper adhesive and create weak spots or air bubbles.

Alligation (Alligator cracks). This web-like cracking, so-named because it resembles alligator skin, occurs when a primer-sealer or adhesive does not bond properly to a wall surface. The usual cause is a contaminant such as grease, wax, or dirt on the wall surface. Proper wall preparation will prevent this problem. Clean the walls thoroughly using a solution of equal parts ammonia and water—never use a cleansing agent that contains phosphorous—and lightly sand the area after it dries. Alligation can also occur as a result of applying a primer-sealer at temperatures below 45 degrees Fahrenheit or by inadequate mixing of the primer-sealer.

Liner paper. The major problem associated with liner paper is in its application to the wall surface. Because liners are used to prepare uneven wall surfaces such as paneling, concrete block, and ceramic tile, it is important that this surface be properly prepared. The major problem is poor bonding to the wall surface. This is frequently caused by poor wall preparation, particularly the failure to remove dirt, grease, wax, or other foreign substances from the wall surface. There are also times when the decorative wallpaper will not properly bond to the liner paper. This is generally caused by using the wrong adhesive (or wrong viscosity) or by an

improper amount of adhesive on prepasted wallpapers. It is sometimes necessary to apply a wallpaper primer-sealer over the liner to prevent it from absorbing too much moisture from the adhesive of the decorative wallpaper.

Mildew and moisture. Mildew appears most often in vinyl, foils, and other nonporous wallcoverings that trap moisture behind them. To prevent mildew from forming, it helps to use a quick-drying adhesive with an added fungicide. Once the gray-green dots of mildew appear, the most difficult solution is to remove the paper, wash the wall with a fungicide, and let it dry completely before resealing the wall and applying new paper.

Sometimes the pattern of mildew signals other problems. If you see mildew concentrated in vertical strips, the cause may be a pipe sweating in the wall cavity. Short of tearing open the wall to insulate the pipes or fix a leak, try drilling a hole near the bottom of the cavity and installing a plug vent—the aluminum grille-type vent normally used to ventilate a soffit in a roof overhang. It will provide an outlet that lets at least some of the moisture escape.

If you have a problem on an exterior wall, consider adding a layer of insulation under the siding or having insulation pumped into the wall cavity itself. Adding insulation reduces the temperature variation of the interior wall surface and makes it less likely to attract the condensation that fosters mildew. Before hanging paper on a wall where mildew is likely to form, several precautions can minimize problems later on. First, keep the area well ventilated. Second, use wallboard panels chemically treated to resist moisture. Third, wash existing walls with a fungicide before hanging paper, or use

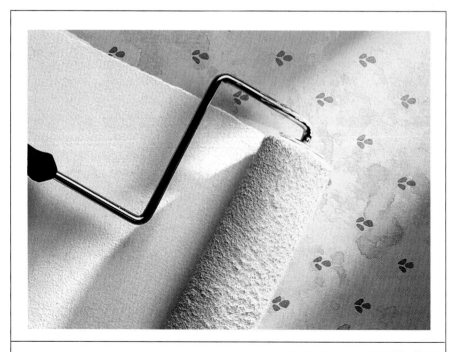

A mildew-stained wall should be washed with a fungicide, then sealed with a wallpaper primer-sealer pigmented to hide stains. Seriously mildewed paper should always be removed.

a homemade brew of three parts water and one part household bleach.

Paint deterioration. In new construction, builders sometimes paint the walls with builder's flat—watered-down drywall mud—or with a poor-quality flat latex paint. Eventually, paper installed over this material falls off or comes loose at the seams. You can confirm the presence of poor-quality paint or builder's flat by the appearance of paint on the backing of the peeling wallpaper. To prevent this problem, apply a high-quality acrylic pigmented wallpaper primer-sealer or an oil-based enamel undercoat (thinned with one quart of paint thinner per gallon) to the wall. The primer-sealer or undercoat will soak into the bad paint and help bond it to the wall surface. *Note: Wall sizing provides uniform porosity on a porous wall surface; however, this product alone will not hold poor latex paint together.*

Paint flaking. When paint flakes from the wall surface, you must scrape it off and repair it before you can install wallpaper. Use a broad knife, scraper, or putty knife. If you don't remove the flaking paint, it will crumble and crack as the adhesive dries and eventually pull away from the wall.

Sand-painted walls. If you want to install wallpaper over a sand-painted wall, the only way to get satisfactory results is to remove the sand finish. You must then apply a wallpaper primer-sealer before installing wallpaper.

Stains. Stains can sometimes appear underneath the wallpaper or in the seams when you use a clay-based adhesive to install semitransparent wallcoverings. Make sure to form seams carefully, and do not allow air to get underneath them, or the adhesive may turn dark brown. Sometimes there are existing problems or wall conditions that a standard wallpaper primer-sealer will not correct. These may include smoke, grease, crayon marks, ink marks, water stains, food stains, graffiti, and nicotine. In these cases, use a special stain-killing primer-sealer. This product secures or prevents these types of stains from bleeding through a wallpaper primer-sealer or an application of paint. However, it is not a wallpaper primer-sealer by itself—apply a wallpaper primer-sealer over the stain-killing primer-sealer as well as the rest of the wall before you install the new wallpaper. Mildew problems also can form beneath the wallpaper. When this happens, they commonly show up as green or purple spots and in a circular or starburst shape. Gradually, the spots begin to merge. The only cure for the problem is to remove the wallcovering and eliminate the mildew fungus.

Transparency. Some wallpaper is semitransparent, and any contrasting colors or existing wall images can show through the new wallpaper. To eliminate showthrough, apply a pigmented wallpaper primer-sealer or install a liner paper.

Problems with Seams

Curling seams. You can prevent seam curling by applying a thinned claybased adhesive to the seaming and

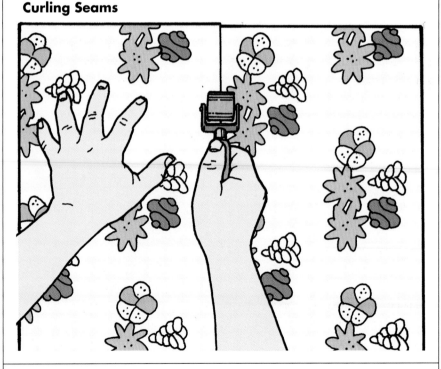

Curling Seams

To fix curling seams right on the wall, brush a little seam adhesive onto the back of the curling edge. With gentle pressure, roll the seam back down on the wall using a seam roller.

trimming areas several hours before the installation. Once the clay-based adhesive dries, it acts as a blotter or sponge within the seaming area. The moisture within the wallpaper's adhesive then soaks into the clay-based adhesive, creating a high tack. The clay-based adhesive also forces the seams or edges to set up much faster than the other sections of the wallpaper strip, preventing shrinkage and gapped seams. To fix a curling edge you can brush seam adhesive onto the back of the edge. Gently press the seam together, and then roll it lightly with a seam roller.

Puckering. This problem usually occurs at the seams as a result of continued expansion of the wallpaper during the installation. The adhesive is still moist enough to force the expansion to the seam rather than in vertical blisters. To eliminate puckers, immediately remove the strip, re-apply extra adhesive (if it is needed), and allow extra relaxing time before hanging. To fix a slightly puckered edge, carefully roll a seam roller over the joined edges. If the puckering is substantial, you might have to overlap one edge or even double-cut the seam using a razor blade. But if you do overlap seams, the overlaps should be in the direction away from the dominant light source in the room, to make them less noticeable. Secure the overlap seam with vinyl-on-vinyl adhesive.

Shrinking. Prepasted wallpaper is especially notorious for seam shrinkage. To compensate for this, some wallpaper manufacturers offer special felt-tip pens or crayons tinted in the same color as the wallpaper background. You simply draw down the seam with

The most careful preparation and installation is needed in baths, where moisture from showers work away at seam adhesive—particularly around windows where there are abrupt temperature changes and more condensation.

the pen to help hide the seam. You can get the same effect by mixing and diluting watercolor paint to match the wallpaper background. Use a small brush to apply the diluted paint to the seam. Wipe off any excess across the seam with a damp cloth. Be sure to use only watercolors or acrylic-based paint. Oil-based paints can cause wallpaper ink to run or smear.

There are several causes of shrinking on nonprepasted papers.

■ Not applying enough adhesive. Wallpaper can expand between 1 and 2 percent of its width, and if you don't put on enough adhesive, it can shrink back to its original size before the adhesion on the wall can stop it.

■ Letting the wallpaper dry out. If you let the wallpaper relax and expand too

long after you paste it, the edges can dry before you hang it on the wall.

■ Allowing excessive moisture, which can cause some types of wallpaper to contract. To help prevent this, install an absorbent liner paper on the wall to soak up the excess moisture from the adhesive.

■ Using excessive pressure. If you apply too much pressure to the seams during installation, they may curl back like springs. If you make a mistake, it's better to remove the entire strip and re-align it to the previous seam.

■ Hanging paper in temperature extremes. Working in temperatures under 50 degrees can result in adhesive crystallization and blisters under the wallcovering. On the other hand,

working in temperatures above 90 degrees can cause the adhesive to evaporate quickly, causing shrinkage.

Stretching. Horizontal stretching occurs when you apply too much pressure to the seams during installation. Vertical stretching occurs when you suspend a long strip without fully adhering it to the wall surface. An extra pair of hands can help relieve any excess weight or pressure on the wallpaper during the installation. Never let a long strip drop or unfold, bearing its own weight, while you are holding the corners of the strip. Instead, lower the strip slowly and gently, one fold at a time.

White seams. The appearance of white seams is usually due to the wallpaper shrinking. Shrinking can occur when the wallpaper soaks too long before you install it. Another cause is improper wall preparation, especially if you fail to prime and seal the walls. Sometimes when a structure settles, white seams appear. For this reason, some pros say it is wise to wait at least a year before you install wallpaper in a newly built house.

Problems with Adhesives

If the pattern you can't live without is not available in a prepasted version, you will have to apply an adhesive to the wallpaper backing. Of course, if you apply too much adhesive, it will take longer to dry and can shrink or result in a nasty mildew problem. Or you could end up with some stain problems as you force extra adhesive out with the smoothing brush. On the other hand, if you don't apply enough adhesive or if you've mixed it too thinly,

seams may come loose and sections may curl away from the wall.

There are three ways to apply adhesives: with a brush, pasting machine, or roller. The brush is the traditional method; it still gives the best results when you need maximum tack, such as when working with heavier products. The trick to using a brush is to work the adhesive well into the wallpaper backing using a figure-8 motion. It's labor-intensive, but it is the most accurate method and gives you the best control over the adhesive, letting you apply a thicker or thinner coat as necessary to meet wall conditions.

Using a roller to apply paste is a good way to spread adhesives on both the wallcovering and the wall, particularly when you're installing wallpaper that doesn't expand or when you don't need additional tack to hold heavyweight papers. If the adhesive beads up on the

wallpaper backing, the wallpaper is defective. Return the wallpaper for credit.

When you mix an adhesive, don't get carried away and apply so much force that you whip air into the mix. The resulting air bubbles can result in tiny blisters forming beneath the wallpaper. Always stir dry adhesive into the water, and stir it well to avoid a lumpy mixture. It's usually a good idea to mix multiple containers of adhesive to an equal viscosity to provide a uniform thickness. This is especially true when using a pasting machine. A large, restaurant-type handheld whisk is the perfect tool for mixing adhesive. Don't use an electric mixer unless it's made specifically for mixing adhesives.

Blisters. Tiny blisters are usually an indication of soured or unstrained adhesives, air in the adhesive, or porous wall conditions caused by improper priming and sealing. Blisters can also result from

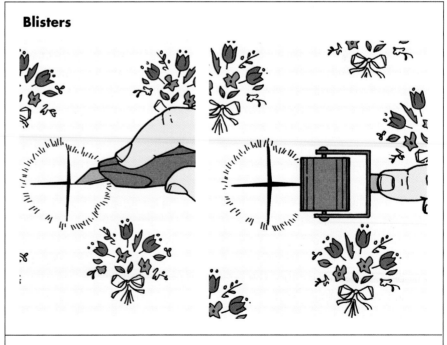

Blisters

Blisters can form when adhesive does not fully cover the paper or when site-mixed adhesive has a few unmixed lumps. To repair a large blister, cut an "X" across the surface, and roll it flat with a seam roller.

installing wallpaper in temperatures under 50 degrees. In this case the adhesive crystallizes on the wall surface, resulting in blisters.

To avoid blisters, always stir dry adhesive into water, but avoid vigorous whipping that will put air into the solution. After you mix the adhesive, strain the mixture through a cheesecloth into a clean bucket. A good alternative to cheesecloth is a filter made from nylon hose. Remember that starch-based adhesive is food to bacteria and fungus. Always mix it fresh, and keep it at room temperature during use. It doesn't hurt to temporarily store leftover adhesive in a refrigerator; just be sure to let it warm to room temperature and stir it gently before using.

When a small blister mars an otherwise perfect job, try these quick fixes before you resort to the major overhaul of removing the defective sheet and hanging a new one. The slickest and least invasive fix is to inject the blister with a shot of adhesive using a wallpaper syringe. You may be able to roll out the blister once the adhesive moistens the paper. If you don't happen to have a syringe in your tool box, use a utility knife to cross-score the blister, peel open the flaps, apply adhesive, replace the flaps, and roll out the surface.

Edge curling. This occurs when the paper backing expands much faster than the decorative surface after you apply the adhesive. There are a few solutions to this problem. The easiest is to first paste, book, and roll the wallpaper strips. After that, place the strips in a plastic bag for about 15 minutes. Another approach is to apply a thin layer of clay-based adhesive to the wall surface a couple of hours before the installation.

This could be the worst possible setting for wallpaper, at least from a maintenance and repair point of view. But the technique of thorough preparation and installation will keep the paper where you want it—even in an alcove with a steamy tub next to a chilly window.

Prepasted wallpaper. In some cases, wallpaper with factory-applied adhesive has either too much or not enough of the chemical that helps the water activate the adhesive. If there is too much of this chemical, the adhesive can wash off the wallpaper backing, resulting in little or no adhesion. To fix this problem, add one teaspoon of vinegar to the water in the tray. If the adhesive does not activate, add one teaspoon of ammonia to the water in the tray.

If you do not let prepasted wallpaper relax and expand properly before installation, it will complete the process on the wall surface. That may sound like a time-saver, but the result is either a series of long vertical expansion wrinkles or small vertical blisters and puckers. These expansion wrinkles will not dry out or dissipate.

If your walls are extremely porous, for example, in an older home with plaster walls, you can apply a diluted adhesive to the back of the prepasted wallpaper to enhance the manufacturer's adhesive. *Note: When you apply diluted adhesive to prepasted wallpaper, you lose the ability to dry-strip the wallpaper later.*

Most professional installers prefer to reactivate the prepasted adhesive by applying a premixed activator or diluted adhesive. This lets them control the viscosity as needed for different types of wall conditions. Be sure to dilute the extra adhesive with 50 percent more water than usually required. This will prevent clogging of the pores in the substrate that results in improper relaxing or adhesive crystallization.

Glossary

Accordion folding: a folding technique used for a booked strip of wallpaper. The paper is folded back and forth to keep pasted sides together and allow relaxing or expanding time. This fold also makes long strips easier to manage during the installation.

Adhesive aeration: a condition where the adhesive is filled with miniature air bubbles. Mixing or whipping the adhesive in too vigorous a manner is usually the cause. These bubbles can cause small blisters to form beneath the wallpaper, especially when installing non-breathable types.

Adhesive penetration: the process where the adhesive soaks into the wallpaper substrate during the relaxing or booking period.

Adhesive viscosity: the internal friction of an adhesive that restricts its tendency to flow or spread. The viscosity controls the amount of adhesive you can spread at a given thickness. Adhesive viscosity also affects drying time.

Adhesive volatility: the evaporation time associated with a particular adhesive. Volatility increases during the hot summer months, especially if you are working on new construction and there is no air conditioning.

Adhesive wrinkles: wrinkles or ridges that occur immediately following the installation of wallpaper, caused by further expansion of the paper. Inadequate booking time is often a cause. Adhesive wrinkles normally dry out within 24 to 48 hours. Wrinkled wallpaper should generally be removed and reinstalled rather than fixed.

Alligation: fine cracks resembling alligator skin that appear in a primer-sealer coat. Alligation can result when there is grease, dirt, or wax buildup on a wall surface, when the temperature is low, or when the product is not thoroughly mixed.

Allowance: the 2 to 3 inches of material for trimming included at the top or bottom of a strip.

Alternating rolls: the technique of working with two separate rolls of wallpaper to minimize waste while installing a drop-match patterned design.

American single roll: an increasingly uncommon unit of wallpaper, usually containing between 34 and 36 square feet. These rolls vary from 20.5 to 36 inches in width and from 4 to 7 yards in length.

Artificial break: the point where the wallpaper or border ends against a decorative wood strip, spindle, or other object. This lets the wallpaper or border end without an obvious mismatch.

Available lighting conditions: the ambient light in a room, including natural light and artificial light. Imperfections in the wall surface or wallpaper are more evident as the ambient light increases.

Backsplash: the perpendicular section at the rear of a countertop, positioned along the wall to prevent spills from leaking down the back of the counter and onto the wall.

Baseboard: the trim that follows the base of the wall next to the floor.

Basket-weave design: a pattern or arrangement that simulates an over-and-under weaving pattern.

Bay window: a window unit consisting of three or more windows and projecting from an exterior wall.

Blister: a small bubble of air that forms under the wallpaper during installation. The cause of blisters includes inadequate soaking or relaxing time, installation temperatures below 50 degrees F, air trapped between the wall and the paper, wallpaper installed on a porous, unsealed wall, and adhesive aeration.

Bolt: a continuous roll of wallpaper equivalent to two or more single rolls and packaged as one unit. Usually 48- and 54-inch commercial wallpapers are packaged in 30-yard bolts. Bolts are packaged this way to increase the usable yield.

Booking: the technique of folding wallpaper and allowing time for the adhesive to penetrate without drying out so that the paper expands. The time period varies with different types of wallpaper. To book wallpaper, fold it pasted side to pasted side, with the edges of the strip in alignment and the ends overlapping about 1/2 inch approximately midway down the strip.

Borders: a strip of wallpaper, usually less than 15 inches wide, that is used as a decorative element along ceiling lines, chair rails, and around doors and windows.

Breathable wallpaper: any wallpaper that has porous surface through which air can pass.

Builder's flat: a mixture consisting of joint compound diluted with water, which is spread on a wall like paint (usually on new construction). It provides a decorative surface, but it is one of the worst enemies of a good wallpapering job. To install wallpaper over builder's flat, first wash it thoroughly with a mixture of ammonia and water, and then seal it with an acrylic primer-sealer or a thinned-down oil-based primer-sealer.

Burnished seam: a seam that has a slick or glossy look caused by excessive pressure from a seam roller.

Butt seam: the most common (and easily achieved) type of seam in wallpapering, in which two strips are placed edge to edge without any overlap. After forming a butt seam, roll it gently with a seam roller to secure it in place. Recheck the seam after 10 minutes, and roll it again

if necessary. See also: Burnished seam.

Casing: decorative trim around door frames, window frames, and other breaks in flat walls.

Cathedral ceiling: angled surfaces of a structure's roof framing that are reflected in the finished ceiling. These are typically found when there is an open floor plan in the first story.

Cellulose paste: odorless, non-staining paste derived from wood pulp, cotton, or other fibrous plant material, used primarily to hang wallpapers made from natural materials such as grasscloths, linens, and stringcloths.

Chalk-line box: a tool used to establish a plumb or horizontal line on a wall. Wallpaper installers sometimes replace the line in a chalk-line box with a cloth fishing line for a more refined line and a minimum of chalk on the wall. For wallpaper applications, a light-colored chalk is preferable.

Clay-based adhesive: a starch adhesive that includes heavy solids to enhance holding power. This type of adhesive can stain or cause the ink to flake off many types of wallpapers. Because clay-based adhesive does not dry as quickly as other types of adhesives, take special care to smooth the wallpaper evenly during installation.

Color way: the different color schemes that are manufactured using the same wallpaper pattern. Manufacturers usually print a wallpaper pattern in two or more different color ways.

Coordinating wallpaper: a wallpaper that blends with another wallpaper, whether by color, design, or other factors. Coordinating wallpapers can visually tie together two rooms or adjacent walls in the same room. Sometimes they are used over and under chair rails as companions.

Cornice: the decorative wood box or molding affixed over a window. It may be painted, wallpapered, or covered with fabric.

Coved ceiling: a ceiling formed in an arched manner at its junction with the side walls.

Creasing technique: the act of making a crease in wallpaper using a trimming tool or putty knife. Creasing is useful to establish a trim mark in tight places, such as around a door frame or along a ceiling line lacking crown molding.

Cross seaming: the lattice-type arrangement that results when you install a wallpaper liner horizontally and a decorative wallcovering vertically.

Crown molding: the molding or other decorative trim that follows the ceiling line around the top of a room.

Curing-out period: the time it takes for a primer-sealer or wallpaper adhesive to completely dry.

Cutting in: the technique of using a brush to apply the primer-sealer or adhesive where a roller cannot reach.

Crystallization: solid matter that forms in an adhesive when the temperature falls below 50 degrees F. Crystallization can also result from installing wallpaper over a porous wall.

Dado: the area of wall surface between the chair rail and the baseboard, usually the lower third of a wall.

Decorative surface: the top layer of the wallpaper. Manufacturers often coat the printed surfaces with a clear solution or laminate to add extra protection.

Deep soffit: a soffit with an underside area that is deeper than the vertical area is high.

Delamination: a condition where wallpaper backing separates from the top or intermediate layer of vinyl. One frequent cause is excessive soaking. Some wallpaper, such as grasscloth and stringcloth, should relax only 3 to 5 minutes before installation.

Depth: an effect that wallpaper creates in a room regarding its size. If a room is papered in light colors, it appears visibly larger. Darker or bolder colors make the room appear smaller.

Design: the decorative composition printed onto wallpaper. The recurring design elements determine the vertical and horizontal repeats within a wallpaper.

Diagonal pattern: a pattern that appears at a slant; an oblique pattern.

Diagonal pattern effect: an effect that becomes noticeable after you install small-scale or some large-scale patterns on a large wall. The effect may not be evident in a small catalog sample or on a single strip of wallpaper.

Diagonal pattern sequence: the diagonal recurrence of a pattern or design across the wall surface. For example, the diagonal sequence of a half-drop match pattern repeats itself at an angle exactly one-half the distance of the vertical repeat.

Directional print: a pattern or design on wallpaper or a border that must be installed in a particular direction in order to appear pleasing.

Disparate patterns: two or more patterns that are each distinct, placed in juxtaposition. An example might be plaids and floral prints. You should carefully consider continuity when you want to install disparate patterns. They could easily clash or distract from the overall appearance of the room.

Dissipation: the process that occurs as adhesive dries. This is what eliminates adhesive wrinkles.

Double-cutting: a technique used to obtain perfectly fitted seams. The installer overlaps the edges of two pieces until the patterns match, uses a razor blade to cut through both layers, and then removes the excess and joins the edges for a perfect seam.

Double roll: a bolt that contains the equivalent of two single rolls of wallpaper in a continuous piece. This packaging reduces waste and permits more usable yield from the wallpaper.

Drop match: sometimes referred to as a half-drop match, a match in which every other strip has the same pattern design at the ceiling line, assuming it is level. This forms a diagonal pattern sequence comparable with the straight-across match.

Drying period: the time that it takes for a primer-sealer to completely dry. Different types of wall conditions, adhesive viscosity, and humidity levels will affect the

drying period. Some conditions may cause the drying to take longer, such as high humidity, a nonporous wall surface, the viscosity of the adhesive, and use of a nonbreathable wallpaper.

Drywall: a gypsum composition sandwiched between two layers of heavy paper. Drywall is the primary wall surface on most new construction.

Dye-lot number: a number, letter, or combination of both, given to a particular batch of wallpaper that is printed at the same time. The dye lot represents the inks, vinyl coating, embossings, and other changeable factors. It is important to record the dye-lot numbers in case you need additional wallpaper to complete a job.

Edge curling: a condition where the edges of the wallpaper curl away from the wall during installation. Causes of edge curling include improper laminating tensions during the manufacturing process, use of an improper primer-sealer or adhesive, or premature drying of adhesive. Sometimes a low-water-content (clay-based) adhesive or an extra relaxing period will help solve the problem.

Embossed paper: wallpaper with a raised, textured pattern. Embossed wallpapers are useful when installing over imperfect wall conditions, as they will camouflage contours on an uneven wall. Do not use a seam roller on embossed papers because it can flatten or burnish the raised effect and cause a shiny streak to appear.

Ending point: the point where the wallpaper stops at an obstacle. Examples include fireplaces, accent walls, and kitchen cabinets.

Etching: Scratching or roughening an existing wallpaper surface to prepare it for the application of a wallpaper-removing solution. The etching of the vinyl-coated surface allows the solution to penetrate through the wallpaper and dissolve the old adhesive to aid in the removal of the existing paper.

Expanded spacer: a full-width, 2- to 3-inch-wide scrap piece of wallpaper used to determine a vertical guideline. The spacer is pasted or soaked and allowed to relax for the same amount of time as the wallpaper being installed. Once on the wall, it will establish the wallpaper's true width.

Extensibility factor: the amount that wallpaper can stretch or extend horizontally, without distorting the pattern or resulting in shrinkage after the installation.

Floating flooring: a vinyl floor covering that is not secured with adhesive. Use extreme care when moving heavy furniture or appliances across the vinyl because it will easily tear.

Floral patterns: any pattern or arrangement of flowers printed as the decorative surface of wallpaper.

Focal point: the first wall you see upon entering a room. To find the main focal wall in a room with multiple entries, you will have to determine the room's dominant flow of traffic.

Gapped seam: a small space between adjacent strips of wallpaper. Causes include improperly prepared walls, excessive force during installation, and improper factory trimming.

Geometric patterns: any pattern or design characterized by straight lines, triangles, circles, and so on.

Grit rating: the coarseness or texture roughness of sandpaper. The higher the number, the finer the grit.

Ground coating: an acrylic coating on the upper surface of the wallpaper substrate. The ground coating is usually an off-white or a colored surface.

Head wall: the wall that faces you when walking down a stairway.

Helix stairway: a stairway that moves in a spiral around a central axis. These structures often have convex or concave walls, difficult to wallpaper.

Horizontal guideline: a line used to align wallpaper or a border on a horizontal plane.

Horizontal pattern sequence: the horizontal recurrence of a pattern or design across a wall surface. A straight-across match has the same pattern at the top of every strip.

Ink flaking: a problem that occurs when the color element of the design begins to come off the decorative surface of wallpaper. Causes include defects in the manufacturing process, adhesive on the decorative surface, and the use of abrasive detergents.

Inside corners: a corner formed when two walls join facing each other, usually at a 90-degree angle.

Inside corner molding: a molding with a concave or convex shape facing the center of a room and flat surfaces on the other sides that attach to the walls, usually at 90-degree angles. Use this type of molding on corners when there is a void space or when the corner is exceptionally out of square. Inside corner molding also helps hide a mismatch of wallpaper in a crooked corner.

Intermediate colors: any color formed by mixing adjacent primary and secondary colors.

Intermediate layer: the middle layer in some types of wallpapers, found between the decorative surface and the substrate. The intermediate layer provides extra opacity, especially if it contains a color other than white or off-white.

Joint compound: Plaster-like substance used to seal seams in gypsum drywall. Also used to repair cracks and holes in a wall surface. A nonshrinking joint compound should always be used under wallpaper to ensure that the repair remains flat.

Kill point: the position where the final strips of wallpaper join together, usually resulting in a mismatch. For this reason, the kill point should fall in an inconspicuous place.

Kneading the wallpaper: the technique of lightly pressing a roll or strip of wallpaper to further minimize the curl factor that originates from the packaging process. To knead the roll, reverse-roll a strip and place it on a work surface; then roll it back and forth while applying slight pressure.

Knee space: the area located underneath a vanity countertop. Don't overlook this space during the estimating and installation.

Knee wall: the lower vertical wall usually below a sloped ceiling, such as in an attic room.

Laminated wallpaper: wallpaper that has a decorative surface bonded to a backing usually made of paper or fabric. Examples include grasscloth, cloth-backed vinyls, and solid sheet vinyls.

Lamination: the process of adhering two thin layers together, such as a wallpaper's intermediate layer and substrate.

Lath: wood strips nailed horizontally to the studs of a wall and used to provide the foundation of plaster.

Light sources: Any device that creates light and any opening that admits light. Consider lighting variables before choosing colors, textures, shiny or dull finishes, etc. Variables include direct or reflected natural, incandescent, or fluorescent light.

Lightweight joint compound: a patching compound that is very light and non-shrinking and requires little effort when sanding. When the joint compound dries, it does not evaporate and, therefore, does not shrink.

Linear feet: a one-dimensional measurement of length.

Liner paper: blank wallpaper stock available in a variety of weights, used to smooth a rough surface or to cover the grooves in paneling or concrete block walls. It is also used under expensive hand-printed murals and foils. Liners minimize the possibility of mildew, as they absorb excess moisture between layers of nonbreathing wallpaper and a non-breathing wall surface.

Matching: the technique of joining two strips of wallpaper so that partial designs will line up suitably or a sequence of designs will line up properly.

Matte finish: a refinement or finish on the decorative wallpaper surface that has very little shine or light reflection; a dull finish.

Memory: the original shape or position that a wallpaper may return to, even after installation on a wall. Wallpaper with a high memory factor can shrink at the seams as it dries.

Metric roll (Euro bolt): an amount of wallpaper containing 28 to 30 square feet per single roll. This is about 25 percent less than the American single roll. The standard metric single roll is usually about 21 inches wide and 16½ feet long; however, some manufacturers are making metric-size single rolls 27 inches wide by 13½ feet long. Metric double rolls contain approximately 56 to 60 square feet.

Mildew: a fungus that grows in dark, moist environments. It appears in different colors such as black, gray, yellow, green, or purple.

Mismatch: a situation where the patterns on wallpaper do not line up evenly from one strip to another.

Moiré: a watered wood grain effect printed or embossed on the decorative surface of wallpaper.

Monochromatic: having only one color or the various tonal values of one color. A monochromatic wallpaper pattern contains same-color blends.

Motif: the duplicated design of vertical and horizontal repeats in a wallpaper pattern. Motif refers to the recurring subject matter.

Mottling: a manufacturing defect consisting of ink spots on the surface of wallpaper.

Multiple-drop match: a drop-match pattern that is neither a half-drop nor a straight-across match. The multiple-drop match will repeat itself at the ceiling line every third, fourth, fifth, sixth, seventh, etc., strip, depending on the distance of the horizontal pattern match drop, as compared with the vertical repeat. If the match is neither a straight-across nor a half-drop, then it is most likely a multiple-drop.

Mural wallpaper: any wallpaper showing a picture or scene, whether of the countryside, a historical event, modern art, or other design. Murals usually come packaged in paneled strips that join together in a particular, numbered order to form the scene.

Netting: this refers to the warp and weft woven materials of grasscloth, rushcloth, jute weaves, etc.

Non-breathing wallpaper: nonporous wallpaper that does not allow air to penetrate the decorative surface. This type of wallpaper usually requires a longer drying time because the adhesive must dissipate into the wall surface. When both the wallpaper and wall surface are non-breathable, liner paper is sometimes used to absorb moisture, in order to prevent a mildew problem.

Oblique patterns: patterns that are neither perpendicular nor parallel to a given line or surface. This refers to patterns that follow a diagonal angle across the wall or to patterns printed on the bias.

Opacity: refers to how transparent or translucent a wallpaper is. If the opacity is poor, it usually means the wallpaper is a light color or does not have an intermediate layer between the decorative surface and the substrate. Primer-sealers that contain titanium dioxide will help prevent show-through from existing wall conditions.

Open doorways: door openings that have no casing or decorative trim placed around them.

Opened seams: seams that have separated between two strips of wallpaper. Causes include poor adhesion, usually because of improper wall preparation, and overworking of the wallpaper during installation.

Out of register: when two or more ink colors on a pattern of wallpaper are printed out of line with one another. This results in a ghost-type image or total misalignment.

Outside corner: a corner formed when two walls join, facing away from each other, usually at a 90-degree angle. Outside corners are typically found in L-shaped rooms or around boxes built around pipes and ductwork.

Outside corner molding: a molding that has been pre-grooved to fit on an outside corner of two walls that meet at a 90-degree angle. These moldings protect corners from abuse and can hide mismatched patterns.

Overlapped seams: a type of seam where one edge of the wallpaper laps over another edge and is not double-cut to form a butt seam. They are rarely used

except when correcting out-of-plumb outside corners, archways, and soffits.

Overtrimmed wallcoverings: the result when too much selvage is removed either at the factory or by the installer. This results in a mismatch on the edges of the wallpaper because part of the print will be missing.

Overworked: the result when a wallpaper strip is stretched or pulled away from the wall too many times. Take care not to overwork wallpaper because you can damage it, causing the seam to gap apart after drying.

Padded double-cut: the technique of inserting a small, thin scrap piece of wallpaper or wax paper between the wall and the two layers of wallpaper before double-cutting. This pads the double-cut area and helps prevent cutting into the wall. This will also help prevent the double-cut seam from separating.

Paint deterioration: a condition where a poor latex paint or builder's flat application breaks down beneath the wallpaper because of improper wall preparation. Any time a poor grade of latex paint is on the wall surface, the paint will not be able to withstand the drying pressures that take place while the wallpaper is drying out. Always make sure to prime wall surfaces with a wallpaper primer-sealer to ensure a satisfactory job and a secure bond.

Pastel colors: any light, delicate shade of color; pale and subdued; a tone of a hue reduced in intensity or strength.

Pattern placement: a particular point or line at which a pattern will follow. Example: Pattern placement would be important when hanging a design that would present a dominant pattern at the ceiling line, border line, or chair rail.

Peelable (strippable) wallpaper: wallpaper that can be removed without damaging the underlying wall. Most peelable wallpapers are paper-backed vinyls, sometimes referred to as solid-sheet vinyls.

Photo murals: wallpaper that reprints photographs, enlarged for placement on a wall or door.

Pieced roll: a roll containing more square footage than an average roll.

During packaging, the roll ended up short, so the manufacturer added several yards to compensate for the splice.

Pigmented primer-sealer: a type of primer-sealer that dries white instead of clear. It blocks existing wallpaper or discolorations on the wall from showing through semitransparent wallpaper.

Plumb bob: a tool used to establish a plumb line, or vertical guideline.

Point of design: a specific detail on a strip of wallpaper's decoration. In a mural, the point of design is the highest or lowest point of the image portrayed.

Popped nails: nails that have backed out of a wall because of vibration or structural setting.

Porosity: permeability to water or air. Consider the porosity of a wall surface before applying a primer-sealer. If it is very porous, seal the wall with an oil-based sealer or a pigmented acrylic primer-sealer. Also consider the porosity of the wallpaper substrate. If it is very absorbent, a second application of adhesive may be required.

Prepasted wallpaper: wallpaper manufactured with a water-soluble adhesive on the substrate.

Pretrimmed wallpaper: wallpaper with the selvage already cut at the factory.

Primer-sealers: an alkyd- or acrylic-based liquid used to prime and seal walls before the wallpaper installation. Most primer-sealers on the market are acrylic-based. These types of primer-sealers soak into a porous wall surface and bond the paint to the wall surface.

Putrefaction: the decomposition of organic matter.

Quality control: inspection of wallpaper before installation to make sure that it meets specifications.

Railroading: the technique of hanging random-textured wallpaper horizontally, rather than vertically, over window or door headers.

Reaction test: a test to predetermine the effect that an adhesive, cleaning solu-

tion, or wallpaper-removing solution may or may not have on a specific wallpaper or wall surface.

Relief cuts: cuts made to take the pressure off a strip when positioning it around an obstacle such as a door or window frame, vanity cabinet, or soffit. Relief cuts are usually made at a mirror angle to the mitered cut of the wood or obstacle.

Reverse-rolling: the technique of reversing a bolt of wallpaper to uncurl or reverse the window-shade effect. This helps the wallpaper lie flat while cutting and pasting it.

Reversing strips: the technique of installing every other strip of wallpaper upside down. This technique ensures that the lighter and darker edges on textured wallpapers will come together and minimize shading.

Roller marks: ridges that result from excess pressure on a roller during the application of paints or adhesives.

Room continuity: the continuous flowing of wallpaper patterns and colors from one room to another.

Sand-painted walls: walls painted with a paint mixed with sand. This finish does not provide a satisfactory surface for wallpaper.

Scarifying/scoring walls: The process of making numerous small holes in the wallpaper surface in preparation for wallpaper removal. These holes allow the wallpaper-removing solution to penetrate the vinyl-coated decorative surface down to the substrate and dissolve the old wallpaper adhesive.

Scrim backing: a cotton or linen fabric of open weave used as a backing on some wallcoverings.

Scrubbable wallpaper: wallpaper with a sprayed or solid vinyl surface, which is durable enough to withstand scrubbing with soap and water. These are ideal for kitchens, baths, children's rooms, and high-traffic areas.

Semitransparent wallpaper: a wallpaper that is usually light in background color and permits darker colors to show through from the wall surface.

Sequence: a continuous or connected series of wallpaper strips, patterns, designs, techniques, etc.

Setup time: the time it takes for the wallpaper and adhesive to dry out. Once the adhesive sets up, you cannot adjust the wallpaper on the wall without completely removing it. Occasionally, attempting removal of wallpaper soon after it has set up will result in severe wall damage.

Settling: a condition in which a structure sinks and shifts over time.

Shade: slight graduation or variation of a color. It usually refers to a darker tonal value of the hue. Wallpaper is considered shaded whenever there is inconsistent tonal value from one strip to another.

Shading: the technique of sorting rolls or strips of wallpaper so that they are uniform in color or tonal values. Wallpapers such as grasscloth, rushcloth, etc., will always contain various inconsistencies in tonal values because this is a natural effect.

Shallow soffit: a soffit whose underside is more shallow than its profile is high. Example: The soffit underside is 3 inches deep and its profile height is 12 inches.

Single roll: an amount or unit of wallpaper used for pricing. The standard metric single roll contains between 28 and 30 square feet. An American single roll contains between 34 and 36 square feet. Although manufacturers' price by the single roll, they customarily package it in double- or triple-roll bolts to minimize waste during installation.

Sizing: a powdered mixture of starch and cornflower or cellulose and pine flower. When applied to a wall surface, these mixtures provide uniform porosity and increase the tack of wallpaper during installation.

Solar light exposure: the angle or directions of direct sunlight and its effect on the color choices within wallpaper. Use cool colors such as blue or silver in a room that receives an east or west exposure. Use warm colors in a room that receives no solar light exposure. Use pastel colors in a southern exposure that receives solar light all day.

Solid-sheet vinyls: wallpaper that has a paper substrate laminated to solid vinyl. These wallpapers are peelable and scrubbable. Solid sheet vinyls are appropriate in heavy wear or traffic areas such as children's rooms, bathrooms, halls, and stairways.

Solid vinyls: wallpapers that contain a woven or non-woven substrate laminated to a solid vinyl decorative surface.

Spacing technique: the technique of using expanded spacers to determine the plumb line placement around inside and outside corners or to establish a vertical guideline past wall obstacles such as windows or doors. Spacers are also used to measure the distance of several strips under a multiple window or to predetermine the pattern placement when hanging around bay windows.

Straight-across match: a type of wallpaper pattern in which the design at the top of each strip is the same.

Straining: pouring an adhesive or primer-sealer through a strainer or nylon-stocking funnel to eliminate foreign matter in the product.

Stress fracture: a crack that forms in a wall during the settling of a structure.

Stretched wallpaper: Horizontal stretching that happens when you force a strip of wallpaper, trying to join it to an adjacent strip after the adhesive has set up. Vertical stretching results from the weight of long strips hanging without being adhered to the wall.

Strippable (peelable) wallpaper: wallpaper that can be removed without damaging the underlying wall surface.

Thermal expansion/contraction: the movement within a structure or wall in response to temperature changes.

Tint: a graduation or variety of a color diluted from the maximum purity of the hue.

Trimming: removal of selvage from untrimmed wallpaper or removal of wallpaper allowance from around the door, windows, ceilings, and baseboards.

Unpasted wallpaper: wallpaper that has not been prepasted at the factory.

Install unpasted wallpaper according to the manufacturer's instructions.

Untrimmed wallpaper: wallpaper with selvage intact.

Usable yield: the quantity of wallpaper actually installed on the wall. Waste factors such as allowances, matching patterns, etc., are important in predetermining the usable yield for a room or wall.

Vapor barrier: a plastic film or other product used on exterior walls prevent the formation of vapor behind the adjoining interior walls. A properly installed vapor barrier can prevent the formation of mildew due to water vapor between the wall and wallpaper.

Variegated pattern: any pattern or design that contains different features in character, form, and appearance. Examples: floral and stripes, wide stripes and narrow stripes.

Vertical guideline: a vertical line used as reference when installing wallpaper. The line is commonly plumb, but is sometimes drawn parallel to a door frame or outside corner

Vertical pattern repeat: the distance from one point on a pattern design of wallpaper to the identical point vertically. Every patterned wallpaper, except for murals and random patterns, has a vertical repeat.

Wainscoting: traditionally, paneling or woodwork that covers the lower third of a wall.

Wall preparation: the various techniques used to prepare a wall surface for wallpapering. Includes wallpaper removal, sanding and washing walls, spackling, removing fixtures, and priming and painting.

Wastage: the amount of wallpaper cut from a roll to match one strip with another. See also: Usable yield.

Working time: the time an installer has to work with a strip of wallpaper from pasting to positioning on the wall. Consider the time factor before attempting to paste too many strips of wallpaper. If you exceed the working time, the wallpaper may delaminate, or the adhesive may dry out.

Index

A

Adhesives, 67–69
    problems with, 134–135
Alligation, 131
Allowance edges, trimming, 77
Anaglypta, 26, 72
Archways, hanging wallpaper around,
    117–118

B

Black and white block prints, 10–11
Black edges, 125–126
Bleach, 16
Blisters, 134–135
Blueprints, estimating wallpaper from, 37
Borders, 97–105
    estimating for, 36
Brick walls, hanging wallpaper on, 47,
    120–121
Business supplies, 21
Butt seams, 62

C

Canvas tool bags, 21
Cathedral walls
    estimating for, 34–35
    hanging wallpaper on, 105–106
Caulk, 18
Ceilings
    estimating for, 35–36
    hanging wallpaper on, 86–88, 103–104,
        105–106
    unlevel, as problem, 81
Cellulose, 68
Cellulose-and-pine-flower sizing, 42
Cement block walls, hanging wallpaper on,
    47, 120–121
Ceramic tile, installing wallpaper over, 47
Chair rails, 81
    using borders as, 102
Chalk-line box, 18
Clamp light, 18
Clay-based premixes, 68
Cleaning supplies, 21
Clear acrylic primer sealers, 41
Clearing and cleaning, 42–45
Clear premixed adhesives, 68
Coloring seams, 69
Commercial vinyl, removing, 49
Commercial wallcoverings, estimating for, 36–37
Companion wallpaper, 101
Concave walls, hanging wallpaper on, 82
Contact paper, installing wallpaper
        over, 47
Convex walls, hanging wallpaper on, 82
Cork veneer, removing, 49–50
Corner guard, repairing, 44
Corners
    hanging wallpaper around, 104–105
    inside, 77–79
    outside, 79–80
Count-strip method of estimating, 32–34, 35

Curling seams, 132–133
Current tester, 16
Custom-mixed adhesives, 69

D

Delamination, 126
Door frames, hanging wallpaper around,
    82–84, 102–103
Dormers, hanging wallpaper around, 118–120
Double-cut seam, 62–63
Double-cutting, 92–93
Dropcloths, 16
Dry-hanging, 90–91
Dry-trimming, 91–92
Drywall
    installing wallpaper over, 47
    repairing damaged, 44–45, 46
Drywall knife, 20
Dye-lot numbers, 29

E

Edge curling, 135
Electrical plates, hanging wallpaper on, 85–86
Electrical tape and wire nuts, 16
Embossment, uneven, 130
Estimating materials, 23–37
Extension cords, 21
Extension shields, 21

F

Fabric-backed vinyl, 27
Fabric fraying, 126
Fans, 18–19
Fast-drying alkyd, 41
Felt paper, removing, 49–50
Fiberglass mesh tape, 17
Fiberglass weaves, 26
First-aid kit, 16
Fixtures
    hanging wallpaper around
        permanently mounted, 86
    removing, 42–43
Flat latex paint, 45
Flat oil paint, 45
Flocked papers, 11, 27
    removing, 50
Foam rubber padding, 21
Foil paper, 27–28
    removing, 50
Framing square, 17

G

Glossy enamel paint, 45, 47
Glue, 67
Grasscloth, 15
    removing, 50
Grease stains, 127
Guidelines, 80–82

H

Half-drop match, 56–58, 65
Hammer and nail set, 17

Heated vinyl, removing, 50
Heat gun, 19
Heavy-duty acrylic, 41
Heavy-duty papers, 26
Hemp, removing, 50
Homemade sizing, 42

I

Ink flaking, 127
Inside corners, 77–79
Installation, 71–93

J

Jute weave, removing, 50

L

Ladder, 19
Laminate, installing wallpaper over, 48
Large pattern repeats, 31–32
Latex enamel paint, 45
Levels, 19
Light bulbs, 21
Lincrusta, 26, 72
Liner papers, 88, 131
    removing, 50
Liquid dish-washing detergent, 16

M

Masking tape, 16
Material inspections, 93
Metal surface, installing wallpaper over, 47
Mildew problems, 44, 131–132
Mitered seam, 63
Moiré, removing, 50–51
Moisture problems, 44, 131–132
Mollys, 21
Multiple drop, 58–60
Multiple-mitered relief cuts, 77
Murals
    estimating for, 37
    hanging, 107–109
    removing, 51
Mylar, removing, 51

O

Obstructions, hanging wallpaper around,
    82–86
Offset screwdriver, 21
Oil stains, 127
Out-of-square printing, 127–129
Outside corners, 79–80
Overlap seam, 63
Over-worked paper, 127

P

Paint brushes, 19
Paint deterioration, 132
Painted wall surfaces, 45, 47–48
Paint flaking, 132
Painting over wallpaper, 48
Palette knife, 21
Paneling nails, 21

Paper-backed vinyl, 27
Paper weave, removing, 50
Parallels, 80–82
Paste, 68
Paste bucket, 19–20
Pattern matches, 54–60
Pattern numbers, 29
Pattern repeats, 30–32
  inconsistency in, 127
Percentage method of estimating, 32
Photo mural. See Murals
Pigmented acrylic, 40–41
Plaster wall, installing wallpaper over, 47
Plywood walls, installing wallpaper over, 48
Prefinished paneling, installing wallpaper over, 47, 121
Prepasted wallpaper, 65–67, 88–90, 135
Priming, 40–42
Printing on the bias, 127–129
Puckering of seams, 133

R
Raised vinyl, removing, 50
Random match, 54
Random texture, 54–56
Recessed windows, hanging wallpaper around, 113–117
Reedcloth, removing, 50
Ridge seam, 62
Rollers, 18
Rushcloth, removing, 50

S
Safety, 5
Sanding, 43
Sand-painted walls, 132
  installing wallpaper over, 48
Scaffold planks, 21
Scalloped edges, 129
Scarifiers, 17
Scrapers, 17
Screen marks, 129–130
Seam roller, 20
Seams, 60–65, 132–134
  butt, 62
  coloring, 69
  curling, 132–133
  double-cut, 62–63
  mitered, 63

overlap, 63
  placement of, 64–65
  protecting, 93
  puckering, 133
  ridge, 62
  shrinking, 133–134
  stretching, 133
  white, 134
  wire, 62
  wrap and overlap, 63, 80
Selvage, 91–93, 130
Shadows, concealing, 43–44
Shredding, 79–80
Shrinking seams, 133–134
Silkscreen prints, removing, 51
Size and packaging variables, 28–29
Sizing, 42
Small pattern repeats, 30
Smoothing brush, 20
Soffits, hanging wallpaper on, 109–113
Solid sheet vinyl, removing, 51
Special areas, 95–121
Special surfaces, installing wallpaper over, 47–48
Sponges, 20
Spot-patching, 43
Square-foot method of estimating, 31–32
Stain-killing primer-sealers, 41–42
Stains, 132
  concealing, 44
Stairways
  estimating for, 34–35
  hanging wallpaper on, 106–107
Standard paper, removing, 51
Starch-and-cornflower sizing, 42
Starch-based adhesives, 67
Steamers, 17–18
Straight-across match, 56, 64–65
Stretching seams, 133
Stringcloth, removing, 50
Strip
  installing first, 74–76
  planning first, 72
Suede, removing, 49–50
Supaglypta, 26, 72
Swatching, 69

T
Textiles, 27

Toggles, 21
Tongue-and-groove boards, installing wallpaper over, 47–48
Tools and supplies, 15–21
Transparency, 132
Trim guide, 21
Troubleshooting, 123–135

U
Uneven embossment, 130
Untrimmed wallpapers, 91–93

V
Vaulted ceilings, hanging wallpaper on, 105–106
Vertical guidelines, 81–82
Vinyl-coated papers, removing, 51
Vinyl-on-vinyl adhesives, 68–69
Vinyls, 27

W
Wallpaper
  adhesives for, 67–69
  changing, at a corner, 80
  companion, 101
  hanging new over old, 96
  history of, 9–13
  painting over, 48
  pattern matches in, 54–60
  prepasted, 65–67, 88–90, 135
  removing, 48–51
  seams and seaming techniques, 60–65
  size and packaging variables, 28–29
  types of, 26–28
  untrimmed, 91–93
Wallpaper adhesive, applying, 72–74
Wall preparation, 39–51
  problems with, 130–132
Washington, George, 13
Water box, 21
Wet look, removing, 51
Wet-trimming, 92
White seams, 134
Windows, hanging wallpaper around, 82, 102–103, 113–117
Wire seam, 62
Wire whisk, 21
Wrap and overlap seam, 63, 80
Wrenches, 17, 21

Photo credits

page 1: Thibaut Historic Homes page 2:Thibaut Historic Homes page 5: Seabrook Wallcoverings Inc. page 6: Imperial Wallcoverings Inc. page 8 Library Company of Philadelphia page 9: New York Public Library page 10: New York Public Library (left); Gross & Daley, New York, NY (right) page 11: New York Public Library (left); Crown Berger (right, right inset) page 12: Harriet Beecher Stowe House Hartford, CT (left); Bradbury & Bradbury, Benicia, CA (photo by Douglas Keister) (right) page 13: Index Stock Imagery (left); Bill Rothschild, Wesley Hills, NY (right) page 14: Eisenhart Wallcoverings page 22: Eisenhart Wallcoverings page 24: Eisenhart Wallcoverings (top left, bottom left, bottom right); York

Wallcoverings (top right) page 25: Eisenhart Wallcoverings (top left, top right); Waverly (bottom left); Essex (bottom right) page 26: Crown Berger (left); Tasso (right) page 27 Eisenhart Wallcoverings (left); Seabrook Wallcoverings (right) page 28: Tom Yee, New York, NY (left); International Wallcoverings (right) page 36: Bradbury & Bradbury, Benicia, CA (photo by Douglas Keister) page 37: Tom Yee, New York, NY page 38: Eisenhart Wallcoverings page 40: William Zinsser & Co. page 49: William Zinsser & Co. page 51: William Zinsser & Co. (top); Sterling (bottom) page 52: Eisenhart Wallcoverings page 66: Brewster Wallcovering page 67: David Arky/CHP page 68: William Zinsser & Co. (top);

David Arky/CHP (bottom left) page 69: David Arky/CHP page 70: Eisenhart Wallcoverings page 72: Brewster Wallcovering page 88: William Zinsser & Co. page 91: Brewster Wallcovering page 94: Eisenhart Wallcoverings page 96: Seabrook Wallcoverings page 99: Brewster Wallcovering page 108: International Wallcoverings page 121: William Zinsser & Co. page 122: Eisenhart Wallcoverings page 131: William Zinsser & Co. page 133: Gencorp Wall Covering page 135: Eisenhart Wallcoverings

All wallpaper borders appear courtesy of Eisenhart Wallcoverings.

Have a home improvement, decorating, or gardening project? Look for these and other fine **Creative Homeowner Press books** at your local home center or bookstore. . .

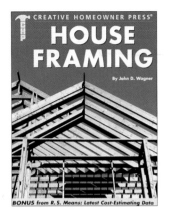

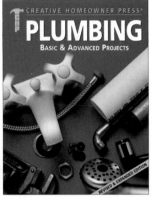
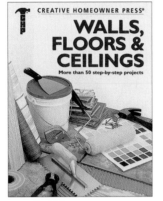